"Perhaps no political leader of such magnitude ever subjected himself publicly to the introspection and analysis that Robert McNamara has. In *The Fog of War*, we see a man struggling with momentous decisions and consequences, a remarkable tour of past and future horizons of great significance for how the United States conducts its foreign policy. James Blight and janet Lang stimulated the creation of this unique treasure, and now they have brought us a version with revealing context and depth, wrought with clarity, intelligence, and urgency. In all ways, it is an important and rewarding book."—**John Tirman,** executive director of the MIT Center for International Studies.

"Jim Blight and janet Lang invented critical oral history in the 1980s as an application of psychology to history, and as a way out of the trap of retrospective determinism—the false belief that things had to turn out the way they did. In Robert McNamara, Jim and janet found one of the all-too-few high officials not yet entrenched behind the fortifications of memoir and the fossilization of memory, remarkably willing at long last to try on other peoples' shoes. The extraordinary result, in addition to winning an Oscar for Errol Morris's film, is here in this book, a 'greatest hits' collection that shows how critical oral history has rewritten what we thought we knew about the closest the world ever came to suicide (the Cuban Missile Crisis), and about the war in Vietnam (echoes resound today in Baghdad)." —**Thomas S. Blanton,** director of the National Security Archive at George Washington University, which won the U.S. journalism's 2000 George Polk Award

"Essential reading for anyone interested in drawing lessons from the Vietnam War."—**Robert K. Brigham,** Shirley Ecker Boskey Professor of History and International Relations, Vassar College, and the author of *Guerrilla Diplomacy: The NLF's Foreign Relations and the Vietnam War*

"In his Academy Award®-winning film, Errol Morris transformed the popular vision of Robert McNamara from a creator and cold accountant of death and destruction into an agonized, thoughtful, sympathetic public servant. For their part, James Blight and janet Lang have documented the challenges Robert McNamara faced throughout his seven years as America's Secretary of Defense. They have provided fascinating, often chilling selections from correspondence with and between Kennedy, Khrushchev, Castro, Johnson and other players during the Cuban missile crisis and the Vietnam War. This previously classified material, together with thoughtful commentary from scholars and observers, and the helpful views of Blight and Lang, provide a valuable background to the lessons McNamara draws from 'The Fog of War.' Just as Morris's documentary is 'must' seeing for all thoughtful Americans, the Blight/Lang book is 'must' reading."—**Chester L. Cooper,** former CIA, State Department and White House specialist on Vietnam, and the author of *The Lost Crusade: America in Vietnam*

"It is difficult to imagine a book more terribly relevant than *The Fog of War.* James Blight and janet Lang weave together a compelling narrative, important historical documents from the Cuban missile crisis and the Vietnam war, and gripping exchanges of old adversaries met in dialogue in order to offer readers Robert McNamara's darkly prophetic 'lessons.' In so doing, they brilliantly engage the turbulent, complex, endlessly fascinating life of this remarkable public figure. The book is certainly one of the surest guides through the fog, and we would be wise to pay attention."—**Edward T. Linenthal,** author of *The Unfinished Bombing: Oklahoma City in American Memory*:

"This excellent book is more than a companion volume to the Oscar-winning documentary. The historical case-studies, declassified documents, and vivid photographs shed important new light on Robert Mc-Namara and his efforts to learn from the triumphs and tragedies of his public life."—**Scott D. Sagan,** professor of political science, Stanford University, and the author of *The Limits of Safety: Organizations, Accidents and Nuclear Weapons*

"Jim Blight and janet Lang's book is a novel achievement. The documentation, and their enormously helpful commentary, complement the film in an incredibly valuable way. This book should be read by anyone who wants to understand the perilous world we live in."—**Paul L. Wachtel,** CUNY Distinguished Professor of Psychology, and former director of the Colin Powell Center, City College of the City University of New York

THE FOG OF WAR

Lessons from the Life of
Robert S. McNamara

James G. Blight and
janet M. Lang

ROWMAN & LITTLEFIELD PUBLISHERS, INC.
Lanham • Boulder • New York • Toronto • Oxford

ROWMAN & LITTLEFIELD PUBLISHERS, INC.

Published in the United States of America
by Rowman & Littlefield Publishers, Inc.
A wholly owned subsidary of The Rowman & Littlefield Publishing Group, Inc.
4501 Forbes Boulevard, Suite 200, Lanham, Maryland 20706
www.rowmanlittlefield.com

PO Box 317
Oxford
OX2 9RU, UK

Copyright © 2005 by Rowman & Littlefield Publishers, Inc.

All rights reserved. No part of this publication may be reproduced, stored in a retrieval system, or transmitted in any form or by any means, electronic, mechanical, photocopying, recording, or otherwise, without the prior permission of the publisher.

British Library Cataloguing in Publication Information Available

Library of Congress Cataloging-in-Publication Data
Blight, James G.
  The fog of war : lessons from the life of Robert S. McNamara / James G. Blight and Janet M. Lang.
        p. cm.
  Companion book to the documentary film The fog of war.
  Includes bibliographical references and index.
  ISBN 0-7425-4220-3 (cloth : alk. paper)—ISBN 0-7425-4221-1 (pbk. : alk. paper) 1. McNamara, Robert S., 1916- 2. McNamara, Robert S., 1916—Political and social views. 3. McNamara, Robert S., 1916—Interviews. 4. Cabinet officers—United States—Biography. 5. United States. Dept. of Defense—Biography. 6. Vietnamese Conflict, 1961-1975. 7. United States—History, Military—20th century. 8. United States—Military policy. I. Lang, Janet M., 1948- II. Title.

  E840.8.M46B58 2005
  327.73'009'04—dc22

                                                                          2004029787

Printed in the United States of America

♾ The paper used in this publication meets the minimum requirements of American National Standard for Information Sciences-Permanence of Paper for Printed Library Materials, ANSI/NISO Z39.48-1992.

In memory of
Carmella Vertullo Lang (1915–2003)
and
Martha Schaard Blight (1922–2003)

&

In gratitude for our "stolen season" …

We all make mistakes. We know we make mistakes. I don't know any military commander, who is honest, who would say he has not made a mistake. There's a wonderful phrase: "the fog of war." What "the fog of war" means is: war is so complex it's beyond the ability of the human mind to comprehend all of the variables. Our judgment, our understanding, are not adequate. And we kill people unnecessarily.

[Woodrow] Wilson said: "We won the war to end all wars." I'm not so naive or simplistic to believe we can eliminate war. We're not going to change human nature anytime soon. It isn't that we aren't rational. We are rational. But reason has limits.

ROBERT S. McNAMARA, in "The Fog of War"

Man proceeds in a fog. But when he looks back to judge people of the past, he sees no fog on their path. From his present, which was their far away past, their path looks perfectly clear to him, good visibility all the way. Looking back, he sees the path, he sees the people proceeding, he sees their mistakes, but not the fog.

MILAN KUNDERA, in *Testaments Betrayed*[1]

CONTENTS

Authors' Note   xi

PROLOGUE   *Critical Oral History*: Robert McNamara's
Road to "The Fog of War"   3

1 LESSON ONE:
"Empathize with Your Enemy"   27

2 LESSON TWO:
"Rationality Will Not Save Us"   59

3 LESSON THREE:
"Belief and Seeing, They're Both Often Wrong"   87

4 LESSON FOUR:
"Proportionality Should Be a Guideline in War"   113

5 LESSON FIVE:
"Be Prepared to Reexamine Your Reasoning"   139

6 CRITICAL ESSAYS:
"I'd Rather Be Damned If I Don't"   173

EPILOGUE   Wilson's Ghost   219

Appendix A: Chronology of the Life and Times of
Robert S. McNamara   243

Appendix B: Further Reading and Exploration   249

Credits   262

Endnotes   265

Acronyms   295

Acknowledgments   296

Index   302

About the Authors   308

"Documents"

"Dialogues"

"Dilemmas"

WAR AND PEACE IN "3-D": Documents, Dialogues, and Dilemmas

Over a twenty-year period, Robert McNamara has been a key participant in two of our research projects, one on the Cuban missile crisis and another on the Vietnam War. Errol Morris read this research as part of his own investigation into these episodes in McNamara's life. We met Errol Morris in 2001, shortly after he began interviewing McNamara, and we have worked with Morris (and his team of talented researchers) and with McNamara throughout the production and distribution of the film.

Our research, such as that incorporated by Errol Morris into "The Fog of War," was carried out using a method called *critical oral history*. We developed the method to build a bridge between the confusion of raw experience and the relatively cut-and-dried rendering of that experience in histories, memoirs, etc. Critical oral history combines, in structured conferences, (1) decision-makers, (2) scholars, and (3) declassified documents (which provide added accuracy and authenticity to the conversation). The decision-makers, whose knowledge comes from their experience (for example, of having had responsibility for managing events in the Cuban missile crisis, or the war in Vietnam), are thus able to confront scholars, whose knowledge of the events is after-the-fact, obtained from documents or interviews. The declassified documents provide a level playing field, on which these groups can ask, and begin to answer, questions about the events under scrutiny.

The structure of this book mirrors, to the extent possible, the method of *critical oral history*, in the following way: chapters 1–5 contain excerpts from *documents,* often formerly classified, that bear on the issues and events; and *dialogues* between former decision-makers in the events—with many taken from critical oral history conferences in the U.S., Russia, Cuba and Vietnam. Chapter 6 contains excerpts from critical essays written about McNamara, Morris and "The Fog of War." All chapters, 1–6, conclude with *dilemmas* that we believe must be faced by all who would try to learn from this history of the 20th century and apply the lessons to the 21st.

The text also has the following characteristics:

- We begin all chapters, including the "Prologue" and "Epilogue," with an excerpt from "The Fog of War" that embodies a central point in the chapter. There are also graphics from the film throughout the book. Each bears a caption from the film.
- Chapters 1–6, as well as the "Prologue" and "Epilogue," include introductions in which we identify key issues, and provide context within which to interpret the material immediately following.
- Chapters 1–5 each take up one of the lessons drawn by Errol Morris in "The Fog of War" that deals with issues of war and peace.
- Chapter 6 contains a selection of reviews of "The Fog of War." We provide introductions to the chapter as a whole and to each critical review.
- The "Prologue" and "Epilogue" focus on Morris' subject, Robert McNamara: his life and times, and his role in the principal events addressed in "The Fog of War"—the firebombing of Japan in the Second World War, the Cuban missile crisis, and the escalation of the war in Vietnam.
- Two appendices are provided which readers may find helpful: (A) a brief "Chronology of the Life and Times of Robert S. McNamara"; and (B) "Further Reading and Exploration," which directs readers to specialized sources related to the issues highlighted in each of the "Dilemmas."

In "The Fog of War," Morris and McNamara have fused their talents to make history come alive. The importance of this process of enlivening history is fundamental. The Second World War, the

Cuban missile crisis, and the Vietnam War are among the pivotal events of the 20th century. The shadow of each looms large in contemporary policy-making. Ignoring this history would be unwise.[1] But learning this history, and applying its lessons, is a formidable task. In 1843, the philosopher and theologian Søren Kierkegaard identified the difficulty: "It is perfectly true, as philosophers say, that life must be understood backwards. But they forget the other proposition, that it must be lived forwards."[2] We must look *back* on events of the 20th century to understand the *forward-moving* perceptions of people who did not know at the time (as we do now) the outcome of those events, and who shared the responsibility for constructing the outcome. This is no easy task under the best of circumstances.

Soon our knowledge of these pivotal events will come only from documents and other records that are at least once removed from the actual experience of bearing some responsibility during (and for) the events themselves. We believe it is the duty of scholars, novelists, filmmakers, poets, and others with the necessary creativity to try to enliven this secondhand knowledge into a more intimate acquaintance, face-to-face, as it were, with the lived experience of these pivotal events of the 20th century. Collectively, these efforts can provide the next generation with a *vicarious* experience that conveys the horror any rational human being ought to feel when confronted with the carnage of the 20th century. "The Fog of War"—the film and the book—provides complementary ways to build that *vicarious* experience. If the film and book are successful, you are *there* in March 1945, trying to decide whether to bomb hundreds of thousands of innocent Japanese civilians, in order to try to end the Pacific War; you are *there* in October 1962, trying to avert a nuclear holocaust over Soviet missiles in Cuba; and you are *there* in 1963 and 1964, trying to avoid escalating the war in Vietnam, while preventing a Communist takeover of the entire country.

Good reading to you!
JGB and jML

To further investigate these events, see our website, http://watson institute.org/criticaloralhistory/.

THE FOG OF WAR

"What 'the fog of war' means is war is so complex it's beyond the ability of the human mind to comprehend all the variables."

CRITICAL ORAL HISTORY:
Robert McNamara's Road to
"The Fog of War"

Historians don't really like to deal with counterfactuals—with what might have been. They want to talk about history. "And how the hell do you know, McNamara, what might have been? Who knows?" Well, I know certain things. What I'm doing is thinking through with hindsight, but you don't have hindsight available at the time. I'm very proud of my accomplishments. And I'm very sorry that in the process of accomplishing things, I've made errors.

ROBERT S. McNAMARA, in "The Fog of War"

Errol Morris' *Academy Award®-winning documentary, "The Fog of War" confronts viewers with a singular fact about the 20th century: roughly 160 million human beings were killed by other human beings in violent conflict. It was the bloodiest century in human history. The film challenges us to look closely at that tragic century for clues as to how we might avoid a repetition of it in the 21st century.*

The film takes the form of a one-on-one conversation between Morris (who is behind the camera) and former U.S. Secretary of Defense Robert S. McNamara (who is on camera). The conversation traces McNamara's experiences from the end of World War I, through the course of World War II, and the unfolding of the Cold War in Cuba, Vietnam and around the world. We are encouraged to experience the 20th century vicariously as the filmmaker and his subject walk us through the experiences of leaders involved in these seminal events. Extensive archival footage and recently declassified tape recordings of presidential conversations help the viewer to place McNamara, who was eighty-five years old when Morris interviewed him, in the chapters of the history he discusses.

Cut from more than twenty hours of dialogue, the 107-minute film is organized around eleven distinct "lessons" which Morris distills from McNamara's experience. In this book, we focus on the five that apply most directly to U.S. foreign and defense policy.[1] These lessons underline the importance of: (1) empathy toward one's adversary; (2) the limits of rationality in foreign policy decision-making; (3) the role of misperception and misjudgment leading to war; (4) the painful moral choices necessary in a wartime environment; and (5) the significance of remaining flexible in pursuit of any nation's most important objective—the prevention of war. We deal with these lessons in chapters, 1–5 of this book. Ultimately, the lessons are cautionary tales for future generations.[2]

America's most eminent film critic, Roger Ebert, called "The Fog of War" a "masterpiece."[3] Stephen Holden of The New York Times wrote: "If there is one movie that ought to be studied by military and civilian leaders around the world at this treacherous moment, it is 'The Fog of War,' Errol Morris's portrait of former United States Defense Secretary Robert S. McNamara."[4] "The Fog of War" has reached an audience much larger than that which typically pays to see documentaries in movie theaters. Between its opening in theaters on December 19, 2003, through May 11, 2004, when the DVD of the film became available, more than one million people saw it in hundreds of theaters across North America. The film quickly came to be regarded as both an artistic triumph and a significant contribution to the public discussion of some of the most pressing issues of our time.

The film is a brilliant work of art, but it is not only a work of art. Via the lessons Morris draws from McNamara's experience, the film also offers clues as to how to prevent the kind of disasters, and near disasters, McNamara describes in the film. This is why we would expand Stephen Holden's suggested audience for the film: it should include not just political and military leaders, but also ordinary citizens, of whatever age, who seek a more peaceful world. This quest must begin, we believe, with an understanding of the foreign and defense policy of the United States of America, the world's remaining superpower, and unavoidably the proverbial "600-pound gorilla" in every discussion and action affecting global security. Errol Morris' film, "The Fog of War," contributes significantly to this understanding. We hope you find this book a worthy complement to it.

"Behind the Scenes"

In the 1980's we studied the problem of nuclear danger. Nuclear war was "unthinkable," but it was not impossible. If it was not impossible, how might it happen? One hazardous route was via a crisis between nuclear nations. The world had traveled this route only once—in the Cuban missile crisis of 1962. Though much research existed on the missile crisis, it seemed to us that another look—a look from a more human angle—had the potential to yield information with contemporary policy relevance. While weapons and command and control systems had changed markedly since the 60s, human nature hadn't. And so, our question was "What was it like to be a decision-maker during the crisis, when, literally, 'the fate of the earth' hung on your decisions?" Decision-makers are the target of our research. They are the people who have a special kind of knowledge that comes from participating in an event, when it is your decisions that shape the event, and when you don't know how things will turn out. But this question—about the details of the look and feel of nuclear danger—is not a simple question either ask or to answer.

The Danish theologian and philosopher Søren Kierkegaard pointed out the difficulty long ago. We live life forward, groping in the dark, unaware of its ultimate outcome, yet we are forced to understand events in reverse, working our way retrospectively backward to their supposed causes. This creates a profound disconnect between lived experience and our understanding of that experience.[5] Caught in the moment—in the crisis—decision-makers often feel confused, unsure, and sometimes even afraid. But the scholarly (after the fact) study of their decision-making usually removes the confusion and fear, focusing simply on explanations of outcomes.

We developed *critical oral history* to build a bridge between the confusion of lived experience and the relatively cut-and-dried rendering of that experience. It does so by combining, in structured conferences, (1) decision-makers (who lived the events "forward"), (2) scholars (who understand the events "in reverse"), and (3) declassified documents (which provide added accuracy and authenticity to the conversation). We held our first critical oral history conference on the Cuban missile crisis in 1987. Most of the men who advised President Kennedy during that crisis participated, along with eminent scholars of the crisis. Since then, we have organized five more critical oral history conferences on the missile crisis. In these conferences we broadened our inquiry to include the look and feel of nuclear danger not just in Washington, DC, but also in Moscow and Havana. Robert McNamara participated in all of them; several of his colleagues from the Kennedy Administration, and their Russian and Cuban counterparts participated in one or more of the conferences. McNamara himself suggested applying critical oral history to the Vietnam War. He participated in three of the five critical oral history conferences that we organized.

Critical oral history often yields rich and surprising insights into what it was really like for decision-makers, then and there, thus affording more accurate analyses and applicable lessons for decision-making, here and now.[6] It can also reveal information and perspectives so startling that the participants can scarcely comprehend what they are being told. Such a moment occurred at our January 1992 conference in Havana, Cuba on the Cuban missile crisis.[7]

General Anatoly Gribkov revealed that the Soviets had deployed short-range tactical nuclear warheads in Cuba, and that if the expected U.S. attack and invasion had come, the Soviet commander would probably have used them. Cuban President Fidel Castro, who also participated in the conference, added that he had urged the Soviets to do just that. Upon hearing this, several U.S. participants, led by Robert McNamara, literally went pale and temporarily speechless, their eyes wide with disbelief. The Americans knew that the attack may have been just hours away, but they did *not* know that ships carrying the invading forces would likely have been destroyed and any U.S. Marines making it to the beaches of Cuba would likely have been incinerated in nuclear fire. It was a rare moment: decision-makers on all three sides were thrown into a figurative "time machine" and the others present, including ourselves, could watch and palpably feel, as if watching an "instant replay" thirty years later, some of the horror, revulsion and despair the leaders felt at the time, as the clock seemed to tick down toward nuclear holocaust.

The decision-makers who come to the table for a critical oral history conference take risks in doing so. At any time, revelations can indicate that they were mistaken in critical respects, even that their mistakes led to tragedy. To agree to participate, their curiosity about what they might learn must overwhelm their fears about the effects possible revelations might have on their reputations. One such moment occurred in our June 1997 conference in Hanoi, Vietnam.[8] Vietnamese general Dang Vu Hiep revealed that an attack on U.S. forces in the Central Highlands at Pleiku, on February 7, 1965, was *not* ordered by Hanoi, as Americans had always believed.[9] In this short statement, General Dang Vu Hiep (who was present at the attack site in 1965) refuted the American rationale for initiating the bombing of North Vietnam, bombing that was begun in response to the Pleiku raid, and thus inadvertently forced the Americans to shoulder a greater share of the burden for the more than three million people killed in that war. U.S. leaders, including Robert McNamara (who led the U.S. delegation to the Hanoi conference) had been mistaken, and the mistake had tragic consequences.

McNamara's remarks in "The Fog of War" are inspired in large measure by the 2001 book he co-authored with James Blight, *Wilson's Ghost: Reducing the Risk of Conflict, Killing and Catastrophe in the 21st Century*.[10] In *Wilson's Ghost*, McNamara and Blight outline the lessons of McNamara's experience in public life and combine them with the lessons learned in the critical oral history projects on the Cuban missile crisis and Vietnam War that we have directed.[11] Errol Morris initially approached McNamara for an interview in connection with a series he had undertaken for a cable TV show. Part of Morris' preparation for the interview was reading *Wilson's Ghost*. But during the first half hour on camera, McNamara told Morris that if the U.S. had lost the Second World War in the Pacific, he had no doubt that he and his superiors would have, and should have, been tried for crimes against humanity due to their role in the firebombing of more than sixty Japanese cities, killing an estimated one million civilians—mainly women, children and elderly men. Morris, startled by McNamara's directness and energy, immediately concluded that this topic warranted a full-length documentary. McNamara agreed, giving Morris nearly twenty-four hours of interviews, over three long sessions.[12] As Morris has often said, "The Fog of War" is in essence a conversation between two Robert McNamaras—a forty-something decision-maker and an eighty-something scholar—about the meaning of his experience with violent conflict in the 20th century.[13]

Critical Oral History's "FAQ"

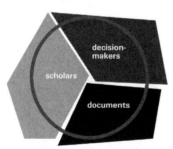

critical oral history

Robert McNamara's "preparation" for the interviews with Errol Morris was accomplished primarily via his participation in critical oral history projects on the Cuban missile crisis (between 1987 and 2002), and on the escalation of the Vietnam War (from 1995 to the present). Because of the centrality of this somewhat unusual research method in McNamara's evolution, it may be worthwhile dwelling momentarily on how it works, by focusing on some questions that have come up over the years—questions which may in fact have already occurred to some readers of this book, especially those familiar with the film.

The method of *critical oral history* has by now generated a more or less standard list of what is now called, on website homepages, "*FAQ*"—"frequently asked questions," along with brief answers. Underlying the FAQ of critical oral history it is possible to detect this overriding concern: how can those of us who use this method be *certain* that statements made by decision-makers are actually *true*? Why should we trust them to tell us the truth? To put the matter less charitably (as it has occasionally been put to us by skeptics): aren't we worried about being bamboozled by people who may have a long history of playing fast and loose with the truth? The shortest, truthful answer is: *yes!* We worry about it all the time.

A somewhat longer, more informative answer is that "certainty" is in most cases an unattainable historical objective, whether one uses critical oral history or any other method of inquiry into the past. What we are looking for is not certainty, but credible additions or corrections to the historical record. These may include important factual revelations such as the startling news that tactical nuclear weapons were present in Cuba by October 1962. But often our findings involve something less newsworthy, perhaps, but just as important in the long run—a thickening of the texture of the historical narrative concerning how decisions actually were made—the *look and feel* of the situations to those who actually lived through them in positions of significant responsibility. This has been especially true, in our own work, of decision-making on the "other" side—decisions made by the Russians, Cubans, or Vietnamese, for example—where much less is known than in the West, where the paper trail is often thin to nonexistent, and where even the various roles played by participants in the events in question are often unclear, at least at the outset.

Here, then, are the most frequently asked questions about our hybrid method of critical oral history, and brief answers to each:

1. MEMORY.

Question: How can we be certain that participants recall events accurately, assuming they desire to do so?

Answer: While we can't be sure, the memories of all participants must be compared with the memories of former colleagues and adversaries, with the documentary record, and with the best guesses of participating scholars who are familiar with the record of the events.

2. AGENDAS.

Question: How can we be certain that participants don't harbor hidden agendas—for instance, to enhance the importance of their roles or to denigrate the roles of others?

Answer: While we can't be certain this won't happen, all participants are screened prior to the conferences, and their responses to our questions are compared to other sources of information on the same issues. As always, arriving at a "final" answer to the most interesting questions is an unrealistic objective. All answers, no matter how well documented, are (or should be) regarded as tentative, and the act of arriving at even tentative conclusions is more a matter of art than science.

3. HINDSIGHT.

Question: How can we be certain that we are able to disentangle retrospective hindsight from foresight during the actual events in question?

Answer: While it is theoretically possible to confuse the two, in practice it rarely happens, primarily because recollections are tightly constrained by both the documentary record and the recollections of the others present. In fact, we have noticed over the years a significant difference between oral testimony given in private interviews—which tends to mimic previous interviews on the subject by each interviewee—and interventions given in a critical oral history setting—which tend to be less defensive, more carefully documented, and more generous to those with whom one may have disagreed or mistrusted during the events under investigation.

4. POLITICS.

Question: How can we be certain we have taken adequate account of the current political context in which the dialogues about history occur?

Answer: The most important fact for Americans to keep in mind is
that Americans almost invariably participate as individuals, while
others—whether Russians, or Cubans or Vietnamese, in the
cases we know best—often do not. Many of them may be "retired," in the sense that they are receiving pensions, no longer
hold any official position, etc. But in many societies, participants
constitute a "team," with fixed instructions from their government as to what can and cannot be said. A deep and detailed
awareness of the particulars of the individual political situation
must be obtained during the preparatory phase of a conference.
The organizers' mantra must be "everything is political"—the
conference agenda, the list of participants, the documentation,
even the fact that the conference is occurring at all.

5. DOCUMENTS.

Question: How can we be as certain about the "other" side's statements as we are of those made by Americans, given the usually
huge discrepancy in available documentation on the side of the
U.S.?

Answer: Usually, we cannot. Yet it is often possible to begin to approximate information contained in the U.S. data base by combining previously published foreign sources, and in-depth interviews with participants who are especially keen to get their
country's side of the story on the record in the West. We have
found that such individuals exist in greater numbers than one
might suppose. One must be resourceful, but the problem is
usually not insurmountable.

6. PARTICIPANTS.

Question: How can we be sure that we have invited the "right"
people, from among those who are available, to participate?

Answer: We can never claim, after the fact, that a better group of
conference participants was not possible to assemble. Nevertheless, we try to put the teams together methodically, filling in
gaps in both civilian and military positions (for example), and
trying to insure that each person "at the table" is willing to do
the extensive preparation necessary for full participation, and is
also comfortable with the highly informal format, in which
cross-questioning is to be expected. This process is made much

more challenging, but also potentially much more important, in the case of meetings between former enemies. Often the non-U.S. team is designated by their government, which means that we need to have developed a working relationship with government officials, at many levels, in order to understand the possibilities and limitations posed by the identity of the participants.

7. ABSENTEES.

Question: How can we be certain that we have not been totally (though inadvertently) misled because many central figures cannot participate, simply because they have died? To put it another way: how would our outlook have been altered if John F. Kennedy and Nikita Khrushchev had been available to participate in the critical oral history of the Cuban missile crisis? Or what if Ho Chi Minh and Lyndon Johnson had been available for the Vietnam War conferences?

Answer: Here again, certainty is out of the question. Yet our experience leads us to believe that it is often important to have the chief executive absent, rather than present at the table. In an important sense, the boss will always be the boss, and this can have an inhibiting effect on the former subordinates.[14] In addition, it is usually possible to invite participants from the inner circle of those who are necessarily absent, though one should not expect them to agree in all, or even most, analyses of the decisions and actions of their former bosses.[15]

*   *   *

There is one remaining question which, while not falling into the "FAQ" category, is nevertheless important. In "The Fog of War," Robert McNamara says that "historians don't really like to deal with counterfactuals—with what might have been. They want to talk about history" as it occurred. McNamara is right. This in fact poses a conundrum for all who use the method of critical oral history. Former decision-makers are usually enthusiastic about trying to replay the past, looking for roads not taken, for data that were misinterpreted, for possible outcomes less disastrous than what occurred. Yet historians and other scholarly specialists on the events under investigation are typically wary of "what-ifs." They believe that once they start down the path of "what might have been," they may slide all the way down a very slippery, epistemological slope into a morass of all (supposedly) possible events—in fact, into an inquiry in which the actual constraints of history as it happened are all but forgotten, in the excitement of constructing alternative narratives.

McNamara himself states the essence of the problem in the movie, when he says, "what I'm doing is thinking through with hindsight, but you don't have hindsight available at the time." As a former decision-maker, he is interested in using historical insight to determine whether, or how, he might have made better decisions. His interest is in comparing *then* with *now*. Historians, aided by declassified documents, generally want, on the contrary, to focus strictly on *then*, stripped of the kind of hindsight—"if I knew then what I know now"—that often makes history come alive to former officials. This is one reason why critical oral history was created—to bridge this gap in a way that encourages a productive conversation between officials and historians, who may have read the same documents in their briefing notebooks, but who have conflicting objectives in the inquiry. When critical oral history works well, the former decision-makers gain insight into their errors, and those of former adversaries, permitting them to draw lessons and to apply them. But at the same time, historians are often able to learn some of the previously hidden, often surprising, and sometimes fascinating history of events they may have studied for decades.

"I've Made Errors": An Outline of What McNamara Has Learned

A central concept in critical oral history is *empathy*. You will be reading a good deal about it in this book. Empathy is not sympathy or agreement, but the capacity to understand reality as someone else understands it—to articulate accurately the story others tell themselves, even though it may be uncomplimentary (to you), or even threatening. Lesson number one in this book (chapter 1) is identical to the first lesson in the film "The Fog of War": "Empathize with your enemy." And for good reason. The absence of empathy leads straightaway to misperception, miscommunication and misjudgment—to mistakes—and thus to actions which are in turn likely to be misunderstood by an adversary. Sometimes, as in the Cuban missile crisis and the war in Vietnam, events spiral out of control, seeming to confirm each side's worst fears about the other. When one side carries out actions for defensive reasons, the other side may feel threatened, and vice-versa. When empathy is present, as it was during the climactic phase of the Cuban missile crisis—when the U.S. and Soviet Union locked onto the same wavelength just in the nick of time—a seemingly imminent and unavoidable disaster can be averted.

When critical oral history works well, a degree of empathy is present between former enemies—and sometimes even between former colleagues-that was not present at the time of the events under scrutiny. For the process to yield results, the curiosity of the former decision-makers must overwhelm their fear of entrapment by the other side. But we have found that the method works most successfully when the curiosity of former decision-makers also swamps their fear of being exposed—as having been wrong in ways that contributed to outcomes they wish they could have avoided.

In other words, *courage* is fundamental: putting yourself and your reputation at risk, to an extent, in order to get nearer to an accurate understanding of what happened, and why. Courage, in a critical oral history setting, moreover, most often takes the form of trying to empathize as fully as possible with former enemies. In so doing, participants explicitly or implicitly assume a viewpoint famously described by the radical English Puritan, Oliver Cromwell. "I beseech you," said Cromwell, "think it possible you may be mistaken."[16] Having dealt by now with hundreds of such individuals in a variety of settings over nearly two decades, it is clear that on this key dimension of courage—thinking it possible that he might be mistaken—Robert McNamara has led the way. He has taken risks, to identify mistakes, empathize with former enemies, and try to learn something from them. For people who take the process seriously, as McNamara has, critical oral history is a risky and uncertain business. Yet as is evident in "The Fog of War," and the research on which it is based, there can be substantial rewards for those willing to take the risks.

*   *   *

At the beginning of "The Fog of War," Robert McNamara says something that is so commonplace it might escape our attention altogether. "The conventional wisdom," he says, "is don't make the same mistake twice—learn from your mistakes. And we all do. Maybe we make the same mistake three times, but hopefully not four or five." True enough, but hardly news, we may think. He goes on to point out that in the event of a nuclear war, "you make one mistake and you're going to destroy nations," a statement that is connected with his long-time advocacy of abolishing nuclear weapons. That is the one mistake, as McNamara points out, that you *really* don't want to make, not even once.

It is at this point that he adds the brief comment that is easily missed, and that we want to emphasize here. "In my life," McNamara says, "I've been part of wars." Also true, of course, and (we may feel) equally unnewsworthy, *if* we fail to connect the "conventional wisdom" with his experience as having been "part of wars." But if we make the connection, we may begin to see that he is saying something quite profound. If we try to step into McNamara's shoes, we might paraphrase it somewhat as follows: I, Robert McNamara, have made some terrible mistakes in my life—mistakes that contributed to the deaths of hundreds of thousands, even millions, of my fellow human beings—mistakes that, in addition, nearly led to exactly the kind of irremediable catastrophe alluded to in the comment about the likely outcome of a nuclear war. McNamara reiterates this near the end of the film when he says, "I'm very sorry that in the process of accomplishing things, I've made errors." We should note that it is highly unusual for former officials, especially top-level officials, to admit having made significant mistakes.

Some have discounted such statements by McNamara as constituting merely an awkward public relations gimmick meant to improve his public image, perhaps even his standing among historians. We know better, however. We have been the organizers of the critical oral history projects, in the course of which McNamara, in our view, has *earned* the right (as have others—he is far from alone in this) to be taken seriously when he makes such statements. We have been present on many occasions when he has learned how profoundly he was mistaken, and how tragic were the consequences of his mistakes, with regard to both the Cuban missile crisis and the war in Vietnam. Of course, he (and we) have learned of the mistakes of others as well—Americans, Russians, Cubans, Vietnamese. We may find it easy to dismiss such findings if we have never had anything like the responsibility that McNamara had to bear as a lieutenant colonel in the Second World War, let alone as secretary of defense from 1961 to 1968—if we have not, as McNamara has, "been part of wars." We may instead be tempted to conclude, in effect: "Well, okay, sure: so the guy made some mistakes, and via this critical oral history process, he discovered what they were. Good. Better that he learns late rather than not at all, I guess." Or something of the sort.

What's missing in such a dismissive attitude is an appreciation for the *emotion*—the feeling of overwhelming responsibility for tragedies, real and potential, the magnitude of which is almost impossible to articulate. As we have seen and heard time and again, for those who *have* been "part of wars," the discovery that one has been mistaken in crucial situations can be shattering-not just to one's reputation or presumed historical legacy, but also deeply upsetting in a very personal way.

To get a sense of why this might be the case, we list a few things that McNamara has learned over nearly two decades of his participation in the critical oral history projects—on the Cuban missile crisis and the war in Vietnam. All will be dealt with in detail later in this book. Here, however, rather than becoming immersed in the details, we hope readers will try to empathize with a person such as McNamara—try to "become" McNamara, nonjudgmentally, for a moment—as we tick off some of his mistakes in the missile crisis and Vietnam. For now, don't worry about the details or documentation, or even whether McNamara is "correct" to believe he was mistaken in the ways we describe. That comes later in the book. For now, we ask that you try to put yourself in his place, sitting at a conference table in (say) Havana or Moscow or Hanoi, as you are bombarded with written documentation and oral testimony concerning what you got—in the phrase McNamara himself has now made famous—"wrong, terribly wrong."[17]

Here is a representative list of his mistakes, and their actual or

"It wasn't until January, 1992, . . . that I learned . . . nuclear warheads . . . were on the island at the time of this . . . crisis."

potential consequences. Imagine that *"you,"* in each case, are (vicariously) Robert McNamara.

THE CUBAN MISSILE CRISIS

- *Destroying Castro's Regime.* The Cubans and Soviets tell you in Moscow in January 1989 that, fearing an imminent invasion of Cuba following the Bay of Pigs fiasco of April, 1961, they had agreed to the deal to put nuclear missiles on the island. Yet you know no invasion was intended. So you, and your colleagues in Washington, via continuing threats to intervene and remove the Castro regime, inadvertently helped to cause the most dangerous crisis in recorded history.

- *Nuclear Danger.* You and your colleagues believed that Soviet nuclear warheads never reached Cuba; thus an airstrike and invasion of the island was unlikely to pose any danger to the American homeland. Yet you learn in Havana in January 1992 that the warheads were present, ready to be used. So the attack and invasion of Cuba, which you and your colleagues came within hours of ordering, would likely have escalated, killing millions of people, including many Americans. If that had happened—and it was mainly luck that prevented it, as McNamara emphasizes in the film—you would have borne some of the responsibility.

- *How Close Was Armageddon?* You firmly believed in October 1962, during the Cuban missile crisis, that no leader of any of the three involved countries would seek a nuclear war, under any circumstances. Yet Fidel Castro tells you, face to face, in Havana in January 1992 that he did in fact ask the Soviets to launch an all-out nuclear strike on the U.S., if Cuba was attacked with the intent of destroying the Cuban Revolution. So now you know that you and your colleagues had so cornered Castro, so stripped him of viable options, that he believed nuclear war was his least worst option, one that might well have been implemented had the crisis erupted into war. Note that *this* Cuban missile crisis is far from Kennedy's (and your) "finest hour," as it is often portrayed in lore. In fact, you (remember: you are still in character, as "McNamara") nearly participated actively, if unwittingly, in the total destruction of your society and, but for "luck," you would have done just that, and been in part responsible for the worst disaster in history.

THE VIETNAM WAR

- *Casualties and Punishment.* You (you are still McNamara, don't forget) firmly believed—why would anyone not?—that some upper bound, some threshold of casualties and sheer punishment must exist, beyond which the Vietnamese communist adversaries would seek to end the war, thus ending their U.S.-inflicted misery. Yet you are told by credible interlocutors in Hanoi in June 1997 that the Vietnamese adversaries, in both North and South Vietnam, had resolved to accept a level of punishment far beyond what they actually received, including nuclear attacks and a U.S. invasion of North Vietnam. So you must conclude that all the bombing you ordered, all the troops you deployed, all the death and de-

"And no amount of bombing, no amount of U.S. pressure would ever have stopped us."

struction inflicted, was pointless. Your strategy would *never* have worked.

- *Civil War.* You believed that the fundamental fact of the Vietnam conflict was that it exemplified the Cold War between East and West, and that Hanoi therefore exerted tight control over its allies, the National Liberation Front (the NLF, or "Vietcong") in the South; and that Moscow and Beijing directed Hanoi's actions in a similar fashion. Yet you learn from declassified Vietnamese documents, and from discussions in Hanoi, that Hanoi exerted no such control, that the NLF in fact resisted being controlled, and that if you had only known this, it might have been clear that the U.S. need not get involved at all in Vietnam. The outcome would have likely been the same—a unified Vietnam under Hanoi's leadership. The difference? Millions of people would been spared, including nearly 60,000 Americans killed in action.
- *Missed Opportunities.* You recall that you initiated many probes of Hanoi between 1965 and 1967, each of which was a serious attempt, in your mind, to find a way to end the killing and move to a negotiated settlement. All of them failed.

Hanoi blamed it on you and your colleagues, for refusing to agree to stop the bombing *first*, before talks could begin. But you learn from well-placed sources in Hanoi of detailed plans by the North Vietnamese government to respond favorably to an American overture, *if* you and your colleagues would only stop the bombing first. These sources say their government could not, as the weaker nation, risk being thought weak, ready to cave into U.S. pressure. So the war went on, year after year, unnecessarily. The Vietnamese communists had a name for the bombing campaign against North Vietnam: "the war of destruction," so-called because its purpose, as they understood it, was simply and only to destroy North Vietnam, its communist government, and most or all of its people, if necessary. In effect, the basic assumption was that the U.S. was willing to commit *genocide* against North Vietnam, if that's what it took to "win," a motive so repugnant, so unthinkable, that you might be inclined to regard statements to that effect as simple propaganda. Now, however, you can begin to see the logic behind their name for that war. What other purpose could the U.S. have, other than "destruction?" You remember the answers you gave at the time—stopping communists; preserving noncommunists; protecting the "Free World," etc. But these motives begin to ring very hollow, once you become convinced that you were mistaken in the ways just listed.

[You are free now to assume your actual identity.] Do you see now why former decision-makers and scholars may have very different reactions to the process of critical oral history, as it unfolds? As scholars, we are pleased to have the information, and the documentation and oral testimony supporting it, in the above listing of the errors of Robert McNamara. But if you were McNamara wouldn't you have to factor in the cost of obtaining such knowledge? In other words, extending empathy to others can be done cheaply by scholars, who had no significant responsibilities in the events in question. But for people like McNamara, empathizing with your former enemy means that you "think it possible you may be mistaken," and that your enemies may have been justified to think and act as they did, in many cases. Which means, of course, that you—

Robert McNamara, say—are in some significant measure responsible for events that, at the time, you were inclined to attribute more
or less completely to *them*. What's more, this insight has been obtained in a setting which, in one form or another, will yield public
knowledge of what transpired. To engage in empathy of this sort,
and to do so over and over again, is what we call courage. And, in
critical oral history, empathy is the pivot upon which everything
turns.

"The Fog of War's" Tale of Two Warriors

On Wednesday, March 19, 2003, James Wolfensohn, president of
the World Bank, hosted a dinner for Robert S. McNamara, who
had served as the Bank's president from 1968 to 1981. Testimonials
were given by many people who had worked with McNamara at the
World Bank—brief speeches emphasizing his determination to
move the Bank's focus from building public and private infrastructure in the developing world, toward a concern for the (often)
abysmal state of its public health, and its improvement. Although
we had worked with Bob McNamara for nearly twenty years—on
scholarly projects on the Cuban missile crisis and the Vietnam
War—we knew relatively little about his tenure at the World Bank,
which in fact lasted nearly twice as long as his service in the
Kennedy and Johnson administrations as secretary of defense
(1961 to 1968). As is typical of such occasions, the praise for the
guest of honor was lavish and abundant; jokes told at his expense
evoked laughter, whether or not they were funny; and a congenial
evening was had by all present, including ourselves.

To us, however, the most memorable comment about McNamara that evening was not given by a present or former World Bank
employee. It was instead a simple, short declarative sentence spo-
ken by Theodore C. Sorensen, President John F. Kennedy's Special
Counsel, who had served with McNamara in the Kennedy administration. Sorensen asked rhetorically: how and why does Bob McNamara, a man eighty-six years old, still travel the world, working
harder than most people half his age or even younger, on the problems that most concern him? What drives him to continue to seek
to reduce the danger of both conventional and nuclear war, as well

as continuing to tackle other aspects of U.S. foreign and defense policy?

Sorensen's explanation for McNamara's commitment and energy was this: "Bob McNamara," he said, "is a *warrior!*" Like many who have worked with McNamara, we had posed versions of Sorensen's rhetorical questions to ourselves on countless occasions, but without ever arriving at a satisfactory answer. One of our favorite ways of shrugging off the question had been simply to assert the obvious: "Bob McNamara is a mutant—he is just different from everyone else!" While demonstrably true, this merely restated the obvious. After Sorensen's remark, however, we looked at one another, smiling from Sorensen's insight. A "warrior." Of course. McNamara is as fierce and determined and controversial now, as a "warrior" for peace, as he was in the 1960s, when he was President Lyndon Johnson's principal executive officer for the escalation of the U.S. war in Vietnam—a war, McNamara wrote in 1995 to a storm of critical controversy, that he now believes was "wrong, terribly wrong."[18]

In "The Fog of War," both warriors-McNamara the war-making lieutenant colonel in World War II and defense secretary in Vietnam, and McNamara the peace-seeking "retiree"—appear in the film, via archival footage from decades ago, juxtaposed with the interviews McNamara gave to Morris in 2001 and 2002. The journey McNamara has made as a warrior (from one who wages war, to one who seeks peace) places his own fallibility, even his culpability, at the center of his quest. He has admitted fundamental mistakes, drawn lessons, and attempted to apply them to the dangerous world of the 21st century. His "reward" has been attacks from the political left, the right and the center, especially (but not only) on issues related to the Vietnam War, which remains a deep wound in the American psyche that (some critics of McNamara claim) he has reopened via his very public, very personal, recent writing on Vietnam and its lessons.[19]

Above all, this journey, which we have witnessed at close range since we began working with him in 1984, has been a journey of self-discovery for Robert McNamara. In "The Fog of War," his journey is presented to the viewer in a phenomenally compact 107 minutes of words and images that powerfully convey in outline the path traveled by McNamara. The film moves at the rate of a little more than one minute of film for every year of his long, eventful life, beginning with his witnessing the end of the First World War, at age two and a half, down to the present. (He was eighty-five when Morris interviewed him.)

This is not the place for psychological speculation about what this journey of "self-discovery" means personally to McNamara. But perhaps something of what he has been through can be gleaned from the recent commentary by British scholar Philip Dunn on the ancient Chinese treatise on strategy, Sun Tzu's *The Art of War*, regarded by many as the most insightful book ever written on the subject. According to Dunn's reading of Sun Tzu, avoiding war altogether must be the primary objective. It is in this sense that Sorensen's remark about McNamara being a "warrior" for peace is especially apt. According to Dunn:

> The peaceful warrior learns first about himself. Before all else, self-knowledge must be found, for this brings an appreciation of sensitivity and vulnerability. When you know yourself, you are automatically sensitive and vulnerable—there is no other way. When you do not know yourself, you are insensitive and living in the false belief of invulnerability—an entirely unnatural state that sooner or later brings conflict, disease and pain. . . .
>
> It is impossible to know anything real unless you have known yourself. And the only way to know yourself is to live a life of vulnerability and openness to possibilities. Don't live in a closed cell. Don't hide yourself behind your mind. Come out.[20]

Has any former high-ranking official ever "come out" to the extent that McNamara has? Has any former official ever made himself more vulnerable to criticism? We doubt it. He has instead become a "peaceful warrior" in Sun Tzu's sense of the term.

We hardly need add that McNamara's path of self-discovery bears little resemblance to any of the well-known monastic routes to self-knowledge, involving long periods of solitary contemplation and other forms of isolation from the world of war and politics. Rather, McNamara's trajectory involves a comprehensive effort on his part to engage as fully as possible with the historical reality as it was—as he formerly helped to shape it; and with the dynamic reality that is emerging daily in the dangerous and uncertain world of the 21st century. He has accomplished this via his participation in the various *critical oral history* projects alluded to in this "Prologue," and discussed in more detail throughout this book.

In essence, "The Fog of War" represents the culmination of McNamara's effort to understand the great events in which he was involved, to identify mistakes—especially his own mistakes—to draw lessons from the mistakes, and to apply the lessons so as to lower the odds of their occurring again. The film, we believe, especially when combined with this book, permits viewers/readers a considerable degree of vicarious participation in McNamara's extraordinary journey. You are thus encouraged to reach your own conclusions regarding the three seminal 20th-century events dealt with in the film and in this book: the bombing of Japan in the Second World War, the Cuban missile crisis, and the U.S. war in Vietnam.

*   *   *

At the conclusion of the March 19, 2003, World Bank testimonial, Bank President James Wolfensohn returned unexpectedly to the podium, after Bob McNamara had thanked the speakers for the generosity of their comments. To a suddenly hushed audience, Wolfensohn announced that the U.S. invasion of Iraq had begun earlier in the evening, during dinner—and that he had not mentioned it earlier in order to avoid the interruption of the happy occasion with such news. Seldom has a celebratory dinner ended on so somber a note. Yet the invasion of Iraq, initiating a war and occupation so reminiscent in the minds of many to the U.S. involvement in Vietnam a generation earlier, only reinforced in our own minds the need to find ways to create more "peaceful warriors," vicariously, via an examination of McNamara's journey.[21] "The Fog of War"—the film and this book—represents efforts toward that end.

The need for such a project seems to us only to have increased since March 19, 2003. As we write this "Prologue," on December 28, 2004, at least 1,324 American soldiers, and perhaps as many as 100,000 Iraqis (mainly women and children), have died as a result of the war.[22] Richard Horton, editor of *The Lancet*, the preeminent British medical journal that published the study of Iraqi casualties, concludes his introductory editorial this way: "The evidence that we publish today must change heads as well as pierce hearts."[23] This has long been the objective of McNamara, the peaceful warrior. It was Errol Morris' overriding objective in making "The Fog of War." It is ours as well, in writing this book.

"In the Cuban Missile Crisis, at the end, I think we did put ourselves in the skin of the Soviets. In the case of Vietnam, we didn't know them well enough to empathize."

CHAPTER 1

LESSON ONE:
"Empathize with Your Enemy"

That's what I call empathy. We must try to put ourselves inside their skin and look at us through their eyes, just to understand the thoughts that lie behind their decisions and their actions.

. . .

In the Cuban missile crisis, at the end, I think we did put ourselves in the skin of the Soviets. In the case of Vietnam, we didn't know them well enough to empathize. And there was total misunderstanding as a result. They believed that we had simply replaced the French as a colonial power, and we were seeking to subject South and North Vietnam to our colonial interests, which was absolutely absurd. And we, we saw Vietnam as an element of the Cold War. Not what they saw it as: a civil war.

ROBERT S. McNAMARA, in "The Fog of War."

Empathy has nothing to do with sympathy, *with which it is often confused. This point has been made by Robert McNamara, and it is a central claim made by Ralph K. White, the foremost exponent of the deployment of empathy in international affairs. White, in addition to having the credentials of both a political scientist and a psychologist, also had a successful career in government, as an official with the U.S. Information Agency. White's work has had a considerable impact on McNamara's views of two historical events in which he played a pivotal role—the Cuban missile crisis and the escalation of the Vietnam War. According to Ralph White:*

> Empathy is the *great* corrective for all forms of war-promoting misperception. . . . It [means] simply understanding the thoughts and feelings of others. It is distinguished from sympathy, which is defined as feeling with others. Empathy with opponents is therefore psychologically possible even when a conflict is so intense that sympathy is out of the question. . . . We are not talking about warmth or approval, and certainly not about agreeing with, or siding with, but only about realistic understanding.[1]

White goes on to explain the implementation of empathy in the cause of reducing the risk of conflict:

> How can empathy be achieved? It means jumping in imagination into another person's skin, . . . imagining how you might feel about what you saw. It means *being* the other person, at least for a while, and postponing skeptical analysis until later. . . . Most of all it means trying to look at one's own group's behavior honestly, as it might appear when seen through the other's eyes, recognizing that his eyes are almost certainly jaundiced, but recognizing also that he has the advantage of not seeing our group's behavior through the rose-colored glasses that we ourselves normally wear. He may have grounds for distrust, fear, and anger that we have not permitted ourselves to see. That is the point where honesty comes in. An honest look at the other implies an honest look at oneself.[2]

White identified three critical mistakes in foreign policy making that prevent empathy from occurring: (1) not seeing an opponent's longing for peace, (2) not seeing an opponent's fear of being attacked, and (3) not seeing an opponent's understandable anger.[3]

In "The Fog of War," Robert McNamara applies the concept of empathy to this question: why, on the one hand, were he and his colleagues in the Kennedy administration able to escape the Cuban missile crisis without a catastrophic war; while, on the other hand, virtually the same group of advisers in the Kennedy and Johnson administrations led the U.S. into the worst foreign policy disaster in American history—the war in Vietnam? His answer? In the missile crisis, leaders in Washington empathized successfully with Nikita Khrushchev and his colleagues in Moscow—as he says, "we did put ourselves in the skin of the Soviets." In regard to Vietnam, however, he says in the film, "we didn't know them [the Vietnamese communists] well enough to empathize." As a result, Kennedy was able, with the crucial assistance of Soviet specialist Llewellyn Thompson, to offer Khrushchev a deal he could accept. Yet despite the efforts of several presidents, and many (otherwise) able advisers, U.S. leaders appear not even to have fathomed the basic assumptions of their Vietnamese adversary, at least not until the war had escalated to catastrophic proportions.

Below are selections from declassified documents and from retrospective dialogues that buttress and expand on McNamara's fundamental emphasis on empathy in the "The Fog of War." We believe these materials fully justify the decision by Errol Morris to make "empathize with your enemy" lesson number one in "The Fog of War."

THE CUBAN MISSILE CRISIS
Documents

President Kennedy is angry at Khrushchev and at his own advisers. The Soviet leader has sent him, on October 26, a private letter with terms of a deal that could end the standoff: the U.S. would pledge not to invade Cuba; the Soviets would pledge to remove the missiles from Cuba. But before he can respond, another letter comes in from Khrushchev, this one a public announcement, adding a contingency to the deal previously proposed: that the U.S. also pledge to remove NATO missiles from Turkey. Kennedy's advisers have told him that the Turks, staunch NATO allies, will be furious if the removal of NATO missiles in Turkey were to become part of the deal. Kennedy, however, tells his advisers point blank that, because of the NATO missiles in

Turkey, that country will likely be a target in any Soviet retaliation for a U.S. attack on the Soviet missiles in Cuba. It is clear that, in Kennedy's mind, attacks on both Soviet missiles in Cuba and NATO missiles in Turkey are likely if the crisis is not resolved quickly.

[Transcript of a secret tape recording of a meeting of President Kennedy and his advisers, 10:00 AM, Saturday, October 27, 1962, Cabinet Room.][4]

Dean Rusk [Secretary of State]: We haven't talked with the Turks. The Turks have talked with us—in NATO.

President Kennedy: Well, have we gone to the Turkish government before this came out this week? I've talked about it now for a week. Have we had any conversations in Turkey, with the Turks?

Rusk: We've asked [Ambassador to NATO, Thomas] Finletter and [Ambassador to Turkey, Raymond] Hare to give us their judgments on it. We've not actually talked with the Turks.

George Ball [Undersecretary of State]: We did it on a basis where, if we talked to the Turks, I mean, this would be an extremely unsettling business.

President Kennedy: Well, *this* is unsettling *now*, George, because he's got us in a pretty good spot here. Because most people would regard this as not an unreasonable proposal. I'll just tell you that. In fact, in many ways—

McGeorge Bundy [National Security Adviser]: But what *most* people, Mr. President?

President Kennedy: I think you're going to find it very difficult to explain why we are going to take hostile military action in Cuba, against these sites, what we've been thinking about. [I'm] saying that he's saying: "If you'll get yours out of Turkey, we'll get ours out of Cuba." I think we've got a very touchy point here.

Bundy: I don't see why we pick that track when he's offered us the other track within the last 24 hours. You think the public one is serious?

President Kennedy: I think you have to assume that this is their new and latest position, and it's a public one.

The following excerpt from Kennedy's secret audio tapes of the missile

Thompson:

I don't agree Mr. President.

crisis deliberations illuminates one of the most momentous and piv-otal decision points in this most dangerous crisis of the Cold War. Kennedy believes the public letter must be Khrushchev's official posi-tion. He would like to respond only to the first (private) letter, which omitted mention of the Turkish missiles. But as a politician, he is convinced that a leader's public pronouncement carries more weight than a private feeler. But then Llewellyn ("Tommy") Thompson dis-agrees with the president and challenges him to go ahead and re-spond to the first (private) letter, more or less as if the second (public) letter did not exist. It is difficult to say which act is more timely or courageous: Thompson's, in opposing his president, or Kennedy's in accepting the counterintuitive advice of his adviser.

[Transcript of a secret tape recording of a meeting of President Kennedy and his advisers, 4:00 PM, Saturday October 27, 1962, Cabinet Room.][5]

President Kennedy: It seems to me we ought to—to be reason-able. We're not going to get these weapons out of Cuba, proba-bly, anyway. But I mean—by negotiation. We're going to have to take our weapons out of Turkey. I don't think there's any doubt he's not going to, now that he made that public.

Tommy, he's not going to take them out of Cuba if we—

Llewellyn Thompson: I don't agree, Mr. President. I think there's still a chance that we can get this line going.

President Kennedy: That he'll back down?

Thompson: Well, because he's already got this other proposal which he put forward [to remove missiles for a pledge not to invade Cuba].

President Kennedy: Now, this other public one, it seems to me, has become their public position, hasn't it?

Thompson: This may be just pressure on us. I mean to accept the other, I mean so far—we'd accepted non-invasion of Cuba. [Unclear group discussion.]

Thompson: The important thing for Khrushchev, it seems to me, is to be able to say: "I saved Cuba. I stopped an invasion."
And he can get away with this if he wants to, and he's had a go at this Turkey thing, and that we'll discuss later. And then, in that discussion, he will probably take—

President Kennedy: All right. . . .

McNamara says in "The Fog of War" that Khrushchev's letter to Kennedy of October 26, 1962, seemed at the time to have been "written by a man who was either drunk, or under tremendous stress." But in retrospect, we can see that the letter is also one of the most profound statements in the nuclear age of the awful power of nuclear weapons, and the terrible responsibilities of those who have custody of them.[6] It is reported that when Kennedy read this letter late on October 26, he concluded that Khrushchev understood their mutual predicament in the same way he (Kennedy) did—they must not let a war of any kind break out under these circumstances, for fear of escalation to catastrophic nuclear war.[7] In other words, Khrushchev, like himself, was truly terrified, as befitted someone who understood what could happen if together they did not, as Khrushchev put it, "display statesmanlike wisdom."

[Letter from Nikita Khrushchev to John F. Kennedy, October 26, 1962.][8]

Dear Mr. President:

I can see, Mr. President, that you also are not without a sense of anxiety for the fate of the world, not without an understanding and correct assessment of the nature of modern warfare and what war entails. What good would a war do you? . . . Should war break out, it would not be in our power to contain or stop it, for such is the logic of war. I have taken part in two wars, and I know that war ends only when it has rolled through cities and villages, sowing death and destruction everywhere.

. . .

I do not know whether you can understand me and believe me. But I wish you would believe yourself and agree that one should not give way to one's passions; that one should be master of them. And what direction are events taking now? If you begin stopping vessels it would be piracy, as you yourself know. If we should start doing this to your ships you would be just as indignant as we and the whole world are now indignant. Such actions cannot be interpreted otherwise, because lawlessness cannot be legalized. Were this allowed to happen, then there would be no peace; nor would there be peaceful coexistence. Then we would be forced to take the necessary measures of a defensive nature which would protect our interests in accordance with international law. Why do this? What would it all lead to?

. . .

If people do not display wisdom, they will eventually reach the point where they will clash, like blind moles, and then mutual annihilation will commence.

Let us therefore display statesmanlike wisdom. I propose: we, for our part, will declare that our ships bound for Cuba are not carrying any armaments. You will declare that the United States will not invade Cuba with its troops and will not support any other forces which might intend to invade Cuba. Then the necessity for the presence of our military specialists in Cuba will be obviated.

. . .

These, Mr. President, are my thoughts, which, if you should agree to them, could put an end to the tense situation which is disturbing all peoples.

These thoughts are governed by a sincere desire to alleviate the situation and remove the threat of war.

Respectfully,

N. Khrushchev

In "The Fog of War," Robert McNamara reports that, at the time, the following letter from Khrushchev seemed to have been written "by a bunch of hard liners." It certainly lacks the almost poetic, tragic and urgent sense conveyed in the letter of the previous evening. Moreover, in proposing to make the Turkish missiles part of the deal, Khrushchev had unwittingly thrust upon Kennedy the possibility of a "Turkish missile crisis," to accompany the Cuban missile crisis. In addition, by juxtaposing the Turkish missiles pointed at the Soviet Union on its southern border with Cuban missiles pointed at the U.S. on its southern border, Kennedy felt that Khrushchev had scored points on the moral dimension, as judged by the court of world opinion. After all, wouldn't people say what was permissible for one superpower to do was permissible for the other?[9]

[Letter from Nikita Khrushchev to John F. Kennedy, October 27, 1962.][10]

Dear Mr. President:

. . .

I think it would be possible to end the controversy quickly and normalize the situation, and then the people could breathe more easily, considering that statesmen charged with responsibility are of sober mind and have an awareness of their responsibility, combined with the ability to solve complex questions, and not bring things to a military catastrophe.

I therefore make this proposal: we are willing to remove from Cuba the means which you regard as offensive. We are willing to carry this out and to make this pledge in the United Nations. Your representatives will make a declaration to the effect that the United States, for its part, considering the uneasiness and anxiety of the Soviet State, will remove its analogous means from Turkey. . . . Of course, the permission of the governments of Cuba and of Turkey is necessary for the entry into those countries of these representatives, and for the inspection of the fulfillment of the pledge made by each side. . . . The Soviet government gives a solemn promise to respect the inviolability of the borders and sovereignty of Turkey. . . . The United States government will make a similar statement within the framework of the Security Council regarding Cuba.

. . .

These are my proposals, Mr. President.

Respectfully yours,

N. Khrushchev

The following is Kennedy's response to the first private letter written, as Llewellyn ("Tommy") Thompson had recommended, as if the second one was never received. This maneuver has come to be known as the "Trollope ploy," so named by Kennedy's national security adviser, McGeorge Bundy. "Trollope ploy" refers to the British Victorian novelist, Anthony Trollope, whose stories are replete with young maidens in search of husbands, and who are often impelled to say "yes" to what they understand (often erroneously) to be hints of offers of marriage from eligible bachelors. Likewise, in this letter, Kennedy says "yes" to the very first offer of Khrushchev's, hoping the Soviet leader is desperate enough to settle for the deal, even though he would obviously rather have the Turkish missiles removed as well. (In fact, the Turkish missiles were part of the eventual agreement, though the pledge of their removal was kept secret, so as not to offend the Turks or other NATO allies. The missiles were dismantled the following spring, and replaced in the NATO arsenal by nuclear missiles aboard the nuclear-powered Polaris submarines, which had recently become available to U.S. and NATO forces.)

[Letter from John F. Kennedy to Nikita Khrushchev, October 27, 1962.][11]

Dear Mr. Chairman:

I have read your letter of October 26 with care and welcomed the statement of your desire to seek a prompt solution to the problem. The first thing that needs to be done, however, is for work to cease on offensive missile bases in Cuba and for all weapons systems in Cuba capable of offensive use to be rendered inoperable, under effective United Nations arrangements.

Assuming this is done promptly, I have given my representatives in New York instructions that will permit them to work out this week and—in cooperation with the Acting Secretary General [of the UN, the Burmese diplomat, U Thant] and your representative—an arrangement for a permanent solution to the Cuban problem along the lines suggested in your letter of October 26. As I read your letter, the key elements of your proposals—which seem generally acceptable as I understand them—are as follows:

1. You would agree to remove these weapons systems from Cuba under appropriate United Nations observation and supervision; and undertake, with suitable safeguards, to halt the further introduction of such weapons systems into Cuba.

2. We, on our part, would agree—upon the establishment of adequate arrangements through the United Nations to ensure the carrying out and continuation of these commitments—(a) to remove promptly the quarantine measures now in effect and (b) to give assurances against an invasion of Cuba; and I am confident that other nations of the Western Hemisphere would be prepared to do likewise.

If you will give your representative similar instructions, there is no reason why we should not be able to complete these arrangements and announce them to the world within a couple of days.

. . .

. . . I hope we can agree quickly along the lines in this letter and in your letter of October 26.

John F. Kennedy

Khrushchev was, in fact, as desperate for a way out of the crisis as any maiden in a Trollope novel might be for a husband. Events were beginning to spin out of control. For example, an American U-2 spy plane was shot down over Cuba on October 27, and the pilot killed. The U.S. leadership was convinced that Khrushchev had ordered the shootdown. But Khrushchev himself was mystified by the event, because he knew he hadn't ordered it, but he also knew the Americans would assume he had, and thus the crisis might reach the boiling point, or even beyond. Also, Khrushchev knew, as did Kennedy, that the U.S. nuclear forces were far superior to the Soviet forces. (The ratio of U.S. nuclear warheads to those of the Soviets was approxi-

mately 17–1 at the time of the crisis.) Khrushchev also knew (though Kennedy did not) that some Soviet nuclear warheads had reached Cuba before the quarantine was in place. This raised the risk of a Soviet nuclear response in Cuba to an American attack. The U.S. and the Soviet Union would then be in a nuclear war. Where would it stop? Nobody knew. Thus did Khrushchev reply at once to Kennedy's offer—not via the usual channels, but over Radio Moscow, in a public broadcast, in Russian, which took only minutes to translate. (In those days, sending messages through official channels could take as long as twelve hours or more.) On the morning of Sunday, October 28, the following message was received in Washington by a greatly relieved group of nearly—exhausted leaders in the White House.

[Communique from Nikita Khrushchev to John F. Kennedy, October 28, 1962, broadcast over Radio Moscow.][12]

Esteemed Mr. President:

I have received your message of October 27, 1962. I express my satisfaction and gratitude for the sense of proportion and understanding of the responsibility borne by you at present for the preservation of peace throughout the world which you have shown. I very well understand your anxiety and the anxiety of the United States people in connection with the fact that the weapons which you describe as "offensive" are not. . . . Both you and I understand what kind of weapons they are.

In order to complete with greater speed the liquidation of the conflict dangerous to the cause of peace, to give confidence to all people longing for peace, and to calm the American people, who I am certain want peace as much as the people of the Soviet Union, the Soviet government, in addition to previously issued instructions on the cessation of further work at building sites for the weapons, has issued a new order on the dismantling of the weapons which you describe as "offensive," and their crating and return to the Soviet Union.

. . .

I regard with respect and trust your statement in your message of October 27, 1962 that no attack will be made on Cuba—that no invasion will take place—not only by the United States, but also by other countries of the Western Hemisphere, as your message pointed out.

. . .

In this way, if one is to rely on your assurances which you have made and on our orders to dismantle, then all necessary conditions for liquidation of the conflict which has arisen appear to exist.

. . .

With respect for you, Khrushchev,
October 28, 1962

Kennedy's response is to the point: he is delighted that the intense phase of the crisis seems to be abating. But it is also possible to see in Kennedy's response a glimpse of the future, of the direction in which he wishes to take the relationship between the superpowers, and the world at large, toward nuclear disarmament—even, it seems in this moment of relief and hopefulness, toward a possible end of the conditions that have created the Cold War itself.

[Letter from John F. Kennedy to Nikita Khrushchev, October 28, 1962.][13]

Mr. Chairman:

I am replying at once to your broadcast message of October twenty-eight even though the official text has not yet reached me because of the great importance I attach to moving forward promptly to the settlement of the Cuban crisis. I think that you and I, with our heavy responsibilities for the maintenance of peace, were aware that developments were approaching a point where events could have become unmanageable. So I welcome this message and consider it an important contribution to peace.

. . .

Both of our countries have great unfinished tasks and I know that your people as well as those of the United States can ask for nothing better than to pursue them free from the fear of war. Modern science and technology have given us the possibility of making labor fruitful beyond anything that could have been dreamed of a few decades ago.

I agree with you that we must devote urgent attention to the problem of disarmament, as it relates to the whole world and also to critical areas. Perhaps now, as we step back from danger, we can together make real progress in this vital field. I think we should give priority to questions relating to proliferation of nuclear weapons, on earth, and in outer space, and to the great effort for a nuclear test ban. But we should also work hard to see if wider measures of disarmament can be agreed and put into operation at an early date. The United States government will be prepared to discuss these questions urgently, and in a constructive spirit, at Geneva or elsewhere.

John F. Kennedy

THE CUBAN MISSILE CRISIS
Dialogues

For a quarter century after the Cuban missile crisis, U.S. scholars still had no clear idea why Nikita Khrushchev would have taken such a gargantuan risk, in deploying Soviet strategic nuclear missiles in Cuba, a mere ninety miles south of Key West, Florida. The feeling among Western historians was that only a desperate leader would resort to such a scheme—someone who felt his back was to the wall. The vast majority had concluded that Khrushchev must have been driven by the fear of falling even further behind in the nuclear arms race, and that he could score both strategic and psychological points against a (presumably) shocked Kennedy administration if he could get away with such a deployment.

But in October 1987, on the 25th anniversary of the crisis, former members of the Kennedy administration learned that Khrushchev had another motive, one that was perhaps even more powerful than the urge to try to catch up quickly with the U.S. in nuclear forces. That motive was the fear of an imminent U.S. invasion of Cuba, the overthrow of the Cuban government of a new and popular Soviet ally, Fidel Castro, and the replacement by a hand-picked group of Cuban exiles waiting in Miami for orders from their U.S. sponsor, the CIA. Former Defense Secretary Robert McNamara, former National Security Adviser McGeorge Bundy, and former Kennedy Special Counsel Theodore C. Sorensen agreed to participate in a conference held in Cambridge, Massachusetts, as did several knowledgeable Soviets.

The former U.S. officials are told that Moscow had been convinced that a U.S. invasion of Cuba was virtually inevitable and, by the spring and summer of 1962, imminent. Sergo Mikoyan, a former aide to his father Anastas Mikoyan, the first deputy premier under Khrushchev, and Georgy Shakhnazarov, a top-level official under the (then) Soviet Chairman Mikhail Gorbachev, tell their U.S. interlocutors that Soviet leaders in 1962, especially Khrushchev, felt that the rapid, clandestine and deceptive deployment of Soviet missiles in Cuba seemed the only way to avert a U.S. overthrow of the Castro regime. The former Kennedy administration officials are stunned by this revelation, principally because they recall vividly that after the Bay of Pigs fiasco of April 1961, Kennedy had ruled out any effort to overthrow Castro via U.S. military intervention.

[A discussion in Cambridge, Massachusetts, October 1987, between U.S. and Soviet policymakers, and scholars of the Cuban missile crisis.][14]

Sergo Mikoyan: I think all the [Soviet] participants in the discussion agreed that the United States was preparing for the liquidation of the Castro regime . . . there were invasion plans.

Joseph S. Nye, Jr. [Moderator]. There was also a covert operation at the time code-named "Mongoose," whose aim was to destablize or overthrow the Castro regime. I don't believe the public knew about it, but the Soviets certainly would have. Mac?

McGeorge Bundy: I remember that in the fall of '62 there was great frustration about Cuba and considerable confusion about what we should do. In my opinion, covert action is a psychological salve for inaction. We had no intention to invade Cuba, but it seems from what you say there was a very solid picture in Moscow that we were going to do something more than we were.

Robert S. McNamara: Let me say we had no plan to invade Cuba, and I would have opposed the idea strongly if it ever came up.

Theodore C. Sorensen: Well, that's the wrong word.

McNamara: Okay, we had no intent.

Georgy Shakhnazarov: But there were subversive actions.

McNamara: That's my point. We thought those covert operations were terribly ineffective, and you thought they were ominous. We saw them very differently.

Nye: That's an important point for our discussion of lessons. Small

actions can be misperceived in important ways, with dispropor-
tionate consequences.

McNamara: That's absolutely right. I can assure you that there
was no intent in the White House or in the Pentagon—at least
in my Pentagon—to overthrow Castro by force. But if I were on
your side, I'd have thought otherwise. I can very easily imagine
estimating that an invasion was imminent.

Shakhnazarov: I do not wish to turn the meeting into reciprocal
accusation. I am inclined to believe you. . . .

*In January 1989, at a conference in Moscow, an epochal confronta-
tion occurred, due to the first-ever participation of a high-level Cuban
delegation in the ongoing U.S.-Soviet discussions of the Cuban missile
crisis. The Cuban group was led by Jorge Risquet, a volatile cigar-
smoking revolutionary, who was then the Cuban Politburo member responsible for Cuba's relations with socialist countries, including of
course the Soviet Union. Just prior to the conference, the Cubans had
acquired from the U.S. sponsors of the conference the just-declassified
plans for Operation MONGOOSE, the program of covert operations
against Cuba, carried out by Cuban exiles in the employ of the CIA.*

*In reading over the documents as the conference is about to begin,
Robert McNamara sees clearly why the Cubans (and the Soviets) believed that a U.S. invasion of Cuba was imminent. At the outset of
the meeting, McNamara asks to speak first, so that he can address
preemptively the issue he knows will be foremost on the minds of the
members of the Cuban delegation: the planning for a U.S. invasion
of Cuba, and the role of Operation MONGOOSE in that planning.
McNamara's surprising intervention elicits an unexpectedly agreeable
response from the fiery Jorge Risquet.*

**[A discussion in Moscow, USSR, in January 1989 with policymakers and
scholars of the missile crisis from the U.S., USSR and Cuba.][15]**

Robert S. McNamara: I want to state quite frankly that with hindsight, if I had been a Cuban leader, I think I might have expected a U.S. invasion. Why? Because the U.S. had carried out
what I have referred to publicly as a debacle-the Bay of Pigs invasion—we'd carried it out in the sense that we'd supported it.
We did not support it militarily—and I think this should be rec-

ognized and emphasized, as it was specifically the decision of President Kennedy *not* to support it with the use of U.S. military force—but in any event we'd carried it out, and after the debacle, there were many voices in the United States that said the error was not in approving the Bay of Pigs operation; the error was in the failure to support it with military force, the implication being that at some point in the future, force would be applied. . . . There were [also] covert operations. The Cubans knew that. There were covert operations extending over a long period of time . . . from the late 1950s into the period we're discussing, the summer and fall of 1962 . . . [Finally] there were important voices in the United States—important leaders in the Senate, important leaders of our House—who were calling for an invasion of Cuba.

The second point I want to make—and I think it shows the degree of misperception that can exist in the nuclear age, the danger to all of us—it was a misperception on the part of the Cubans and Soviets . . . I can state this categorically, without qualification, and with the certainty that I am speaking not only of my own knowledge, but of my understanding—and I think it was complete—of the mind of President Kennedy . . . we had *absolutely no intention* of invading Cuba . . . therefore the Soviet action to install missiles . . . was, I think, based on a misconception—a clearly understandable one, and one that we, in part, were responsible for. I accept that.

. . .

Jorge Risquet: I am amazed at Mr. McNamara's frankness in acknowledging that if he had found himself in the Cubans' shoes, the Cuban side had every right to think that there could be a direct invasion by the Americans.

■

THE VIETNAM WAR
Documents

By early 1967, President Lyndon Johnson and his advisers had deployed a half million Americans in South Vietnam. In addition, the

"In the case of Vietnam, we didn't know them well enough to empathize."

U.S. continued to bomb North Vietnam (the Democratic Republic of Vietnam—the DRV) and suspected routes of the so-called Ho Chi Minh Trail, along which the Hanoi government supplied their allies in the South, the insurgents of the "Vietcong" (the National Liberation Front—NLF), with men and arms. Yet Hanoi refused all overtures from the U.S. for a deal by which the U.S. would cease its bombing of the North, if the Hanoi government stopped supplying the southern insurgents, who were engaged in a bloody struggle against the U.S.-backed government in Saigon. Johnson was aggravated by what he saw as North Vietnamese intransigence, but he was also mystified by it. It was obvious, as he saw it, that the U.S. was inflicting severe damage on North Vietnam—damage which could easily be halted, if only Hanoi would agree to stop supplying the NLF, and come to the negotiating table. Hanoi, however, disdained all U.S. offers from mid-1965 onward. Then unexpectedly on January 28, 1967, the North Vietnamese Foreign Minister, Nguyen Duy Trinh, made this announcement: "It is only after the unconditional cessation of U.S. bombing and all other acts of war against the DRV that there could be talks between the DRV and the U.S."[16]

   To test whether Trinh's statement means that Hanoi is finally willing to come to the negotiating table, Johnson takes the unprecedented *step of sending a personal letter to Hanoi's leader, Ho Chi Minh, with an offer to begin peace talks, as soon as "infiltration" to the South is halted. The letter is sent a little over a week after Nguyen Duy Trinh's announcement. Johnson is anxious to begin peace talks, obviously, but to do so on terms that prevent the Vietnamese communists, both North and South, from taking advantage of any truce to strengthen their position. The letter is a moving testament to Johnson's sincerity in seeking an end to the war, but also to his utter inability to grasp the way the Vietnamese communists understood the conflict.*

[Letter from Lyndon B. Johnson to Ho Chi Minh, February 8, 1967.][17]

Dear Mr. President:

I am writing to you in the hope that the conflict in Vietnam can be brought to an end. That conflict has already taken a heavy toll—in the lives lost, in wounds inflicted, in property destroyed, and in simple human misery. If we fail to find a just and peaceful solution, history will judge us harshly.

. . .

In the past two weeks, I have noted public statements by your government suggesting that you would be prepared to enter into direct bilateral talks with representatives of the U.S. government, provided that we ceased "unconditionally" and permanently our bombing operations against your country and all military actions against it. In the last day, serious and responsible parties have assured us indirectly that this is in fact your proposal.

Let me frankly state that I see two great difficulties with this proposal. In view of your public position, such action on our part would inevitably produce worldwide speculation that discussions were under way and would impair the privacy and secrecy of those discussions. Secondly, there would inevitably be grave concern on our part whether your government would make use of such action by us to improve its military position.

With these problems in mind, I am prepared to move even further towards an ending of hostilities than your government has proposed in either public statements or through private diplomatic channels. I am prepared to order a cessation of bombing against your country and the stopping of further augmentation of U.S. forces in South Vietnam as soon as I am assured that infiltration into South Vietnam by land and sea has stopped. These acts of restraint on both sides would, I believe, make it possible for us to conduct serious and private discussions leading toward an early peace.

. . .

The important thing is to end a conflict that has brought burdens to both our peoples, and above all to the people of South Vietnam. If you have any thoughts about the actions I propose, it would be most important that I receive them as soon as possible.

Sincerely,

Lyndon B. Johnson

Ho Chi Minh responds to Johnson's overture a week later. It is in many respects a remarkable document. For instead of a direct response to Johnson's formulation of the conditions under which the U.S. would be willing to stop bombing North Vietnam, Ho Chi Minh issues forth with a bitter, withering attack on the very idea of negotiating under such conditions. In response to what Johnson no doubt felt was a sincere "peace feeler," he is told by Ho Chi Minh that the Americans should not be in Vietnam, that the Americans are totally responsible for the war, that the Americans are guilty of war crimes and crimes against humanity, and that Hanoi will never negotiate with the U.S. under the conditions laid out by Johnson. Instead, after listing the "crimes" he believes the U.S. has committed in Vietnam, Ho Chi Minh restates the essence of Nguyen Duy Trinh's message of January 28, 1967: Hanoi will agree to negotiate only after the Americans cease all bombing. But Ho Chi Minh also adds: talks can begin only after all U.S. troops leave Vietnam. In other words, the U.S. must surrender unconditionally its basic objective in Vietnam, which is to help insure the survival of an independent, anticommunist South Vietnam. This is the irony of Ho Chi Minh's message: one of the poorest, most backward countries in the world demands the surrender of the world's greatest superpower. No wonder Johnson was mystified.

[Letter from Ho Chi Minh to Lyndon B. Johnson, February 15, 1967.][18]

Lyndon B. Johnson
President of the United States
Your Excellency:

On February 10, 1967, I received your message. Here is my reply:

Vietnam is thousands of miles away from the United States. The Vietnamese people have never done any harm to the United States, but contrary to the commitments made by its representative at the Geneva conference of 1954, the United States government has constantly intervened in Vietnam, has launched and intensified its aggression against South Vietnam for the purpose of prolonging the division of Vietnam and of transforming South Vietnam into an American colony and an American military base. For more than two years now, the American government, using its military planes and its navy has been waging war against the sovereign and independent Democratic Republic of Vietnam [North Vietnam].

The U.S. government has committed war crimes and crimes against peace and against humanity. In South Vietnam, a half million American soldiers and soldiers from satellite countries have used the most inhuman and barbaric methods of warfare such as napalm, chemicals and toxic gases to massacre our compatriots, destroy their crops and level their villages. In North Vietnam, thousands of American planes have rained down hundreds of thousands of tons of bombs destroying towns, villages, factories, roads, bridges, dikes, dams, and even churches, pagodas, hospitals and schools. In your message you seem to deplore the suffering and the destruction in Vietnam. Allow me to ask you: who is perpetrating these awful crimes? It is the American and satellite soldiers. The United States government is entirely responsible for the critical situation in Vietnam.

. . .

The Government of the United States is aggressing against Vietnam. It must stop this aggression as the only way leading toward the reestablishment of peace. The Government of the United States must stop the bombing, definitively and unconditionally, and all other acts of war against the Democratic Republic of Vietnam, withdraw from South Vietnam all its troops and those of its satellites, recognize the National Liberation Front of South Vietnam [the "Vietcong" guerrillas] and allow the people of Vietnam to settle their problems by themselves.

. . .

The Vietnamese people will never yield to force nor agree to talks under the menace of bombs.

Our cause is entirely just. It is our hope that the Government of the United States acts with reason.

Sincerely yours,

Ho Chi Minh

After waiting nearly two months after receiving the letter from Ho Chi Minh, Johnson sends the following, half-hearted invitation to engage in a discussion of how to end the war. In between the lines, it is possible to detect Johnson's supreme perplexity at his exchange with the North Vietnamese leader. In Johnson's view, he had offered to halt the punishing bombing carried out by the U.S.—surely, he thought, this would be welcomed by the North Vietnamese people and government—if only Hanoi would first cease their resupply of the rebel NLF forces in the South. To Johnson, Ho Chi Minh seems positively irrational, even masochistic; while to Ho Chi Minh, Johnson appears to be patronizing and condescending. Meanwhile, the war continues to escalate, and casualties on both sides continue to multiply.

[Letter from Lyndon B. Johnson to Ho Chi Minh, April 6, 1967.][19]

Dear Mr. President:

I was, of course, disappointed that you did not feel able to respond positively to my letter to you of February 8.

. . .

You and I will be judged in history by whether we worked to bring about this result [peace in Vietnam] sooner rather than later.

I venture to address you directly again in the hope that we can find the way to rise above all other considerations and fulfill that common duty. I would be glad to receive your views on these matters.

Sincerely,

Lyndon B. Johnson

[This letter received no reply.]

THE VIETNAM WAR
Dialogues

In June 1997, the first-ever historical conference with high-level former North Vietnamese and U.S. officials was held in Hanoi to discuss the escalation of the American war in Vietnam. That conference initiated a fruitful process, during the course of which a half-dozen other such meetings occurred: in Vietnam, in Italy, and in the U.S. By the second meeting, in February 1998, some of the participants began to shed the formality that sometimes marks international meetings of this sort, as they began to probe one another more deeply about the assumptions and decisions of each side during the escalation of the war in the 1960s. Two such people were the men who came to be referred to by the other participants simply as "the colonels": Col. Quach Hai Luong, the former commander of anti-aircraft batteries protecting Hanoi during the war, and now the deputy director of a military think tank in Hanoi; and Col. Herbert Y. Schandler, a former infantry commander in Vietnam, now a professor in the Department of Grand Strategy at the National Defense University in Washington, DC.

The following conversation takes place in a crowded restaurant in central Hanoi, facilitated by young interpreters from each side: Mr. Le Hong Truong, from the Vietnamese Foreign Ministry, and Ms. Kathy Ngan Ha Le, from Brown University's Watson Institute for International Studies. Note that the informality extends even to a willingness on the part of "the colonels" to be interrupted by their young aides. The vast chasm between the U.S. and North Vietnamese conceptions of the war is painfully obvious throughout.

[A discussion in Hanoi, Vietnam, in February 1998, between two former adversaries—army colonels, one American, one Vietnamese.][20]

> **Col. Herbert Schandler:** Do you think the war might have ended more favorably to the Americans if we had brought in a lot more combat troops, and maybe attempted to take the land war north of the 17th parallel?

Col. Quach Hai Luong: No. In that case, I believe you would have lost the war sooner.

Col. Herbert Schandler: You do? Why?

Col. Quach Hai Luong: Because you would have done exactly what the French had done years before. You would have spread yourselves out widely and put yourselves in an unfavorable position. You see, just as we saw Vietnam as one country, we saw the battlefield as *one and only one* battlefield. Now, the U.S. had tremendous military strength, of course. We could not deny this. If you concentrated your strength in only a few areas—like the French did, at the last, in the three major cities—then you would have an advantage in those areas.

But if the war is a *war of attrition*, which the war between our countries definitely was, and you have to maintain your forces all over the country, then we will last longer than you. We know this. We have not the slightest doubt about this. Military strategists always try to avoid being spread out in a war of attrition, which is, in a way, a Vietnamese type of war.

Col. Herbert Schandler: But suppose we had also concentrated our bombing, early in the war, on critical targets in the North— targets closely associated with your war effort. Would that have made a difference?

Col. Quach Hai Luong: But how would you know where such targets are located? How would you know where to send your pilots?

Col. Herbert Schandler: I think we had reasonably good intelligence from aerial reconnaissance and other sources on where your physical war resources were located. We held back on the bombing primarily because we wanted to try to give you an incentive to halt your assistance to the war in the South. And of course, we were also concerned about the possibility of a Chinese intervention, if the air war in the North was carried too close to the Chinese border.

Col. Quach Hai Luong: I understand that there are Americans who believe that early, massive air strikes on the North would have won the war for the U.S. Maybe this would have been a good strategy for you in World War II, against heavily industrialized countries like Germany and Japan. But when you are bombing an almost totally agricultural country like Vietnam, then your bombs just hit the ground and kill a little rice. In the 1960s, our country ran much like it had run 100 or 500 years before. Not entirely, of course. But even today, we are more than 80% rural.

Col. Herbert Schandler: I understand that. But as you know, our strategy for the air war was based on the belief that we could destroy the will of the people in North Vietnam to continue to support the war in the South.

Mr. Le Hong Truong [*Vietnamese interpreter*]: May I intervene? When I studied in the United States, I took a course in which my professor taught the Vietnam War as a case study. He said that if the U.S. had bombed more aggressively, more actively, the U.S. might have succeeded in breaking the will of the people. So I stood up and had to disagree with him. I had to explain: no, it did not work like that. The more you bombed, the more the people wanted to fight you.

Ms. Kathy Ngan Ha Le [*U.S. interpreter*]: And at the June 1997 conference [in Hanoi], several of the Vietnamese participants compared the U.S. bombing of North Vietnam to the German air raids on London during World War II. They pointed out that the bombing only served to strengthen the resolve of the British to fight.

Col. Quach Hai Luong: You see? These two young people have already answered your question. [Laughter.]

Col. Herbert Schandler: Yes. It bodes well for the future. [Laughter.] Let me ask about the reprisals. The signal we were trying to send to Hanoi was this: if you increase your participation in the war in the South, we will bomb you. So if you want us to stop the bombing, all you have to do is decrease your support for the war in the South. We said that, in effect, *you* controlled the level of bombing by your level of support for the NLF in the South.

Col. Quach Hai Luong: Let me give you our understanding of your "reprisal" bombing you have mentioned. When you were losing in the South, you bombed the North with more intensity. We noticed this. Of course, we had to alter our tactics some-

what, moving things around and so on. But it did not affect our
strategy. You see, we understood *your* message, turned it around,
and used it against you. Every time you bomb the North, we
said, we know we are succeeding in the South. More than this:
every time *you* escalate the bombing in the North, in our understanding, we in the North are forcing you to use resources that
you cannot expend in the South.

Let me put it another way, using your concept of "reprisal."
We said, in a way, that *you* controlled the amount of support we
would give to our friends in the South. How? By the level of
your bombing. By the use of your troops. If you stop bombing
and withdraw your troops, we will be pleased to cease assistance
to the South. But that is the only way you can get us to do it.

Col. Herbert Schandler: It really was a war of attrition all the way
around, wasn't it? We both said "we'll stop if you only quit first."

Col. Quach Hai Luong: Until you quit. Then we stopped.

Col. Herbert Schandler: Yes.

*Robert McNamara began to suspect that the American war in Viet-
nam was unwinnable as early as November 1965, less than six
months after President Johnson decided to send large numbers of
combat troops to assist the Saigon government. Due in large part to
his conviction that the Vietnam conflict had no strictly military solution, McNamara spearheaded many efforts to probe the Hanoi government—to determine the conditions under which the fighting
could be ended, and the warring parties moved to the negotiating
table. Several dozen initiatives of this sort were undertaken between
mid-1965 and the end of 1967. They all ended in failure, however.
In the thirty-year interval between the 1960s and the historic June
1997 conference on the war in Hanoi, McNamara recalls often want-
ing to ask leaders in Hanoi why they spurned offers to negotiate an
end to the war, offers that he, as the U.S. Defense Secretary, authorized and that he obviously regarded as serious. So McNamara, sitting
at last across from his counterparts from Hanoi, leads off with a question he has been waiting three decades to ask: why did the leadership
of North Vietnam not take the U.S. overtures seriously?*

The stage is set for one of the most emotional and pivotal moments of the conference, and in fact of the entire (by now) nearly decade-long research process. Mr. Tran Quang Co, the former First Deputy Foreign Minister, understands McNamara not to be asking a question primarily about the U.S. peace probes, which was his intent, but rather to be subtly accusing the Hanoi leadership of crimes against their own people—of supreme insensitivity to the pain and suffering of the Vietnamese people. Working up to a fever pitch of emotion, Tran Quang Co suddenly switches from Vietnamese into English and accuses McNamara of being "wrong, terribly wrong," a phrase made famous by McNamara himself in his 1995 memoir of the war.[21] Tran Quang Co's intervention ends abruptly, followed by a long and eerie silence.

Mr. Dao Huy Ngoc, who is chairing the session, next adds that the Vietnamese people have suffered from invasions and occupations for more than 4,000 years, but in the end they always prevail. The invaders and occupiers eventually go home, just as the Americans went home. The discussion is concluded by Mr. Nguyen Co Thach, the former Vietnamese Foreign Minister and head of the Vietnamese delegation, who adds that while leaders in Hanoi certainly wanted peace, the Vietnamese have never accepted "peace at any price." (Robert McNamara and Nguyen Co Thach subsequently take up this conversation at lunch following this exchange, an event vividly described by McNamara in "The Fog of War" as the point at which "we almost came to blows.")

[A discussion in Hanoi, Vietnam, in June 1997, between former policymakers from both the U.S. and Vietnamese governments.][22]

Robert S. McNamara: My belief is that there could have been negotiations between the end of '65 and '68 which would have led to a settlement that was roughly the same as the one that eventually occurred, but without that terrible loss of life.

Why didn't it occur? Were you not influenced by the loss of lives? Why didn't it move you toward negotiations? Wasn't there, from your point of view, reason to probe the degree to which you could have "manipulated" the negotiations in ways that

would have been favorable to you? Why didn't you at least probe the degree to which we could have been persuaded to reduce the military pressure, to move toward a unified Vietnam, unaligned. Now in a sense that's what ultimately happened. But at a tremendous cost in human life. Why weren't the negotiations started earlier? I have not heard anything this morning that answers that question.

Tran Quang Co: I would like to answer Mr. McNamara's question. You imply that there was a difference in attitude toward the war between the people of North [Vietnam] and the North Vietnamese leadership. You have this misconception that even though the Vietnamese people were suffering because of the war, still the Vietnamese leadership did not want peace, did not want to proceed to peace.

I must say that this question of Mr. McNamara's has allowed us to better understand the issue. During the coffee break, an American colleague asked me if I have learned anything about the U.S. during the discussions of the past few days. And I responded that I have learned quite a lot. However, thanks to this particular question, I believe we have learned still more about the U.S. We understand better now that the U.S. understands very little about Vietnam. Even now—in this conference—the U.S. understands very little about Vietnam.

When the U.S. bombed the North and brought its troops into the South, well, of course to us these were very negative moves. However, with regards to Vietnam, U.S. aggression did have some positive use. Never before did the people of Vietnam, from top to bottom, unite as they did during the years that the U.S. was bombing us. Never before had Chairman Ho Chi Minh's appeal—that there is nothing more precious than freedom and independence—gone straight to the hearts and minds of the Vietnamese people as at the end of 1966.

But if Mr. McNamara thinks that the North Vietnamese leadership was not concerned about the suffering of the Vietnamese people, with deaths and privation, then he has a huge misconception of Vietnam. That would be [Speaks in English] "wrong, terribly wrong." [Resumes in Vietnamese] There was never any such thing. On the contrary, if at that time we had begun negotiations with the U.S., we would have had to explain to the people why we could negotiate with the U.S., to meet with the U.S., and host the U.S., while bombs fell on us. On the contrary, it must be said that at those moments, when the bombs were falling, there was a complete unity between the leaders and the people. There could be no negotiations under the pressure of the bombing. We have to keep in mind that the war occurred on Vietnamese soil, not in America. Because we suffered a thousand times more than you, we needed and sought peace all the more.

Dao Huy Ngoc: When you look at this question of the sacrifice made by Vietnam in the war, you must also consider the history of our country. When we gained our independence in 1945 we already had four thousand years of history. For one thousand years, we were under the feudalist control of the North [of China]. We had to fight in order to regain our independence. And three thousand years later we had to fight to regain our independence again. Then after independence—after the August Revolution [of 1945, against Japanese occupation]—we had to fight the French for nine years in order to protect our independence. Only then came the fight against the U.S.

So, yes, I would agree with what Mr. McNamara has said. The price that we have had to pay is huge. But it is far larger, and has been going on for much longer, than Mr. McNamara referred to—during the three years of the Vietnam War—1965 to 1968.

Nguyen Co Thach: I ask you: why on earth would Vietnam *not* be serious about peace? The war was on Vietnamese soil. Why would Vietnam not want peace? We wanted the war to end early—as soon as possible—the earlier the better, the less our people would have to suffer. I can assure you, we wanted peace very badly. But not at any price, not if we had to give up what we were fighting for. But still, we wanted—the Vietnamese people wanted—peace.

I wanted to emphasize this because, based on questions from some reporters outside this conference, and some things said by

"There aren't many examples in which you bring two former enemies together, at the highest levels, and discuss what might have been."

the participants here, some may have gotten the impression that Vietnam—that Vietnamese leaders—did not care about the lives of the Vietnamese people—that Vietnam would not think much about those Vietnamese who lost their lives—the many who lost their lives. Let me just say this: those who believe this—if any of you believe this [gestures at U.S. participants]—this is wrong, this is very wrong—a complete misunderstanding of Vietnam.

The Dilemma: Empathy Is Essential But Elusive

Empathy—what it is, how to recognize when it is or is not present in analyzing the affairs of another nation (especially an adversary), how to raise the odds that it is deployed in foreign and defense policy—all this remains as big a mystery as ever. What is becoming clear, however, based on the detailed study of the Cuban missile crisis and the Vietnam War, is that empathy is an absolutely fundamental element in determining success or failure in foreign policymaking. If it is present, as it was *at the end* of the Cuban missile crisis—where there seems to have been just enough of it, just in time—war can be avoided, peace established, understanding achieved. If it is absent, as it was, and to a degree still is absent between Americans and Vietnamese when they are discussing the American war in Vietnam, outcomes are possible that are far worse then even so-called "worst-case" analyses predict.

It is useful to be reminded that no one either wished for, or predicted, anything as dangerous as the Cuban missile crisis eventually became. But due to a three-way empathy void, nuclear war nearly began. Nor would anyone in Washington have believed, even after the introduction of American combat troops into Vietnam in 1965, that a decade later more than two million Vietnamese and more than 58,000 Americans would have died, with the U.S. manifestly losing a war—and losing decisively—for the first time in its history, having been defeated by one of the world's poorest and most backward nations. Lacking empathy, we—as a nation, and as the human race—can therefore expect danger, death, destruction and defeat. With empathy successfully deployed, we lower the odds of such apocalyptic events.

But how do we go about the task of "increasing" empathy? A moment's reflection on family life reveals how difficult it can be to empathize even with individuals who are highly familiar to us. How then do we even conceive the task of increasing empathy among nations, particularly enemies, where empathy is most needed, but where it is also likely to be in shortest supply, and where the dearth of empathy is most likely to lead to conflict, suffering, injustice and war? We state the issue in this stark way not because we have a pat answer—a list of empathy "do's" and nonempathy "don'ts." We don't. We do so rather because we believe empathy has received too little attention from those involved with both the theory and the practice of international relations. Our historical research suggests to us that many, perhaps most, conflicts arise in large part due to misperception, miscalculation and misunderstanding, at the core of which is the inability, or unwillingness, to empathize with an adversary. The world of the 21st century is proving to be a very dangerous and unpredictable place. Will we find a way, as was found in the missile crisis, to inject enough empathy, in time to avoid disaster? Or will the Vietnam War provide the model for what is to come, in which all sides failed to empathize with one another, resulting in the kind of misunderstandings that led to mutual tragedy?

See Appendix B, Lesson One, for further discussion of this dilemma.

". . . the dates when we literally looked down the gun barrel into nuclear war"

CHAPTER 2

Lesson Two: "Rationality Will Not Save Us"

[General Curtis] LeMay believed that ultimately we're going to have to confront the . . . [Soviets] in a conflict with nuclear weapons. And, by God, we better do it when we have greater superiority than we will have in the future.

. . .

It wasn't until January, 1992, in a meeting chaired by Castro in Havana, Cuba, that I learned 162 nuclear warheads, including 90 tactical warheads, were on the island at the time of this critical moment of the crisis. I couldn't believe what I was hearing, . . .

[Fidel Castro] said, number one, I knew the . . . [nuclear warheads] were there. Number two: I would not have recommended to Khrushchev, I did recommend to Khrushchev that they be used. Number three: what would have happened to Cuba? It would have been totally destroyed. That's how close we were.

. . .

I want to say, and this is very important: at the end we lucked out! It was luck that prevented nuclear war. We came that close to nuclear war at the end. [Gestures by bringing thumb and forefinger together until they almost touch.] Rational individuals: Kennedy was rational; Khrushchev was rational; Castro was rational. Rational individuals came that close to the total destruction of their societies. And that danger exists today.

The major lesson of the Cuban missile crisis is this: the indefinite combination of human fallibility and nuclear weapons will destroy nations.

ROBERT S. McNAMARA, in "The Fog of War."

"The Fog of War" *begins with Robert McNamara's account of the Cuban missile crisis, history's closest brush with nuclear holocaust. McNamara's account of his experience is harrowing; the escape from armageddon seemed to him at the time to hang by a thread—especially the wisdom of Kennedy aide Llewellyn Thompson, whose role is dealt with in some detail in "Lesson One: Empathize with Your Enemy." Thompson convinced President John F. Kennedy late in the crisis that Soviet leader Nikita Khrushchev might still be amenable to a diplomatic solution, at a moment when many Kennedy advisers were advocating war. One of the most vehement in urging preemptive war on Kennedy was, as McNamara notes, the Air Force Chief of Staff, Gen. Curtis LeMay. In retrospect, it seems almost miraculous to McNamara that Kennedy followed Thompson's advice and ignored LeMay (and many others who supported LeMay's position, but were less strident in advocating a massive attack on Cuba). Thompson was right. Kennedy was vindicated. Khrushchev removed the missiles. War was avoided.*

But as scary as McNamara's personal narrative of the missile crisis is in "The Fog of War," it pales by comparison to what McNamara says he has learned about the crisis retrospectively, in a seventeen-year research project on the crisis, involving six international conferences, with senior U.S., Russian and Cuban decision-makers participating. (The most recent conferences, in 1992 and 2002, took place in Havana, Cuba, and were chaired by Cuban President Fidel Castro.)[1]

One of the most unsettling moments in the film comes when McNamara delivers his retrospective assessment of October 1962, based on what he has since learned about it via his participation in the missile crisis project: "I want to say—and this is very important—at the end we lucked out! It was luck that prevented nuclear war!" This is without question the most disturbing conclusion McNamara derives from what we now know about the Cuban missile crisis. It seems paradoxical—that it took a stroke of luck to prevent a nuclear war no one wanted—yet it is consistent with the known facts. Rationality alone, it seems, including the quite reasonable abhorrence of nuclear war, may not save us in such situations from nuclear holocaust.[2]

This dire assessment is based on two principal findings: first, the momentum of the crisis was toward something that has come to be called the evolution of situational perversity. This means that being ra-

tional, and being unalterably opposed to the initiation of nuclear war at the outset of the crisis, did not guarantee that such a war would be or could be avoided, after the crisis had begun to escalate—to spin out of control. The situation seemed to become so perverse, in other words, that just a decision or two away, leaders believed they might have to consider moves that could lead directly to disaster. As the crisis evolved, there seemed to the central participants to be fewer and fewer noncatastrophic options. A war that began in this fashion would be called an inadvertent war, in which the evolving crisis itself produced successive situations so shocking, with available options so dreadful, that the formerly unthinkable—initiating a war that could lead straightaway to nuclear war—began to look almost unavoidable.[3]

A second feature of the crisis, which we also have come to appreciate only in retrospect, is the monumental extent to which all three countries, all three leaders, lacked empathy for one another. The mutual misperception and miscalculation was extraordinary. For example, the Soviets and Cubans believed they needed Soviet missiles in Cuba because their intelligence from the Caribbean led them to conclude (understandably but incorrectly) that a U.S. invasion of the island was imminent. The U.S., on the other hand, dismissed growing signs of the possibility of a Soviet deployment of nuclear missiles to Cuba because the Soviets had never before deployed such weapons outside the Soviet Union, and also because it was so obvious (to the Americans, though not to the Soviets) that such a deployment would be totally unacceptable in Washington. And the Soviets believed (though the Cubans tried in vain several times to persuade them that they were wrong) that the missiles could be introduced into Cuba secretly, via a clandestine operation supplemented by a systematic attempt to deceive the U.S. government—a strategy which only inflamed the crisis, once U.S. leaders discovered the scale of the program of lies and deceit.

The documents and dialogues that follow permit the reader a significant degree of insight, we believe, into why Robert McNamara is convinced that, in any future crisis as deep and dire as the Cuban missile crisis, "rationality will not save us." These materials show what the crisis looked and felt like from the "inside" as leaders experienced it, and as they remember it, and thus a way for the rest of us to understand how the unthinkable became almost unavoidable.

Documents

The following conversation takes place three days before President Kennedy's televised October 22 speech which informed the nation and the world about the crisis. Kennedy and his advisers have been discussing three broad options, ever since their first meeting following the discovery of the missile sites in Cuba, on October 16. They are: (1) a "diplomatic option," in which the U.S. would take its case to the UN Security Council, but without first threatening an attack and invasion if diplomacy failed; (2) a "quarantine," or blockade of the island of Cuba, which would prevent Soviet equipment and men from getting to the island, which could be tightened, and which could lead to more decisive military action, if the Soviets still refused to remove the missiles; and (3) an air attack against the missile sites, probably followed by a U.S. invasion and occupation of the island, and the overthrow of the Castro government. The first option had already been rejected, because few believed mere diplomatic action would force the Soviets to remove the missiles. Many also doubted whether the second option, the quarantine, would work, but some (the so-called "doves") favored it because it bought some time, and it could lead to stronger action later. The majority of Kennedy's advisers, however, favored option three: the air strike and invasion.

In this conversation, Kennedy confronts the entire Joint Chiefs of Staff: Gen. Maxwell Taylor, the Chairman; Gen. Earle Wheeler, Army Chief; Gen. Curtis LeMay, Air Force Chief; Gen. David Shoup, Marine Corps Commandant; and Admiral George Anderson, Chief of Naval Operations. They are unanimously in favor of option three: direct military action, as soon as possible. LeMay is asked by Taylor to make the case to the president.

LeMay is blunt, almost rude, with the president. He tells Kennedy there is no realistic alternative to what he calls "direct military action," by which he means the air strike and invasion. None. Kennedy responds by saying he is not unalterably opposed to it, but he worries about a Soviet reprisal, probably in West Berlin, where the U.S. is highly vulnerable. LeMay's response is: all we have to do is warn the Soviets not to make trouble in Berlin, or we'll "fight," that is, use nuclear weapons there. Then we should hit Cuba "right now." The Soviets will be smart enough, according to LeMay, not to engage in any reprisal of any kind, because they know we can and will destroy

"General Curtis LeMay . . . was saying 'Let's go in, let's totally destroy Cuba.'"

them, due to the tremendous U.S. advantage at the nuclear level. Castro and his government will be destroyed. And the Soviets will be taught a lesson they won't soon forget. (Subsequent documentation and testimony suggests LeMay was wrong.[4]) LeMay ends by insulting the president: he tells him that anything less than what he is recommending is like "appeasement at Munich," referring to the failed attempt of the British in 1938 to appease Adolf Hitler. The transcript ends with a discussion among the Chiefs alone, after the president and the others have left the room. Shoup, with LeMay's agreement, berates the president and other doves for their worries over whether an attack on Cuba would lead to "escalation" to global nuclear war.

[Transcript of a secret tape recording of a meeting of President Kennedy with the Joint Chiefs of Staff, 9:45–10:30 AM, Friday, October 19, 1962, Cabinet Room.][5]

> **President Kennedy:** Let me just say a little, first, about what the problem is, from my point of view.
>
> . . .
>
> [W]hat makes our problem so difficult? If we go in and take them [the missiles] out on a quick air strike, we neutralize the chance of danger to the United States of these missiles being used. And we prevent a situation from arising, at least within

Cuba, where the Cubans themselves have the means of exercising some degree of authority in this hemisphere.

On the other hand, we increase the chance greatly, as I think they—there's bound to be a reprisal from the Soviet Union, there always is—of they're just going in and taking Berlin by force at some point. Which leaves me with only one alternative, which is fire nuclear weapons—which is a hell of an alternative—and begin a nuclear exchange, with all this happening.

On the other hand, if we begin the blockade that we're talking about, the chances are they will begin a blockade [of Berlin] and say that we started it. And there'll be some question of the attitude of the Europeans. So that, once again, they will say that there will be this feeling in Europe that the Berlin blockade has been commenced by our blockade. So I don't think we've got any satisfactory alternatives.

. . .

I just wanted to say that these were some of the problems that we have been considering. Now I'd be glad to hear from . . .

General Maxwell Taylor: Well, I would just say one thing and then turn it over to General LeMay. We recognize all these things, Mr. President. But I think we'd all be unanimous in saying that really our strength in Berlin, our strength any place in the world, is the credibility of our response under certain conditions. And if we don't respond here in Cuba, we think the credibility of our response in Berlin is endangered.

President Kennedy: That's right. That's right. So that's why we've got to respond. Now the question is: What kind of response?

General Curtis LeMay: Well, I certainly agree with everything General Taylor has said. I'd emphasize, a little strongly perhaps, that we don't have any choice except direct military action. If we do this blockade that's proposed and political action, the first thing that's going to happen is your missiles [i.e., Soviet missiles in Cuba] are going to disappear into the woods, particularly your mobile ones. Now, we can't find them, regardless of what we do, and then we're going to take some damage if we try to do anything later on.

President Kennedy: Well, can't there be some of these undercover now, in the sense of not having been delivered?

General LeMay: There is a possibility of that. But the way they've lined these others up—I would have to say it's a small possibility. If they were going to hide any of them, then I would think they would have hid them all. I don't think there are any hid. So the only danger we have [is] if we haven't picked up some that are setting [sic] there in plain sight. This is possible. If we do low-altitude photography over them, this is going to be a tip-off too.

Now, as for the Berlin situation, I don't share your view that if we knock off Cuba, they're going to knock off Berlin. We've got the Berlin problem staring us in the face anyway. If we don't do anything to Cuba, then they're going to push on Berlin and push *real hard* because they've got us on the run. If we take military action against Cuba, then I think that the . . .

President Kennedy: What do you think their reprisal would be?

General LeMay: I don't think they're going to make any reprisal if we tell them that the Berlin situation is just like it's always been. If they make a move we're going to fight. Now I don't think this changes the Berlin situation at all, except you've got to make one more statement on it.

So I see no other solution. This blockade and political action, I see leading into war. I don't see any other solution for it. It will lead right into war. This is almost as bad as the appeasement at Munich.

[Pause.]

Because if this . . . blockade comes along, their MiG's [fighter aircraft] are going to fly. The IL-28s [fighter bombers] are going to fly against us. And we're just gradually going to drift into a war under conditions that are at great disadvantage to us, with missiles staring us in the face, that can knock out our airfields in the southeastern portion [of the United States]. And if they use nuclear weapons, it's the population down there [that will suffer the consequences]. We just drift into a war under conditions that we don't like. I just don't see any other solution except direct military intervention *right now*.

. . .

President Kennedy: Well, it is a fact that the number of missiles there, let's say . . . no matter what they put in there, we could live today under. If they don't have enough ICBMs today, they're going to have them in a year. They obviously are putting a lot of—

General LeMay: This increases their accuracy against the 50 targets that we know they could hit now.

But the thing is, if we leave them there, is the blackmail threat against not only us but the other South American countries that they may decide to operate against.

There's one other factor that I didn't mention that's not quite in our field, [which] is the political factor. But you invited us to comment on this at one time. And that is that we [the Joint Chiefs of Staff] have had a talk about Cuba and the SAM [surface-to-air missile] sites down there. And you have made some pretty strong statements about their being defensive and that we would take action against offensive weapons. I think that a blockade and political talk would be considered by a lot of our friends and neutrals as being a pretty weak response to this. And I'm sure a lot of our own citizens would feel that way, too.

In other words, you're in a pretty bad fix at the present time.

President Kennedy: What did you say?

General LeMay: You're in a pretty bad fix.

President Kennedy: You're in there with me. [Slight laughter, a bit forced.] Personally.

. . .

[President Kennedy leaves first, exiting to the South Lawn of the White House, to a waiting helicopter. Robert McNamara and Gen. Maxwell Taylor have a brief discussion, before both depart. Marine Gen. Shoup, Gen. Earle Wheeler, and Gen. LeMay remain. (It is unclear from the recording whether Admiral Anderson departs or remains in the Cabinet Room with the other three Chiefs.)]

General Shoup: You, you pulled the rug right out from under him.

General LeMay: Jesus Christ, what the hell do you mean?

General Shoup: I just agree with that answer, General. I just agree with you. I just agree with you a hundred percent. That's the only goddamn. . . .

He [President Kennedy] finally got around to the word *escalation*. I heard him say *escalation*. That's the only goddamn thing that's in the whole trick. It's been there in Laos; it's been in every goddamn one [of these crises]. When he says *escalation*, that's it. [Pause.]

If somebody could keep them from doing the goddamn thing piecemeal. That's our problem. You go in there and friggin' around with the missiles. You're screwed. You go in and frig around with anything else, you're screwed.

General LeMay: That's right.

General Shoup: You're screwed, screwed, screwed. And if some goddamn thing, some way, he could say: "Either do this son of a bitch and do it right, and quit friggin' around." That was my conclusion. Don't frig around and go take a missile out.

General Earle Wheeler: Well, maybe I missed the point.

General Shoup: . . . Goddamn it, if he wants to do it, you can't fiddle around with taking out missiles. You can't fiddle around with hitting the missile sites and then hitting the SAM sites. You got to go in and take out the goddamn thing that's going to stop you from doing your job.

This next document, one of the most extraordinary of the Cold War, takes us "inside" Fidel Castro's request to Nikita Khrushchev to make Cuba a martyred nation, if the Americans invade and occupy the country. Was Castro "rational" in making this request? In Castro's mind, his options in the event of the imminent total destruction of his nation were: Cuba would be destroyed for no redeeming reason; or Cuba would be destroyed, but her destruction would be redeemed by the total destruction of its nemesis, the U.S., via a Soviet nuclear strike.

By the last weekend of October, 1962, Fidel Castro has concluded that an American air strike and invasion of the island are virtually inevitable. This leads him to request of Nikita Khrushchev, in a cable drafted in the predawn hours of October 26/27, that in the event of an invasion—what Castro in the following letter calls the "second variant"—Khrushchev should launch an all-out nuclear strike against the U.S. "That would be the moment," Castro writes to Khrushchev, "to eliminate such danger forever through an act of legitimate self-defense, however harsh and terrible the solution would be, for there would be no other."[6] Or as the translator of the cable, Soviet

Ambassador Aleksandr Alekseev, puts it in his own cable to the Soviet leader, Castro said: "If they attack Cuba, we should wipe them off the face of the earth."[7] In solidarity with his leader, Castro's colleague Ernesto ("Che") Guevara declares his willingness "to walk by the path of liberation even when it may cost millions of atomic victims."[8] If the temple has to fall—if Cuba is destroyed—the Cuban leadership is asking the Soviets to take the Americans down with them.

[Letter from Fidel Castro to Nikita Khrushchev, October 26, 1962.][9]

Havana, October 26, 1962

Dear Comrade Khrushchev:

From an analysis of the situation and the reports in our possession, I consider that the aggression is almost imminent within the next 24 or 72 hours.

There are two possible variants: the first and likeliest one is an air attack against certain targets with the limited objective of destroying them; the second, less probable although possible, is invasion. I understand that this variant would call for a large number of forces and it is, in addition, the most repulsive form of aggression, which might inhibit them.

You can rest assured that we will firmly and resolutely resist attack, whatever it may be.

The morale of the Cuban people is extremely high and the aggressor will be confronted heroically.

At this time I want to convey to you briefly my personal opinion.

If the second variant is implemented and the imperialists invade Cuba with the goal of occupying it, the danger that that aggressive policy poses for humanity is so great that following that event the Soviet Union must never allow the circumstances in which the imperialists could launch the first nuclear strike against it.

I tell you this because I believe that the imperialists' aggressiveness is extremely dangerous and if they actually carry out the brutal act of invading Cuba in violation of international law and morality, that would be the moment to eliminate such danger forever through an act of clear legitimate defense, however harsh and terrible the solution would be, for there is no other.

. . .

Fraternally,

Fidel Castro

Khrushchev is already in a near panic by the final weekend of October 1962. Events seem to be spinning out of control. An American U-2 spy plane has been shot down over Cuba and the pilot killed, yet Khrushchev has no idea who gave the order to do so, and he mistakenly attributes the shootdown to the Cubans. (The Soviets had shot it down, with encouragement from the Cubans, who celebrated the event.) Khrushchev fears that this action will escalate the crisis in the minds of the U.S. leadership, which it does. The pilot of another U-2, on an air-sampling mission, becomes confused about his route, and accidently overflies Soviet territory in Siberia. The Soviets, believing that the plane may be doing last-minute reconnaissance in preparation for a massive U.S. attack on the Soviet Union, elect (fortunately) not to shoot it down.

Then, just when Khrushchev and Kennedy appear to have reached a deal on Saturday, October 27, a cable arrives in Moscow from Castro, stating that a U.S. attack is imminent, and that Cuba stands ready as a people and nation to pay the ultimate price, and become martyred for socialism. Khrushchev is deeply disturbed by this cable, believing that anyone who would send such a message may be losing his grip on reality. So the Soviet leader counsels his young Cuban ally to settle down and celebrate what Khrushchev implies is a Soviet-Cuban victory in the crisis.[10]

[Letter from Nikita Khrushchev to Fidel Castro, October 28, 1962.][11]

Dear Comrade Fidel Castro:

Our October 27 message to President Kennedy allows for the question to be settled in your favor, to defend Cuba from an invasion and prevent war from breaking out. Kennedy's reply, which you apparently also know, offers assurances that the United States will not invade Cuba with its own forces, nor will it permit its allies to carry out an invasion. In this way, the president of the United States has positively answered my messages of October 26 and 27, 1962.

We have now finished drafting our reply to the president's message. I am not going to convey it here, for you surely know the text, which is now being broadcast, over the radio.

With this motive I would like to recommend to you now, at this moment of change in the crisis, not to be carried away by sentiment and to show firmness. I must say that I understand your feelings of indignation toward the aggressive actions and violations of elementary norms of international law on the part of the United States.

But now, rather than law, what prevails is the senselessness of the militarists at the Pentagon. Now that an agreement is within sight, the Pentagon is searching for a pretext to frustrate this agreement. This is why it is organizing the provocative [reconnaissance] flights [over Cuba]. Yesterday, you shot down one of these, while earlier you didn't shoot them down when they overflew your territory. The aggressors will take advantage of such a step for their own purposes.

Therefore, I would like to advise you in a friendly manner to show patience, firmness and even more firmness. Naturally, if there's an invasion, it will be necessary to repulse it by every means. But we mustn't allow ourselves to be carried away by provocations, because the Pentagon's unbridled militarists, now that the solution to the conflict is in sight and apparently in your favor, creating a guarantee against the invasion of Cuba, are trying to frustrate the agreement and provoke you into actions that could be used against you. I ask you not to give them the pretext for doing that.

On our part, we will do everything possible to stabilize the situation in Cuba, defend Cuba against invasion and assure you the possibilities for peacefully building a socialist society.

I send you greetings, extensive to all your leadership group.

N. Khrushchev
October 28, 1962

Khrushchev and his colleagues in the Soviet leadership clearly expect the Cubans to be: (a) grateful to Moscow for having ended the crisis short of war—a war in which Cuba would have suffered first and foremost; and (b) grateful for having gotten a pledge from Kennedy that the U.S. would not invade Cuba and try to overthrow the Castro government. But instead of gratitude, Castro's response to the resolution of the crisis is a bitter rebuke of the Soviets. In fact, Castro is full of rage; he hates everything about the way the Soviets handled the crisis: they did not consult the Cubans about the withdrawal (Castro hears about it on the radio); the so-called noninvasion "pledge" is, in Castro's view, worthless, and the Americans are already preparing for an invasion, this time without any fear of a Soviet response; and the Soviet Union, far from being a dependable friend of Cuba, is instead a selfish superpower that has betrayed its Cuban ally by abandoning it when the chips were down.

Finally, Castro orders his anti-aircraft gunners to try to shoot down U.S. planes, which continue to overfly Cuba in an attempt to verify the Soviet withdrawal of the missiles. Khrushchev, concerned that the Cubans will shoot down some American planes, or in other ways torpedo the agreement with Kennedy, sends his deputy, Anastas Mikoyan, to Cuba to try to assuage Castro and the Cubans. Mikoyan prevents a deepening of the crisis, and gets Castro's reluctant agreement to allow the Soviet withdrawal to continue. But the two agree on little else. After nearly three weeks in Cuba, Mikoyan is told by Castro, "the people's hatred for the imperialists is so great that it is as if they would prefer even death."[12] Mikoyan, who is both mystified and troubled by what he regards as Cuban "emotionalism" responds, "But we do not want to die beautifully."[13] And even two years after the crisis, Castro's colleague Ernesto ("Che") Guevara told a friend, "I will never forgive Khrushchev for the way he resolved the missile crisis."[14]

[Letter from Fidel Castro to Nikita Khrushchev, October 31, 1962.][15]

Havana
October 31, 1962
Mr. Nikita S. Khrushchev
Prime Minister of the Soviet Union
USSR

Dear Comrade Khrushchev:

I received your letter. . . . You understand that we were indeed consulted before you adopted the decision to withdraw the strategic missiles. You base yourself on the alarming news that you say reached you from Cuba and, finally, my cable of October 27. I don't know what news you received; I can only respond for the message I sent you in the evening of October 26, which reached you the 27th.

What we did in the face of events, Comrade Khrushchev, was to prepare ourselves and get ready to fight. In Cuba, there was only one kind of alarm, that of battle stations.

. . .

Danger couldn't impress us, for danger has been hanging over our country for a long time now and in a certain way we have grown used to it.

The Soviet troops which have been at our side know how admirable the stand of our people was throughout this crisis and the profound brother-hood that was created among the troops from both peoples during the deci-sive hours. Countless eyes of Cuban and Soviet men who were willing to die with supreme dignity shed tears upon learning about the surprising, sudden and practically unconditional decision to withdraw the weapons.

Perhaps you don't know the degree to which the Cuban people was [sic] ready to do its duty toward the nation and humanity.

I realized when I wrote them that the words contained in my letter [of October 26–27] could be misinterpreted and that was what happened, per-haps because you didn't read them carefully, perhaps because of the trans-lation, perhaps because I meant to say so much in too few lines. However, I didn't hesitate to do it. Do you believe, Comrade Khrushchev, that we were selfishly thinking of ourselves, of our generous people willing to sacrifice themselves, and not at all in an unconscious manner but fully assured of the risk they ran?

No, Comrade Khrushchev. Few times in history, and it could even be said that never before, because no people had ever faced such a tremen-dous danger, was a people so willing to fight and die with such a universal sense of duty.

We knew, and do not presume that we ignored it, that we would have been annihilated. . . . However, that didn't prompt us to withdraw the mis-siles, that didn't prompt us to ask you to yield. Do you believe that we wanted that war? But how could we prevent it if the invasion finally took place? The fact is that this event was possible, that imperialism was ob-structing every solution and that its demands were, from our point of view, impossible for the USSR and Cuba to accept.

And if war had broken out, what could we do with the insane people who unleashed the war? You yourself have said that under current conditions, such a war would inevitably have escalated quickly into a nuclear war.

. . .

There are not just a few Cubans, as has been reported to you, but in fact many Cubans who are experiencing at this moment unspeakable bitterness and sadness.

The imperialists are talking once again of invading our country, which is proof of how ephemeral and untrustworthy their promises are. Our people, however, maintain their indestructible will to resist the aggressors and per-haps more than ever need to trust in themselves and in that will to struggle.

Fraternally,
Fidel Castro

To understand how Cuba viewed its interests in the resolution of the missile crisis, and how different their view was from that of its Soviet ally, one need look no further than the Cuban government's statement of its "Five Points," issued in response to learning of the Kennedy–Khrushchev agreement. The Soviets seemed satisfied: they received a U.S. non-invasion pledge, in return for removal of Soviet missiles and other weapons. The Cubans were enraged rather than satisfied. Cuba's requirements were, in fact, worlds apart from those of the Soviets. The Cuban Five Points were, in sum:

1. An end to the U.S. economic embargo against Cuba.
2. An end to U.S.-backed subversion in Cuba.
3. An end to naval attacks by CIA-backed Cuban exiles.
4. An end to U.S. overflights of Cuban territory.
5. An end to U.S. occupation of the Guantanamo base.[16]

This is the deeper reason for Cuban rage at the way the Soviets agreed to resolve the crisis: none of the interests of Cuba, as determined by Cuba, were taken into account. Even now, more than four decades later, the U.S. embargo remains in place, as do U.S. forces at the Guantanamo naval base. In an important sense, what the Cubans refer to as the "October crisis" was never resolved at all.[17]

In the following letter to Acting UN Secretary-General, U Thant, Fidel Castro informs the UN of Cuba's intention to act decisively on point four-the only point on which Cuba can act effectively and alone: they will try to shoot down all U.S. planes overflying Cuba, in spite of the fact that the Kennedy—Khrushchev agreement allowed the U.S. to do so.

[Letter from Fidel Castro to U Thant, November 15, 1962.][18]

15 November 1962
His Excellency, U Thant, Acting Secretary-General of the United Nations

Your Excellency,

. . .

I should like to refer solely to the following matter: we have given you-and we have also given it publicly and repeatedly—our refusal to allow unilateral inspection by any body, national or international, on Cuban territory.

In doing so, we have exercised the inalienable right of every sovereign nation to settle all problems within its own territory in accordance with the will of its government and its people.

The Soviet government, carrying out its promise to Mr. Kennedy, has withdrawn its strategic missiles, an action which was verified by the United States officials on the high seas.

. . .

What have we obtained in exchange? The violations have increased in number; every day the incursions of war planes over our territory become more alarming. . . . [T]o the extent of the fire power of our anti-aircraft weapons, any war plane which violates the sovereignty of Cuba, by invading our air space, can only do so at the risk of being destroyed.

. . .

We believe in the right to defend the liberty, the sovereignty and the dignity of this country, and we shall continue to exercise that right to the last man, woman or child capable of holding a weapon in this territory.

May I reiterate to you the expression of my highest consideration.

Fidel Castro
Prime Minister of the Revolutionary
Government

Dialogues

The Castro–Khrushchev cables exchanged during the missile crisis became publicly available in late November 1991. At once, they were interpreted by many as confirming that the (then) young, high-strung Fidel Castro, and his equally youthful colleagues in the Cuban leadership, had actually recommended to Khrushchev that he launch a preemptive nuclear strike on the U.S.—an act that would very likely have resulted in national suicide for both Cuba and the Soviet Union, given the huge advantage over the Soviets the U.S. then enjoyed in strategic nuclear weapons (approximately 17:1). In the following intervention of Castro's, at the January 1992 conference in Havana, he attempts to explain why he sent his controversial cable of October 26/27, and what he hoped it would accomplish.

In Castro's telling of the story, on the evening of Friday, October 26, 1962, he came to the Soviet embassy from a meeting with the So-

viet military leadership on the island. (He has just been told that "all is ready"—meaning not only the Soviet troops equipped with conventional weapons, but also the Soviet forces with responsibility for the nearly ninety short-range, tactical nuclear weapons that could be used against a U.S. invasion force.) Thus, Castro recalls, he and his Soviet colleagues on the island were absolutely convinced that any war initiated by the Americans would be a nuclear war in which Cuba will be destroyed. Nuclear war is, he believes, absolutely inevitable, if the Americans invade, as it seems to him they will.

In his cable to the Soviet leader, he tries valiantly to explain himself, within the constraints of very difficult conditions—it is the wee hours of the morning, Spanish–Russian translators are few and poorly trained, and the composition is hurried due to the onrush of events. He wants to encourage Khrushchev not to hesitate, not to cave in, on Cuba's behalf, because all of Cuba is ready to pay the ultimate price, as are the Soviet forces in Cuba. (We learned at the October 2002 conference in Havana that on the morning of October 27 the Soviet forces, 42,000-strong, who had previously worn Cuban uniforms in an attempt to disguise the size of the Soviet presence, changed into their Soviet uniforms. They believed they were about to die, and they wished to die honorably, in their own uniforms.)[19]

[An intervention by Fidel Castro in Havana, Cuba, January 1992, at a conference of Cuban, U.S. and Soviet policymakers, and scholars of the Cuban missile crisis.][20]

> **Fidel Castro:** Now, to know why this confusion around my letter of the 26th [of October, 1962] started, we should recall the way the letter was dictated. The letter was written and dictated at the Soviet embassy and sent from there. We almost didn't have translators. I'd write and dictate, and then I'd revise it again. I'd say, for example, "Delete this word, add this, change that." This was in the wee hours of the morning of the 27th, the night between the 26th and the 27th. It was almost dawn when we finished. I did that after my meeting with the Soviet . . . [military leaders in Cuba].
>
> I asked myself, "After almost five days of intensive work, what is there still left to do? We've done everything in terms of

military preparation. Well, the only thing that remains to do is to send a letter to Khrushchev." To understand this, we have to keep in mind that on the night of the 26th, we saw no possible solution. We couldn't see a way out. Under the threat of an invasion, of an attack, with enormous propaganda using all the mass media, and an international campaign talking about this very serious problem, we couldn't really see any solution. . . . And I dared to write a letter to Nikita, a letter aimed at encouraging him. That was my intention. The aim was to strengthen him morally, because I knew that he had to be suffering greatly, intensely. I thought I knew him well. I thought I knew what he was thinking and that he must have been at that time very anxious over the situation.

. . . You see, I had other fears, really: I was afraid that there'd be mistakes, hesitations, because I was already seeing that mistakes were being made, and there were signs of hesitation. I proposed some ideas as to what should be done in the event, not of an air strike, but of an invasion of Cuba in an attempt to occupy it. That is in my letter of the night of between the 26th and 27th, written and sent from the embassy.

Throughout most of the nuclear age, specialists in international security worried most about three scenarios under which a nuclear war between major nuclear powers might begin: (1) a nuclear nation achieves a huge advantage over its nuclear adversary, and its leaders decide to launch a preemptive nuclear strike to destroy all the weaker state's nuclear arsenal, without fear of a catastrophic response; (2) the leader of a nuclear state becomes irrational and, in some sort of delusionary state, launches the nuclear weapons under his command; and (3) a series of accidents involving nuclear weapons (for example, faulty radar which mistakes geese for incoming missiles) results in a nuclear launch.[21] During the Cold War, enormous efforts were made by both Moscow and Washington to lower the risk that any of these scenarios would actually occur.

Toward that end they: (1) sought to achieve and maintain a rough parity in their nuclear capabilities; (2) built many safeguards into the launch procedures of the U.S. and USSR, in order to help prevent an irrational leader from initiating a nuclear holocaust in a fit of para-

*noia, rage or another irrational state of mind; and (3) the surveil-
lance technology became highly sophisticated, with multiple, independent checking capabilities, in an effort to prevent accidental or
mistaken assessments of one another's actions. The underlying assumption all along was: rationality, augmented with sophisticated
technology can, in fact, save us from nuclear catastrophe.*

*Robert McNamara learns from Fidel Castro at the January 1992
Havana conference that rationality will not save us, in circumstances
such as occurred in the Cuban missile crisis. For in Castro, McNamara confronts a leader who, in October 1962, had no nuclear
weapons at all under his control, and only a few dozen in his country,
controlled by Soviet forces; who seemed as sober and rational as could
be; and who did not fear the onset of war with the Americans, a war
in which, as he says, "we were going to disappear."*

*McNamara (along with many others present) is deeply shocked by
Castro's recollection of his state of mind during the peak of the missile crisis. For McNamara knows that U.S. policies were, to a significant extent, responsible for the situation in which Castro had found
himself in October 1962. And as former U.S. Defense Secretary, he
knows that the invasion which, in all likelihood, would have provoked a nuclear response from Soviet forces in Cuba, may have been
only a day or two away. Thus, McNamara arrives at a frightening conclusion, which he would later state forcefully in "The Fog of War":
But for luck, "Rational individuals [including himself and Castro]
came . . . close to the total destruction of their societies."*

**[A discussion between Robert McNamara and Fidel Castro, at a January
1992 conference of Cuban, U.S. and Soviet policymakers, and scholars of
the Cuban missile crisis.][22]**

Robert McNamara: Mr. President [addressing Fidel Castro] . . . I,
as one of the participants in the crisis, want to congratulate you
on the candor and thoughtfulness with which you [have] expressed your understanding of events as they evolved. It is with
particular reference to one of those circumstances, which I was
unaware of until this meeting, that I wish to put a question.

. . . [T]he Soviet Union anticipated the possibility of a large-
scale U.S. invasion of the type that we were equipped for by

"Rational individuals came that close to total destruction of their societies."

October 27 . . . something on the order of 1,190 air sorties the first day, five army divisions, three Marine divisions, 140,000 U.S. ground troops. The Soviet Union, as I understand it, to some degree anticipated that, and equipped their forces here— the 42,000 Soviet troops—with . . . tactical nuclear warheads.

. . . My question to you, sir, is this: Were you aware that the Soviet forces (a) were equipped with [short-range] *Luna* launchers and nuclear warheads; and (b)—something I never could have conceived of—that because the Soviets were concerned about the ability of the Soviet troops and the Cuban troops to repel the possible U.S. invasion using conventional arms, the Soviets authorized the field commanders in Cuba, without further consultation with the Soviet Union—which of course would have been very difficult because of communication problems—to utilize those nuclear launchers and nuclear warheads?; (a) Were you aware of it? (b) what was your interpretation or expectation of the possible effect on Cuba? [And (c)] How did you think the U.S. would respond, and what might the implications have been for your nation and the world?

Fidel Castro: Now, we started from the assumption that if there was an invasion of Cuba, nuclear war would erupt. We were certain of that. If the invasion took place in the situation that had been created, nuclear war would have been the result. Everybody here was simply resigned to the fate that we would be forced to pay the price, that we would disappear. We saw that danger—I'm saying it frankly—and the conclusion, Mr. McNamara, that we might derive is that if we are going to rely on fear, we would never be able to prevent a nuclear war. The danger of nuclear war has to be eliminated by other means; it cannot be prevented on the basis of fear of nuclear weapons, or that human beings are going to be deterred by the fear of nuclear weapons. We [Cubans] have lived through the very singular experience of becoming practically the first target of those nuclear weapons: no one lost their equanimity or their calm in the face of such a danger, despite the fact that the self-preservation instinct is supposed to have been more powerful. . . .

You want me to give you my opinion in the event of an invasion with all the troops, with 1,190 sorties? Would I have been ready to use nuclear weapons? Yes, I would have agreed to the use of nuclear weapons. Because, in any case, we took it for granted that it would become a nuclear war anyway, and that we were going to disappear. Before having the country occupied—totally occupied—we were ready to die in defense of our country. I would have agreed, in the event of the invasion you are talking about, with the use of nuclear weapons. . . .

I wish we had had the nuclear weapons. It would have been wonderful. We wouldn't have rushed to use them, you can be sure of that. The closer to Cuba the decision of using a weapon effective against a landing, the better. Of course, after we had used ours, they would have replied with, say, 400 tactical [nuclear] weapons—we don't know how many would have been fired at us. In any case, we were resigned to our fate. So, the idea of withdrawing the weapons simply didn't cross our minds.

Robert McNamara and Fidel Castro find common ground in the principal lesson each draws from the Cuban missile crisis: that nuclear weapons should be eliminated as soon as is safely possible. But they draw the lesson for different reasons, reflecting their respective roles as representatives of a rich superpower and a small, relatively weak and poor country. Without nuclear weapons, as McNamara points out in "The Fog of War," fallible human beings will be unable to destroy entire nations, perhaps even the human race itself, as it seems almost to have done in October 1962. This is his principal motive in advocating the elimination of nuclear weapons by any credible and verifiable means: to prevent nuclear powers from destroying themselves and human civilization as well.

Castro, on the other hand, responds to McNamara's endorsement of a nonnuclear world by reminding him that "the use of nuclear weapons is a desperate act." The implication is that the behavior of great powers like the U.S., Russia and others must change—must cease to create desperation in small countries like Cuba. Otherwise, a desperate, though fully rational, leader of a small country (or perhaps a transnational terrorist organization), who may have access to nuclear weapons, might just come to the same conclusion that he (Castro) drew in October 1962: that the only viable option left is to die honorably, to undertake the ultimate suicide mission—what McNamara refers to in "The Fog of War" as the inclination to "pull the temple down on our heads."

[A discussion between Robert McNamara and Fidel Castro, at a January 1992 conference of Cuban, U.S. and Soviet policymakers, and scholars of the Cuban missile crisis.][23]

Robert McNamara: . . . [O]ur invasion force, had it invaded, would *not* have been equipped with tactical nuclear weapons. . . . Had the invasion occurred, had it been met with nuclear fire from the [short-range Soviet] *Luna* launchers . . . the U.S. would . . . have very quickly made available tactical nuclear warheads to its forces.

But I come back to the point that . . . this was an added element of danger which some of us . . . (a) had not anticipated, and (b) would have been horrified to think of the consequences of. . . . This is simply another example that human beings are incapable of fully controlling such complex situations as military conflict among nations today. Now, that is dangerous in a world equipped with conventional weapons. It is absolutely potentially disastrous in a world that has as many nuclear weapons as we have today. It horrifies me to think what would have happened in the event of an invasion of Cuba! But it frightens me to think that the world may continue for decades with this risk. And the conclusion I draw is that we must join together in trying, quickly, to reduce the number of nuclear warheads in the world.

Fidel Castro: If you will allow me, I agree with what you've said. I believe that the decision not to authorize the commanders of the [U.S.] expeditionary forces to carry nuclear weapons was wise, because the situation was very different on the American side than on the Cuban side. We would not have rushed into using nuclear weapons from the very beginning if we had been in your shoes. But for us, perhaps an enormous naval flotilla, impossible to stop, might have posed the problem. For the United States, giving these weapons to the troops was not a necessity, since they had those thousands of planes, which could immediately be equipped with nuclear weapons of any kind without posing additional risks to the troops using them or being equipped to use them—if in a matter of minutes there could have been an air retaliation using nuclear weapons, from the political and military point of view, it was wise and correct not to equip American forces with nuclear weapons at the outset. That simply would have increased the risks. The use of nuclear weapons is a desperate act; and while the defenders might have been in a desperate situation, U.S. troops would not, since there was always the possibility of a nuclear counterattack if these weapons were used against them.

In "The Fog of War," the newspaper columnist Walter Lippmann is quoted as saying that Robert McNamara is "not only the best Secretary of Defense, but the first one who ever exerted civilian control over the military." Because of McNamara's success in making the armed services fiscally responsible, and because McNamara understood and attempted to implement Kennedy's strong aversion to armed conflict, McNamara was regarded by Kennedy as perhaps the most important of his cabinet officers, after his brother Robert, the Attorney General. It was no secret, however, that the Joint Chiefs of Staff deeply resented what they felt was McNamara's arbitrary and high-handed manner with them, and his disinterest in consulting them fully. Gen. Curtis LeMay, under whom McNamara had served in the U.S. Army Air Corps in the Second World War, especially chafed under the tight supervision of his former subordinate (and now boss), McNamara.

Even twenty years after his retirement from the Air Force, LeMay was still bitter about the way he felt McNamara ran the Pentagon. In these reflections, collected by his quasi-official biographer and excerpted below, LeMay portrays McNamara as a dictator who ruled with an iron hand. Moreover, in LeMay's view, his boss did not, in a basic sense, know what he was doing when he involved himself in what LeMay and the other chiefs regarded as purely military matters, over which they were accustomed to having a good deal more control than McNamara, with Kennedy's blessing, permitted.

According to LeMay, McNamara's considerable influence on Kennedy seemed to him particularly unfortunate during the Cuban missile crisis. Both McNamara and Kennedy, he believed, failed to appreciate the overwhelming significance of U.S. nuclear superiority over the Soviets in the Cuban missile crisis. In his reflections below, LeMay berates the civilian leadership of the Kennedy administration for being (as he saw it) so unnecessarily frightened during the crisis that they felt they had to "make a trade with Khrushchev." LeMay's colleague, former Chairman of the Joint Chiefs Gen. Maxwell Taylor, agreed. In an interview given twenty years after the crisis, Taylor fumed that "we had Khrushchev over a barrel, but then we offered him a piece of cake."[24] This is the way LeMay, Taylor—in fact all the Chiefs—felt. There was nothing to fear from the Soviets because, according to LeMay et al., the Soviets knew precisely how large was the U.S. nuclear advantage. Being rational, they weren't about to start a nuclear war with the U.S. under any circumstances. Thus, the Chiefs believed there was much to gain, and nothing to lose, from launching a massive air attack and invasion of Cuba.

[Comments by General Curtis LeMay, ed. by Thomas M. Coffey.][25]

We in the military, did not raise a blanket objection to being overruled [by Robert McNamara]. What we did object to was the Secretary saying "no" to something the military wished to do, and giving a *military reason* for his action. Palpably, thus, he and his coterie were setting themselves up as military experts.[26]

The Kennedy administration came in and right from the start we got the back of the hand. Get out of our way. We think nothing of you and your opinions. We don't like you as people. We have no respect for you. Don't bother us.

My quarrel with McNamara was not so much our differences of opinion. I've had differences of opinion with a lot of people. My quarrel with him was—he has the same responsibility as I have, and he's not listening to me. [I'm] trying to do the same thing he is. I'm trying to help him and he doesn't want my help. And he does things I've known all my life are wrong.

[A hospital administrator] can run a good hospital. He doesn't have to be a doctor. But he won't run a good hospital if he dabbles in brain surgery. This is what McNamara and his crew did. They dabbled in brain surgery [i.e., military strategy].[27]

We [the Joint Chiefs of Staff, or JCS] started off trying to talk to him. It was just like talking to a brick wall. We got nowhere. Finally, it was just a waste of time and effort. We would state opinions when we had a chance. That was all. . . . We in the military felt we were not in the decisionmaking process. . . . [McNamara] would tell the Congress that he always consulted the JCS on important matters, and [technically] that could be construed as a true statement. But we'd get papers from the Secretary's office to give an opinion on, and we knew he had already made the decision and issued the orders three days before.[28]

My opinion is, [McNamara] believed if we had a deterrence, if we had forces of equal size [with the Soviet Union], reasonable men could discuss things and solve [their] problems without going to war. This is, to me, too idealistic. First you've got to have two reasonable men. Are you going to have two reasonable men? Or are you going to have an idiot on one side and a smart guy on the other? Or a vindictive individual who won't agree to anything? I couldn't see any guarantee of success in this happening. And who's going to decide if you have equal forces? I just didn't agree with that. To me, it was [necessary] to have strength. If you had that strength and you didn't push your adversary into an impossible situation, you were going to have peace. He wouldn't attack you.[29]

As I remember it, before I went to Europe [on October 2, 1962] I issued orders to fill up the bomb dumps in the Southeast, and the gas storage dumps, and to notify the units there to get ready for other units coming in. . . . [In the Cuban missile crisis] we had a chance to throw the Communists out of Cuba. Even though the Army and Navy weren't ready, the Air Force could have begun the attack. But the administration was scared to death they [the Russians] might shoot a missile at us. We couldn't guarantee they wouldn't. We didn't know whether we had found them all. [But] we were on alert every place and made sure the Russians understood this.

What Kennedy actually did was to make a trade with Khrushchev. If he'd take his missiles out of Cuba, we would take our missiles out of Turkey and Italy. . . . I'm sure that's what happened.[30]

The Dilemma: Rationality Is Necessary, But Insufficient

Bringing his thumb and forefinger so close they almost touch, Robert McNamara states in "The Fog of War" that "rational individuals came "this close" to the total destruction of their societies." It is worthwhile pondering the fact that this statement was made by one of the 20th century's best-known advocates of rationality in human affairs. McNamara helped rationalize—in the sense of making them more efficient—the complex operations that resulted in the firebombing of Japan; he rationalized a helter-skelter accounting system at the Ford Motor Company, after which Ford began turning a profit; and he hired several dozen economists and lawyers in his Defense Department whose task was to rationalize—to subject to the rigors of deductive logic—military acquisition, spending and deployment in the Kennedy and Johnson administrations.

But what McNamara learned via his involvement in the critical oral history of the Cuban missile crisis is that even supremely rational people, at the controls of the machinery of governments, cannot necessarily accomplish even their most fundamental task with rationality alone: the protection of their people and the preservation of their societies. He has learned that, but for the intervention of *luck*, the world may well have been destroyed in October 1962. Has any former high-ranking public official ever admitted learning anything this discrepant from his former beliefs—from the principles on which he based his life and work? We doubt it. Thus when this apostle of rationality tells us in "The Fog of War" that "reason has its limits," we need to pay close attention.

This necessity, yet insufficiency, of rationality in foreign and defense policy leads, we believe, to three troubling conclusions. First, once they are embroiled in a crisis, a disastrous nuclear war can happen even if leaders remain rational, and thus seek earnestly to avoid it. Do we know how to avoid deep crises? We doubt it. Second, the only sure path, therefore, away from the nuclear abyss is via the abolition of nuclear weapons. Yet events in this first decade of the 21st century suggest that interest in acquiring nuclear weapons may be increasing among those nations not already possessing them (for example, North Korea, Iran, and numerous non-state actors, including organizations linked to al-Qaeda), rather than decreasing. Can we stop further nuclear proliferation? Not without a radical overhaul of the United Nations Security Council and other aspects of the international system, which would be required to enforce nonproliferation measures, if they should ever be agreed to by the UN and its member states. Even the U.S., with its vaunted military power, cannot by itself stop nuclear proliferation. Third, and perhaps most disturbing, our research into the missile crisis seems to suggest that fundamental obstacles prevent mutual understanding between the very powerful and the relatively weak. What may *seem* irrational to leaders of Great Powers may seem perfectly rational, honorable, even necessary to leaders of weaker nations. Cuba's rationality manifestly was *not* understood by either the U.S. or Soviet Union in October 1962. Thus, rationality—necessary yet insufficient to prevent the worst catastrophes—has yet to be augmented with empathy on a sufficient scale, so that one nation's rationality can be understood as such by an adversary or even an ally.

See Appendix B, Lesson Two, for further discussion of this dilemma.

Admiral Sharp:

[Admiral Moore] said many of the reported contacts with torpedoes fired appear doubtful....

CHAPTER 3

Lesson Three: "Belief and Seeing, They're Both Often Wrong"

ROBERT McNAMARA: *It was just confusion, and events afterwards showed that our judgment that we'd been attacked that day [August 4th, 1964] was wrong. It didn't happen. And the judgment that we'd been attacked on August 2nd was right. We had been, although that was disputed at the time. So we were right once and wrong once.*

Ultimately, President Johnson authorized bombing in response to what he thought had been the second attack—it hadn't occurred but that's irrelevant to the point I'm making here. He authorized the attack on the assumption it had occurred, and his belief that it was a conscious decision on the part of the North Vietnamese political and military leaders to escalate the conflict and an indication they would not stop short of winning.

We were wrong, but we had in our minds a mindset that led to that action. And it carried such heavy costs. We see incorrectly or see only half of the story at times.

ERROL MORRIS: *We see what we want to believe.*

ROBERT McNAMARA: *You're absolutely right. Belief and seeing, they're both often wrong.*

ROBERT McNAMARA and ERROL MORRIS in "The Fog of War."

On November 26, 1963, *four days after President Kennedy's assassination, President Johnson approved National Security Action Memorandum (NSAM) 273. Washington's objective in southeast Asia, it asserted, was "to assist the people and Government of South Vietnam to win their contest against the externally directed and supported communist conspiracy."[1] In approving NSAM 273, President Johnson also directed that planning begin for a covert action program which later became known as Operational Plan (OPLAN) 34-A, which would play an important role in the July–August 1964 events in the Tonkin Gulf.*

As the plan evolved, South Vietnamese commandos, trained and supplied by the CIA, carried out raids on various targets inside North Vietnam. On occasion, U.S. forces became involved with these missions in a supporting role, for example by shelling facilities from U.S. warships, near locations along the coast of North Vietnam into which the commandos were to infiltrate. By the summer of 1964, Washington regarded the program as a notable military failure; the commandos did little damage and were usually either captured or killed by the North Vietnamese. It was continued, however, mainly because it provided the South Vietnamese forces with missions in which U.S. officials could credibly deny direct U.S. involvement. (In mid-1964, the U.S. still did not officially have combat forces in South Vietnam; they were thus eager to avoid U.S. casualties, while continuing to emphasize that U.S. forces were only acting as advisers.) Hanoi complained loudly about these operations but did not, at first, seek to challenge the U.S. ships and planes supporting the guerrillas involved with OPLAN 34-A.

Then unexpectedly, in the summer of 1964, the North Vietnamese struck back. At 3:40 AM (EDT) on Sunday, August 2, 1964, the U.S. destroyer Maddox was attacked by North Vietnamese patrol boats in the Gulf of Tonkin, off the North Vietnamese coast. The Maddox, joined by aircraft from the U.S. carrier Ticonderoga, damaged two of the attacking boats and disabled another. President Johnson, when informed of the incident, chose not to retaliate, though he issued a protest and warning to the Hanoi government. Maxwell Taylor, the U.S. Ambassador in Saigon, saw a chance to raise morale in the always shaky South Vietnamese government by retaliating against the North. Failure to respond, he cabled to Secretary of State Dean Rusk on August 3, would signal to Hanoi "that the U.S. flinches from direct confrontation with the North Vietnamese."[2] Johnson, however, chose not to retaliate as Taylor (and many other advisers) recommended.

Johnson was running hard for president for the first time, and wanted to be seen as the candidate of peace, especially when compared to the hawkish Republican candidate, Sen. Barry Goldwater. If Johnson was going to order a military response, therefore, it would have to be carefully calibrated, and artfully packaged in its presentation to the American people—as necessary but not more than was necessary, strong, but prudent. Johnson doubtless hoped the incident of August 2 would prove to be just an isolated occurrence, not to be repeated. If it were repeated, then he would have to assume the North Vietnamese, for reasons unfathomable to him, had decided to escalate the conflict in Vietnam by taking on the Americans directly.

Two days later, on the morning of Tuesday, August 4, Robert McNamara called the president to tell him that the Maddox *was again reporting the presence of hostile patrol boats and that, based on information intercepted from North Vietnamese radio communications, an attack might be imminent. This was the beginning of a day long series of trans-Pacific telephone conversations involving a host of people, including McNamara and members of his staff in Washington, and many U.S. military officials in the Pacific. The question—one that assumed immense importance by late in the day—was whether an attack had actually occurred on the* Maddox *and another U.S. ship, the* Turner Joy.

Johnson and his advisers eventually concluded that the attack was "probable but not certain."[3] Having decided that the attack probably had *occurred, he decided that this time it would* not *go unanswered Just before midnight (EDT) August 4, he announced on radio and television that a retaliatory strike was then underway on North Vietnamese port and oil facilities that were believed to be associated with the activities of the torpedo boats that had attacked the U.S. ships. On Friday, August 7, Congress approved the "Southeast Asia Resolution," better known as the Tonkin Gulf Resolution. The House vote was 416–0; the Senate vote, 88–2. This became a de facto go-ahead from Congress for the Johnson administration's deepening involvement in the war in Vietnam.*

In hindsight, these events can be seen to mark a watershed in the escalation of the conflict in southeast Asia to an American war in Vietnam. It marked the first time a U.S. president ordered the bombing of North Vietnam. This decision, in turn, led to a good deal of planning within the U.S. government concerning how to move "up the ladder of escalation," if the North Vietnamese continued to target U.S. assets and personnel. Throughout the summer and fall of 1964, in fact, attacks on U.S. personnel and facilities in South Vietnam increased, which in turn led the Johnson administration to escalate the war, in the belief that the Vietnamese communists, both north and south, would eventually understand that their only means of escape from U.S. retribution was to cease and desist from such activities.

But alas, the bombing was not interpreted by the North Vietnamese as a sign that if they relented, the U.S. would concomitantly relent. Instead, Hanoi concluded that the bombing of 4–5 August, 1964 was a clear signal that they were now irrevocably at war with the United States. Having thus concluded, leaders in Hanoi ordered the North Vietnamese Army to begin preparations for moving in large numbers, for the first time, into South Vietnam to assist the guerrillas of the National Liberation Front (NLF, or "Vietcong"). A deadly war of attrition was about to begin in earnest, a war that would result in the deaths of millions, the destruction of vast tracts of southeast Asia, and which left an inextinguishable blot on the history of America's foreign and defense policy.

How ironical and tragic—how absolutely surreal—that the August 4, 1964 watershed leading to a war in which more than three million people were killed was a result of a double misunderstanding. For high-ranking North Vietnamese officials did not (as Washington concluded) order the attacks on U.S. vessels in the Tonkin Gulf on August 2, 1964. They were the result of a decision by a local commander. Moreover, the August 4 attack never occurred. Thus Hanoi could not have intended by such actions to signal their intention to escalate the war. Nor did the U.S. intend (as Hanoi concluded) that the air strikes on North Vietnamese targets signaled an escalation of the war and a decision to do whatever was necessary to destroy the North Vietnamese regime. Looking back, each side could justifiably say, as Robert McNamara says in "The Fog of War," that "we were wrong . . . and it carried such heavy costs." This does not necessarily mean an American war in Vietnam would have been avoided if the events of August 2, 1964 (and the non-"events" of August 4) had transpired differently. But if one wishes to grasp the way misunderstanding and misperception fed the escalation of the war to its eventual tragic dimensions, the Tonkin Gulf affair is a good place to begin.[4]

Documents

The events in the Tonkin Gulf have put President Lyndon Johnson in an uncomfortable situation. He doesn't want to appear "soft" in response to North Vietnamese actions, fearing attacks from the right wing of his own Democratic party and from his Republican challenger in the upcoming November 1964 election, Sen. Barry Goldwater. But neither does he want to appear overly eager to get into a war in Asia, as Goldwater seems intent on doing. So on August 3, the day after the attack on the Maddox, *Johnson tells McNamara to present the administration's case to the Congressional leadership as "firm as hell," but not "dangerous." The following day, August 4, is a case study of "the fog of war," as leaders in Washington attempt to determine what, if anything, actually happened in the Tonkin Gulf. Johnson orders McNamara to prepare for a retaliatory strike, but only if they are sure one or more U.S. ships were actually attacked. Johnson is obviously concerned to be seen as retaliating, rather than initiating combat operations, because the U.S. is not officially at war in southeast Asia. But on August 8, a newspaper story has broken emphasizing Hanoi's claim that their actions were in retaliation for U.S.-backed attacks on North Vietnam (via the OPLAN 34-A covert action program). Johnson asks McNamara for guidance on how to respond to questions about the story, without appearing either to confirm or deny it. This is, as McNamara notes, a "very delicate subject."*

[Transcripts of secret tape recordings of telephone conversations between Lyndon Johnson and Robert McNamara, August 3, 4 and 8, 1964.][5]

Monday, August 3, 1964, 10:20 AM:

President Johnson: I wonder if you don't think it'd be wise for you and Rusk to get the Speaker [of the House, Carl Albert] and [Senate Majority Leader, Mike] Mansfield to call a group of fifteen or twenty people together from the Armed Services, Foreign Relations [Committees]. Tell 'em what happened.

Robert McNamara: Right. I've been thinking about this myself.

President Johnson: They're gonna start an investigation if you don't. . . . You say, "They fired at us; we responded immediately and we took out one of their boats and put the other two running and we're putting out boats right there and we're not running 'em in."

McNamara: . . . We should also at that time, Mr. President, explain this OPLAN 34-A, these covert operations. There's no question that that had bearing on it. On Friday night, as you probably know, we had four PT boats from [South] Vietnam manned by Vietnamese or other nationals attack two islands. . . . Following twenty-four hours after that, with this destroyer [the *Maddox*] in that same area—undoubtedly led them to connect the two events.

President Johnson: Say that to [Senate Minority Leader, Everett] Dirksen. You notice Dirksen says this morning that "we got to reassess our situation—do something about it." I'd tell him that we're doing what he's talking about.

McNamara: You want us to do it at the White House or would you rather do it at State or Defense?

President Johnson: I believe it'd be better to do it up on the Hill. . . . I'd tell 'em awfully quiet though so they won't go in and be making a bunch of speeches. . . .

Now I wish you'd give me some guidance on what we ought to say. I want to leave an impression on background . . . that we're gonna be firm as hell without saying something that's dangerous. . . . The people that're calling me up . . . all feel that the Navy responded wonderfully. And that's good. But they want to be damn sure I don't pull 'em out and run. . . . That's what all the country wants because [Sen. Barry] Goldwater is raising so much hell about how he's gonna blow 'em off the moon. And they say that we oughtn't to do anything that the national interest doesn't require, but we sure ought to always leave the impression that if you shoot at us, you're gonna get hit.

McNamara: I think you would want to instruct [Presidential Press Secretary] George Reedy this morning . . . to say that you personally have ordered the Navy to carry on the routine patrols off the coast of North Vietnam, to add an additional destroyer to the one that has been carrying on the patrols, to provide an air cap, and to issue instructions to the commanders to destroy any force that attacks our force in international waters.[6]

. . .

Tuesday, August 4, 1964, 11:06 AM:

McNamara: Mr. President, we just had word by telephone from Admiral [U. S. G.] Sharp that the destroyer is under torpedo attack.[7]

President Johnson: [Almost inaudible sound.]

McNamara: I think I might get Dean Rusk and Mac Bundy and have them come over here and we'll go over these retaliatory actions and then we ought to—

President Johnson: I sure think you ought to agree to that. Yeah. . . . Now where are these torpedoes coming from?

McNamara: We don't know. Presumably from these unidentified [craft] that I mentioned to you a moment ago. We thought that the unidentified craft might include one PT boat, which has torpedo capability, and two Swatow boats, which we don't credit with torpedo capability, although they may have it.

President Johnson: What are these planes of ours doing around while they're being attacked?

McNamara: Presumably the planes are attacking the ships. We don't have any word from Sharp on that. The planes would be in the area at the present time. All eight of them.

President Johnson: Okay, you get them over there and then you come over here.[8]

Saturday, August 8, 1964, 8:24 AM:

McNamara: I do think that if you have a press conference today you're going to get questions on the claim of the North Vietnamese that their strike on the 2nd against the *Maddox* was retaliation for U.S. participation in the strike of July 30th and 31st against those islands. . . . This is a very delicate subject.

President Johnson: What's the net of it?

McNamara: The net of it is that you state categorically that U.S. forces did not participate in, were not associated with, any alleged incident of that kind. . . .

President Johnson: Is this the outgrowth of [CIA Director] John's [McCone's] briefing?

McNamara: It's the outgrowth of a lot of conversation . . . in the press . . . and I think it's one you have to disassociate yourself from and certainly not admit that any such incident took place. But neither should you get in a position of denying it. Because the North Vietnamese have asked the ICC [International Control Commission] to come in there and examine the site and it would be very unfortunate if they developed proof that you in effect had misstated the case.[9]

President Johnson: Did the South Vietnamese launch an attack that period?

McNamara: On the night of the 30th and continuing into the morning of the 31st, the South Vietnamese ran one of these patrol boat raids against these two North Vietnamese islands. Part of that covert operational plan [OPLAN 34-A]. It was what John [McCone] was alluding to when he talked to the [Congressional] leaders. . . . The *Washington Post* has quite an article on it today . . . "*Maddox* Incident Reexamined—Miscalculation Theory Weighed in Viet Crisis." This is by Murray Marder. He goes on to say that it's now thought it was probably a reprisal action by North Vietnam.[10]

These phone logs contain in microcosm many of the features that led Robert McNamara in "The Fog of War" to conclude that "war is so complex it's beyond the ability of the human mind to comprehend all the variables." Human error, bad weather, bureaucratic red tape, imperfect communication through the chain of command—all these play a role in the events of August 4, 1964. In the early afternoon, the Pacific Fleet Commander, Admiral U. S. G. ("Ollie") Sharp tells Gen. David Burchinal in Washington that he is not really sure that the suspected North Vietnamese attack has occurred. Two hours later, Robert McNamara queries Sharp, saying that they should not begin to execute the retaliatory air attack on North Vietnam until they confirm that, in fact, the U.S. vessel was attacked. Two hours after that, Sharp concludes that the attack "probably" occurred. So at just past 6:00 PM, EDT, the worry shifts to whether Washington will announce that a retaliatory attack is under way before the attacking planes are out of danger, or "off target." Burchinal reassures Sharp that "nothing comes out of here until we know that you're off target." Unfortunately, Sharp has great difficulty confirming either that an attack has occurred, and if it has, whether it is safe for President Johnson to make his public announcement of a retaliatory strike. Able to wait no longer, Johnson goes on radio and television at just past 11:30 PM EDT. As a harbinger of what is to come, Lt. Everett Alvarez, Jr., of San Jose, California, a pilot in the raid, is shot down over Hon Gay, in North Vietnam, and captured—the first of what would become hundreds of Americans, mostly pilots, who would be held throughout the war in the infamous Hoa Lo (or "Hanoi Hilton") Prison in central Hanoi.

"It was just confusion, . . . our judgment that we'd been attacked that day was wrong. It didn't happen."

[Transcripts of telephone logs of Department of Defense conversations during the Tonkin Gulf Episode, at 2:08 PM, 4:08 PM, 6:07 PM, and 11:11 PM (all EDT), August 4, 1964.[11]

2:08 PM EDT:

Admiral U. S. G. Sharp: It does appear now that a lot of these torpedo attacks were torpedoes reported in the water from the sonar men, you see, and probably a lot of them inaccurate because whenever they get keyed up on a thing like this everything they hear on the sonar is a torpedo.

General David Burchinal: You're pretty sure there was a torpedo attack?

Sharp: No doubt about that, I think. No doubt about that. Oh, there is one report here that says they think that maybe one PT was sunk by another. But that's—this is still in the conjecture stage.

Burchinal: Okay, well, that's fine. . . . Thank you, Ollie.

Sharp: Welcome. Bye.

4:08 PM:

Robert McNamara: Hello, Ollie, this is Bob McNamara. What's the latest information on the action . . . ? There isn't any possibility there was no attack, is there?

Sharp: Yes, I would say there is a slight possibility, and that is what I am trying to find out right now, and about 20 minutes ago I told [Admiral] Tom Moorer to get in touch with these people and get a definite report on it.

McNamara: Okay. How soon do you think it will come in?

Sharp: Well, it should come within an hour, but I have a slight doubt now, I must admit, and we are trying to get it nailed down.

. . .

McNamara: We obviously don't want to do it until we are damn sure what happened.

Sharp: That's right.

McNamara: Now, how do we reconcile all this?

Sharp: Well, I would recommend this, sir. I would recommend that we hold this execute until we have a definite indication of what happened.

McNamara: Well, how do we get that?

Sharp: I think I can—I think I will have it in a couple of hours.

McNamara: Okay, well, the execute is scheduled for 7:00 PM our time, which is three hours from now, right?

Sharp: Yes, sir.

McNamara: Alright, so if you have it in two hours, we still have an hour.

Sharp: It's 7:00 o'clock out there?

McNamara: That's right, and that is three hours from now.

Sharp: Yes, sir.

McNamara: If you get your definite information in two hours, we can still proceed with the execute, and it seems to me we ought to go ahead on that basis—get the pilots briefed, get the planes armed, get everything lined up to go.

Sharp: Yes, sir.

McNamara: Continue the execute order in effect, but between now and 6 o'clock get a definite fix and you call me directly.

Sharp: I agree, yes sir, I will do that.

McNamara: Okay, very good.

Sharp: Right, sir. Bye.

6:07 PM EDT:

Sharp: Now the press should not get this story at 1900 [7:00 PM EDT] your time [in Washington].

Burchinal: We are cognizant of that and will probably not—we will insure that nothing comes out of here until we know that you're off target.

Sharp: Alright. That's going to be 2100 [9:00 PM EDT] your time.

Burchinal: We're making plans to have it late.

Sharp: Well, I notice that there is going to be a meeting across the river [at the White House].

Burchinal: It's going on right now, but nothing's coming out of it at the moment. They will delay that until they are sure that there is no possibility of anyone reading it.

Sharp: Okay, I'm not going to call you again on this—this is my telling you that I'm going to execute.

Burchinal: This is my telling you that that's our understanding here firmly.

Sharp: Okay.

Burchinal: Fine, Ollie.

Sharp: Thank you, Dave. Goodbye.

11:11 PM EDT:

Sharp: Yes, sir.

McNamara: Ollie, if you don't launch against those northerly targets because of bad weather—

Sharp: Yes, sir.

McNamara: Is there any reason why the [U.S. aircraft carrier] *Constellation* couldn't launch against the southerly targets, including the oil depot?

Sharp: No, sir. That is exactly what we would do.

McNamara: Is the weather okay down there?

Sharp: It is better down there, sir. It's not good; it's deteriorating now.

McNamara: I think the point is that as a nation we just can't sit here and let them attack us on the high seas and not do something.

Sharp: No, sir.

McNamara: So I think the President has to say that we are going to retaliate.

Sharp: We are going to do it, sir. There is no doubt about that. It is just that I don't think that there is any question that they have launched. It is just the question of getting the doggone report.

McNamara: Okay.

Sharp: I have just blasted them again.

McNamara: Okay, Ollie. Thanks again.

Sharp: Doing my best.

McNamara: Right-oh.

Sharp: Right-oh.

Those Americans who stay up late enough to see President Johnson deliver his statement live from the White House see an exhausted, perspiring, evidently uncomfortable leader. That he slurs some of his words is, in retrospect, hardly surprising, since it is nearly midnight, and he has been attempting for more than twelve hours to craft a policy, and this speech. His statement is somewhat confusing, mostly because he succeeds to a fault in allowing for equal parts toughness and outrage, on the one hand and, on the other, the concerned benevolence of a parent figure, explaining that while the retaliatory strike was necessary, "we seek no wider war," beyond what was done, which he says was "limited and fitting." In other words, a crime was committed by North Vietnam, and the punishment given them by U.S. forces fit the crime. Johnson thus seems equally uncomfortable with either the strong "reply" he has ordered, or with a "wider war" he says he wants to avoid.

Moreover, while he may not be seeking a wider war, he clearly is prepared to pursue one, if the North Vietnamese do not cease their "aggression" against U.S. assets and personnel in and around Vietnam. To accomplish this, he announces that he will urge Congress to pass legislation permitting Washington "to take all necessary measures" in southeast Asia to preserve an independent, noncommunist South Vietnam. The key question on his mind is clearly: will Hanoi cease and desist, under this threat of U.S. retaliation? Johnson, and the world, would get their answer in due course. Hanoi, convinced that the bombing of August 4–5, 1964 indicated that the Americans were bent on destroying them, would decide to escalate the war, rather than bend to U.S. pressure. In fact, the events in the Tonkin Gulf will spur the North Vietnamese to prepare for total war against the world's most powerful country—something that was still scarcely imaginable in official Washington on August 4, 1964.

[President Lyndon Johnson's announcement that air attacks had been carried out against targets in North Vietnam,[12] delivered from the White House, August 4, 1964, at 11:36 PM EDT.]

My fellow Americans:

As President and Commander in Chief, it is my duty to the American people to report that renewed hostile actions against United States ships on the high seas in the Gulf of Tonkin have today required me to take action in reply.

The initial attack on the destroyer *Maddox*, on August 2, was repeated today by a number of hostile vessels attacking two U.S. destroyers with torpedoes. The destroyers and supporting aircraft acted at once on the orders I gave after the initial act of aggression. We believe at least two of the attacking boats were sunk. There were no U.S. losses.

The performance of commanders and crews in this engagement is in the highest tradition of the United States Navy. But repeated acts of violence against the Armed Forces of the United States must be met not only with alert defense, but with positive reply. That reply is being given as I speak to you tonight. Air action is now in execution against gunboats and certain supporting facilities in North Vietnam which have been used in these hostile operations. In the larger sense, this new act of aggression, aimed directly at our own forces, again brings home to all of us in the United States the importance of the struggle for peace and security in southeast Asia. Aggression by terror against the peaceful villagers of South Vietnam has now been joined by open aggression on the high seas against the United States of America.

The determination of all Americans to carry out our full commitment to the people and to the government of South Vietnam will be redoubled by this outrage. Yet our response, for the present, will be limited and fitting. We Americans know, though others appear to forget, the risks of spreading conflict. We still seek no wider war.

I have instructed the Secretary of State to make this position totally clear to friends and to adversaries and, indeed, to all. I have instructed Ambassador [to the United Nations, Adlai] Stevenson to raise this matter immediately and urgently before the Security Council of the United Nations. Finally, I have today met with the leaders of both parties in the Congress of the United States and I have informed them that I shall immediately request the Congress to pass a resolution making it clear that our government is united in its determination to take all necessary measures in support of freedom and in defense of peace in southeast Asia.

I have been given encouraging assurance by these leaders of both parties that such a resolution will be promptly introduced, freely and expeditiously debated, and passed with overwhelming support. And just a few minutes ago I was able to reach Senator [Barry] Goldwater and I am glad to say that he has expressed his support of the statement that I am making to you tonight.

It is a solemn responsibility to have to order even limited military action by forces whose overall strength is as vast and as awesome as those of the United States of America, but it is my stated conviction, shared throughout your government, that firmness in the right is indispensable today for peace; that firmness will always be measured. Its mission is peace.

"The Tonkin Gulf Resolution" is perhaps the most controversial public U.S. document associated with the escalation of the war in Vietnam. It states the U.S. government's case on the Tonkin Gulf events succinctly, and it offers considerable insight into what will become the U.S. rationale for "Americanizing" the war, when combat troops were sent to Vietnam the following year. Here is the argument: (a) North Vietnam is the aggressor, in the Tonkin Gulf and throughout southeast Asia, in that the Hanoi government seeks to overthrow the government in Saigon; (b) the U.S. seeks only to assist "the people of South Vietnam" as they endeavor to resist the "aggression" from the north; (c) and finally, the U.S. has treaty obligations that require it to come to the aid of any member nation in the region being threatened by an outside power, exactly as South Vietnam is threatened. The U.S. must therefore act with force to oppose force, but not more than what is necessary to force Hanoi to cease and desist.

The U.S., in addition, has no imperial aims in the region and will, in fact, leave South Vietnam on its own, to work out its own future, once Hanoi understands that its aggressive behavior toward Saigon will cause it more pain than it is worth. Thus, the U.S., according to this resolution, can and must "take all necessary measures" to preserve an independent, noncommunist South Vietnam. As Lyndon Johnson is said to have remarked, the Tonkin Gulf Resolution is "like Grandma's nightshirt—it covers everything." Neither he nor his advisers ever imagined, however, that within three years of the passage of this resolution, "everything" would involve more than 500,000 U.S. combat troops fighting, dying and (ultimately) losing in Vietnam.

[The "Tonkin Gulf Resolution," signed by President Lyndon Johnson on August 10, 1964.][13]

"Sec. 1. Whereas the naval units of the communist regime in Vietnam, in violation of the principles of the Charter of the United Nations and of international law, have deliberately and repeatedly attacked United States naval vessels lawfully present in international waters and have thereby created a serious threat to international peace;

"Whereas these attacks are part of a deliberate and systematic campaign that the communist regime in North Vietnam has been waging against its neighbors and the nations joined with them in the collective defense of their freedom;

"Whereas the United States is assisting the peoples of southeast Asia to protect their freedom and has no territorial, military or political ambitions in that area, but desires only that these peoples should be left in peace to work out their own destinies in their own way. Now therefore, be it

Resolved by the Senate and House of Representatives of the United States of America in Congress assembled that the Congress approves and supports the determination of the President, as Commander in Chief, to take all necessary measures to repel any armed attack against the forces of the United States and to prevent further aggression.

"Sec. 2. The United States regards as vital to its national interest and to world peace the maintenance of the international peace and security in southeast Asia. Consonant with the Constitution and the Charter of the United Nations and in accordance with its obligations under the Southeast Asia Collective Defense Treaty, the United States is, therefore, as the President determines, to take all necessary steps, including the use of armed force, to assist any member or protocol states [such as South Vietnam] of the Southeast Asia Collective Defense Treaty requesting assistance in defense of its freedom.

"Sec. 3. This resolution shall expire when the President shall determine that the peace and security of the area is reasonably assured by international conditions created by action of the United Nations or otherwise, except that it may be terminated earlier by concurrent resolution of the Congress."

The following chronology of events was reconstructed in the 1980s by the Vietnamese Defense Ministry. It gives a concise outline of Hanoi's point of view toward the Tonkin Gulf events of August 1964. The argument is roughly the following: (a) the U.S. is the aggressor—it has no legitimate business patrolling so close to North Vietnamese territory; (b) the U.S. strategy is to try to intimidate North Vietnam so that Hanoi ceases its efforts to aid the National Liberation Front (NLF) in the south, in the hope of eventually unifying the country under the leadership of the communist government in the north; and (c) the action taken on August 2, 1964, was initiated by a local commander in the area, not from the central authority in Hanoi, as Washington assumed at the time.

One might think that the local commander in question would have been punished in some fashion for initiating an action that resulted in the first U.S. bombing of North Vietnam. However, while they did not order the attack of the North Vietnamese PT boat on the destroyer Maddox, leaders in Hanoi were not displeased. Instead, we find the following comment in Hanoi's official 1988 history of the episode, "August 5, 1964: The Vietnamese People's Navy makes the date of its first merit in defeating the U.S. navy and air force in the North as its tradition day."[14] Why the honor? Apparently for carrying out, on their own initiative, essentially a suicide mission against the Maddox, and thus luring the U.S. into an air attack.

[Hanoi's view of the Tonkin Gulf affair: A chronology of military events.][15]

- On July 30 U.S. warships violated our coastal waters and fired on Hon Ngu Island (Nghe Tinh Province) 4 kilometers from the coast, and Hon Me Island (Thanh Hoa Province), 12 kilometers from the coast.
- On July 31 the U.S. destroyer *Maddox* entered the zone south of Con Co Island to begin its "tour" of reconnoitering and threatening along our coast.
- On July 31 and August 1 1964 U.S. airplanes based in Laos bombed the border defense post at Nam Can and Nong De Village in Nghe Tinh Province, which were situated 7 to 20 kilometers from the Vietnamese-Laotian border.

- Faced with that situation, the local naval commanders adopted the policy of striking back at and punishing the pirates who violated our waters and our people's security.
- At noon on Sunday, August 2 1964, our navy's Squadron 3, consisting of three torpedo boats, was ordered to set out and to resolutely punish the "acts of piracy" of the U.S. imperialists, and to attack the destroyer *Maddox*, which had penetrated deeply into our coastal waters in the area between Hon Me Island and Lach Truong in Thanh Hoa Province.[16]

Dialogues

In November 1995, Robert McNamara becomes the first senior U.S. official during the Vietnam War to visit Hanoi. He does so to inquire as to whether the Vietnamese government wishes to collaborate on an inquiry into key decision points in the escalation of the war, along the lines of the Cuban missile crisis project, which had produced such striking results. During that visit, McNamara meets with his counterpart during the 1960s, Gen. Vo Nguyen Giap, the legendary former defense minister and architect of Hanoi's military strategy.

Supremely confident, dismissive of any suggestion that any of Hanoi's decisions may have been based on false assumptions about the Americans, Giap is the "anti-McNamara." McNamara is remarkably willing to consider the possibility that he was mistaken in ways that contributed to what he calls the "tragedy" of Vietnam. Giap tells McNamara that a Vietnamese-American inquiry would be interesting, though the Vietnamese missed no opportunities, would do nothing different, and were participants in a "noble sacrifice," rather than a tragedy. In their discussion of the Tonkin Gulf incident, with which their discussion began, Giap tells McNamara that he knows that the Americans purposely provoked the affair, because they were anxious to take over the war from the South Vietnamese. Although both of these conclusions are highly questionable at best, McNamara is unable to convince Giap to keep an open mind at least until the planned conference occurs.

Not everyone in Vietnam agrees with Giap. There is plenty of evidence that many Vietnamese feel ambivalent about the war, even questioning whether it should have been fought at all, though in the tightly controlled Vietnamese society, these sentiments are seldom stated directly and publicly. But our own experience in Vietnam suggests that many have a good deal of sympathy for the view of the writer known as Bao Ninh, whose 1993 novel, The Sorrow of War, *became a bestseller. The novel is based on the author's experience in 1969, when all but ten of his brigade (of more than 500) were killed in some of the war's bloodiest fighting. The book rejects Giap's smug triumphalism, and focusses instead on "the horrors of war . . . the cruelties, the humiliations . . . all the ridiculous prejudice and dogma which pervaded everyone's life." According to the author, "each of us had been crushed by the war in a different way."[17] The Vietnamese government permitted the publication of the novel, but placed Bao Ninh under house arrest when it became a bestseller, in Vietnam and abroad. One wonders how long it will be before such views can be put forth in Vietnam without fear of official reprisals.*

[A discussion between Robert McNamara and Gen. Vo Nguyen Giap at a November 1995 meeting in Hanoi, Vietnam.][18]

Robert McNamara: General, I want us to examine our mindsets, and to look at specific instances where we—Hanoi and Washington—may each have been mistaken, have misunderstood each other, such as in the Tonkin Gulf episode we've been discussing.

Gen. Vo Nguyen Giap: I don't believe we misunderstood you. You were the enemy; you wished to defeat us—to destroy us. So we were forced to fight you—to fight a "People's War" to reclaim our country from your neo-imperialist ally in Saigon—we used the word "puppet," of course, back then—and to reunify our country.

Robert McNamara: General, I am interested—and my U.S. colleagues are interested—in putting a claim such as you have just made to the test at our conference. Were we—was I, was Kennedy, was Johnson—a "neo-imperialist" in the sense you are using the word? I would say *absolutely not!* Now, if we can agree on an agenda focussed on episodes like Tonkin Gulf, where we may have misunderstood each other, then. . . .

Gen. Vo Nguyen Giap: Excuse me, but we *correctly* understood you—what you were doing in the Tonkin Gulf. You were carrying out sabotage activities to create a pretext that would allow you to take over the war from the Saigon government, which was incompetent.

Robert McNamara: That is totally wrong, General. I assure you: there was no such intent. None. But this is why we need to re-examine each other's misunderstandings—for two reasons. First, we need to identify missed opportunities; and second, we need to draw lessons which will allow us to avoid such tragedies in the future.

Gen. Vo Nguyen Giap: Lessons are important. I agree. However, you are wrong to call the war a "tragedy"—to say that it came from missed opportunities. Maybe it *was* a tragedy for you, because yours was a war of aggression, in the neo-colonialist "style," or fashion of the day for the Americans. You wanted to replace the French; you failed; men died; so, yes, it was tragic, because they died for a bad cause.

But for us, the war against you was a noble sacrifice. We did not want to fight the U.S. We did not. But you gave us no choice. Our people sacrificed tremendously for our cause of freedom and independence. There were no missed opportunities for us. We did what we had to do to drive you and your "puppets"—I apologize, Mr. McNamara, for again using the term "puppet"—to drive you and your puppets out. So I agree that *you* missed opportunities and that *you* need to draw lessons. But us? I think we would do nothing different, under the circumstances.

At the June 1997 conference in Hanoi, Robert McNamara was told by credible Vietnamese participants that he and the Johnson administration had been wrong on two key issues regarding the Tonkin Gulf episode: first, the attack on August 2 had been ordered by a local commander, not the central authority in Hanoi; and second, the August 4 attack considered by the Johnson administration to be "probable but not certain" never occurred. No wonder, as McNamara says later, that the North Vietnamese believed the whole affair was a pretext cooked up in Washington to facilitate an increased American role in the war. He finds this view completely at variance with his memory and the tale told in U.S. declassified documents. But now he under-

stands why Hanoi had responded as it had, on the (incorrect) assumption that as of August 4–5 1964, the Johnson administration had already decided to try to destroy them.

Sometimes a personal detail can drive home a larger point with great poignancy and power. Mr. Luu Doan Huynh, a former foreign ministry official and now a leading Vietnamese scholar of the war, provides just such a detail in a February 1998 conference in Hanoi. Huynh recounts how, immediately following the August 4–5, 1964 bombing, his own son, like children all over North Vietnam, were evacuated from Hanoi to the countryside, where many would spend their entire childhood. The whole country went on permanent alert. The bombing had started. What became known in the north as the American "war of destruction" had begun.

[A discussion between Robert McNamara, Gen. Nguyen Dinh Uoc, and Luu Doan Huynh, at a June 1997 conference in Hanoi, Vietnam of U.S. and Vietnamese policymakers, and scholars of the Vietnam War.][19]

Robert McNamara: The first question I have is: was there an attack on the *Maddox* on August 2nd, 1964. The answer to that is almost surely "yes." I say this because I have a fragment of a North Vietnamese shell that I took off the deck of the *Maddox,* so I think there had to be an attack. But I'd like this on the record. I see my Vietnamese colleagues nodding agreement. Okay, We'll accept that.

Now, the more important question . . . is: who ordered it? Was it a local commander or did the order come from a central authority?

Gen. Nguyen Dinh Uoc: Now, as to whether or not the North Vietnamese attacked the American ship *Maddox* on the 2nd of August: General Vo Nguyen Giap said that one of the responsibilities of the Vietnamese navy in Thanh Hoa was to guard against any vessels violating the national waters of Vietnam. And if there were violations, the navy had the right to attack in order to protect those waters. That was the general policy adopted by the central authority to defend the country's sea coast, at the time. It was not a decision made centrally. That is the answer.

Robert McNamara: Thank you for a very clear answer. It points to something that certainly we did not understand or anticipate at the time. . . . There was a far greater de-centralization of authority and command with respect to the North Vietnamese military than we understood at the time. I think it's an important point, because it now seems as if we may have drawn unwarranted conclusions, based on our misunderstanding of your command and control arrangements.

Second question: did the presumed second attack occur on August 4th—on the *Turner Joy* and the *Maddox*?

Gen. Nguyen Dinh Uoc: I will give you my opinion. Several days ago, when I met with him, General Vo Nguyen Giap did say very clearly that the August 4th "incident" positively did not occur. And the general also said that his private journal testifies that the August 4th "incident" did not occur. And that is the truth.

· · ·

Luu Doan Huynh: We understood that the bombing [of August 4–5, 1964] was designed to curb the fighting will of North Vietnam; and also to halt supplies to the South. That is true. We did see those motives behind the decision to bomb the North.

But I would add to this that there was something else that we saw—that was indicated by the bombing. This was a signal—as we saw it—showing that you have not only extended the war to the North, but you were also going to expand the war in the South. You were going to "Americanize" the war. Based on this assessment, we believed that very important decisions would soon be made in Washington. So we have to be careful. We have to be ready to face the possibility of an imminent escalation to a big war with the U.S. This worried us a lot.

In fact, we expected the bombing of North Vietnam to begin sometime in 1963. Yes, I said "1963." One of your high officials, according to your documents, claimed in 1963 that we were using "salami tactics" to avoid your bombing. Anyway, so the bombing began. After the bombing started in early 1965, President Ho Chi Minh made a statement calling on all Vietnamese to fight for the liberation of the country. This is a very significant statement—very significant, and I am not sure the Americans understood the meaning of it at the time. It means that since you have extended the war to North Vietnam, we are now saying—officially saying—that we are entering the war in the South.

. . .

I told you before that since 1963, we were anticipating the bombing. I don't mean that we thought the bombing was going to begin in 1963. Maybe yes, maybe no. What I mean is that was when we concluded that *at some point* you will begin the bombing. Why? Because at some point, you will see that you are losing ground in the South. So we decided to stand ready.

Now I am talking about August 5, 1964 and the bombing right after. After August 5, the children in Hanoi were ordered to go to the countryside for dispersal. My young son was among these children who were quickly moved to the countryside, because we knew that the bombing—the real bombing in earnest—could begin at any time. Our Foreign Ministry, and many other ministries, organized boarding houses in the countryside for the children.

So, this means that in 1963 we realized—I would say for the first time—that the bombing is coming, at some point. In August 1964, we went on alert, so to speak, and evacuated children from Hanoi, in anticipation of the bombing. And the bombing began the following February.

The Dilemma: We Remain Prisoners of Our Mindsets

Why did Defense Secretary Robert McNamara, after agonizing over the available information from his sources in the Pacific, finally say to President Lyndon Johnson that the alleged "second" attack in the Tonkin Gulf on August 4, 1964, was "probable, but not certain," knowing that Johnson would subsequently order "retaliatory" air strikes against targets in North Vietnam? One answer, suggested in the text of the documents and dialogues of this chapter, is a combination of otherwise unrelated factors, including domestic political concerns (a decision must be made showing the president, who is running for election against a "hawk," Barry Goldwater, to be forceful), and uncertainty about the weather over North Vietnam (a "window of opportunity" for retaliating was closing, as the cloud cover thickened). In addition, McNamara knew well the palpable confusion among the U.S. officers in the Tonkin Gulf and elsewhere—those who were trying to determine whether or not an attack had actually occurred. As McNamara says in the film, "It was just confusion." Yet a decision had to be made, and he made it—wrongly, as it happened and, as McNamara recognizes now, "it [the mistake] carried such heavy costs."

The fundamental problem, however, was not politics or weather or even the confusion of the sonar analysts. These and other operational factors only exacerbated the fundamental problem—which is that both Washington and Hanoi were imprisoned in mindsets about the adversary that led them to conclusions about the events in the Tonkin Gulf that *seemed* self-evidently true at the time, but were in fact, as McNamara notes in the film (with the benefit of his subsequent research), "absolutely absurd."

Thus, it was simply inconceivable to leaders in Washington that a local North Vietnamese commander might make a decision on his own to attack a U.S. destroyer. A decision of such significance *must* come from Hanoi, or so they mistakenly assumed. Thus, any such attack must, to leaders in Washington, also represent a carefully calibrated escalation of the war against the U.S., by Hanoi's leaders. On the other hand, the mindset of Hanoi's leaders was a mirror image of the Washington mindset. Leaders in Hanoi had for years theorized endlessly about when the U.S. would—not might, or could, but *would*—begin an all-out air war against the North. Thus, *any* bombing of the North publicly announced by the U.S. president could not possibly represent simply an episode, a retaliatory response pure and simple, to provocations, as President Johnson stated. It was, they concluded, the beginning of the U.S. attempt to totally destroy North Vietnam, and they made preparations from that point onward to fight the Americans "to the death."

Thus, the way incoming information was *organized*—not the information itself—proved decisive in both Washington and Hanoi, not the information itself. Each group was imprisoned in a powerfully held, but deeply erroneous mindset. Each side, believing the other had already made an irrevocable decision for all-out war, took actions in defense that seemed, to the other, to confirm their worst-case hypotheses. The misunderstandings of each side led to actions that guaranteed that each side's beliefs would become self-fulfilling prophecies.

In this 21st century, rigid and misguided mindsets affecting decisions related to peace and war seem to be proliferating, with disastrous consequences. Osama bin Laden, for example, apparently believed the 9/11 attacks would spur massive counterattacks by the West, followed by revolution throughout the Islamic world. But as subsequent events proved, this was bin Laden's mindset at work, not reality. Likewise, the U.S. administration of George W. Bush could not conceive of the possibility that Saddam Hussein's Iraq didn't possess weapons of mass destruction (WMD), and was prepared to use them. So in the spring of 2003, a war and occupation of Iraq was undertaken, killing thousands, and infuriating much of the world, but without the discovery of a single weapon of mass destruction. As with the Johnson administration's handling of the Tonkin Gulf affair, these recent mistakes "carried such heavy costs"—costs, we add, not yet calculated in full, as the U.S. "war on terror" continues unabated, and Islamic extremists continue to call for a jihad, or holy war, against the U.S. and its allies.

See Appendix B, Lesson Three, for further discussion of this dilemma.

"*I analyzed bombing operations, and how to make them more efficient . . . in weakening the adversary.*"

CHAPTER 4

Lesson Four: "Proportionality Should Be a Guideline in War"

[Gen. Curtis] LeMay . . . was the only person I knew in the senior command of the Air Force who focused solely on the loss of his crews per unit of target destruction. I was on the island of Guam in his command in March 1945. In that single night, we burned to death 100,000 Japanese civilians in Tokyo: men, women and children.

. . .

I think the issue is: in order to win a war should you kill 100,000 people in one night, by firebombing or any other way? LeMay's answer would be clearly "yes."

"McNamara, do you mean to say that instead of killing 100,000 Japanese civilians—burning to death 100,000 Japanese civilians in that one night—we should have burned to death a lesser number, or none? And then had our soldiers cross the beaches in Tokyo and been slaughtered in the tens of thousands? Is that what you're proposing? Is that moral? Is that wise?"

. . .

Proportionality should be a guideline in war. Killing 50 percent to 90 percent of the people of 67 Japanese cities and then bombing them with two nuclear bombs is not proportional, in the minds of some people, to the objectives we were trying to achieve.

. . .

LeMay said, "If we'd lost the war, we'd all have been prosecuted as war criminals." . . . LeMay recognized that what he was doing would have been thought immoral if his side had lost. But what makes it immoral if you lose and not immoral if you win?

ROBERT McNAMARA in "The Fog of War."

In the United States, *the Second World War has come to be referred to as "the good war": a necessary, unavoidable war in which the U.S. and its allies, at great sacrifice, defeated the evil empires of Nazi Germany and imperial Japan. This increasing tendency to view the war in heroic terms—the forces of light triumphing over the forces of darkness—was given a significant boost by a best-selling oral history of the war, called "The Good War", published by Studs Terkel in 1991. Terkel's book has been followed by the appearance of many subsequent books, movies and television shows celebrating the bravery and sacrifices of what newscaster and author Tom Brokaw calls "The Greatest Generation"—Americans who fought in the Second World War, or who endured hardships on the home front and did so stoically, for the most part, without complaint.[1] A salutary effect of the popularity of "the good war" phenomenon in the U.S. has been to remind generations that followed "the greatest generation" just how much is owed to our parents, grandparents, and great-grandparents.*

There is a danger accompanying this revival of interest in the war, however, and it is this: that in celebrating the courage and forbearance of our elders, we lose sight of the fact that the Second World War was the greatest manmade catastrophe in human history, in which approximately fifty million people died, and which was fought with such bitterness and ferocity that even the victorious Western Allies, led by the U.S. and Great Britain, ultimately resorted to strategies and tactics that many regard as immoral, inhuman, even criminal. It is easy to forget, or perhaps not even to notice, that the phrase "the good war" that provides the title of Terkel's popular book is inside quotation marks. In fact, the war was a spectacle of almost unmitigated horror on an unprecedented scale. There was an overwhelming reason for the famous reluctance of the survivors of "greatest generation" to talk about their experience: they wanted to forget the horror, and the loss of loved ones and friends.

This was particularly the case in the Pacific War, in which Japan was ultimately forced to agree to an unconditional surrender in August 1945. A cartoon published three days after the December 7, 1941, Japanese attack on Pearl Harbor captures succinctly the character of the conflict which would follow. A U.S. sailor is marching resolutely toward a cannon, carrying ammunition under each arm. In the distance we see a blackened Pearl Harbor, and beyond that a blackened, ghastly face in the middle of Japan's symbol, a rising sun. At the top of the cartoon, we read "Throwing in an extra charge." A tag is attached to one of the bags of ammunition, which reads "War without mercy on a treacherous foe."[2] This would indeed by a "war without mercy"—a war fought, especially in its climactic phase, without regard for the generally accepted rules of war: for example, that prisoners of war should be treated humanely; that civilians, or noncombatants, should be immune from attack; and that the scale of attacks on an adversary should be roughly proportional to whatever objectives one is attempting to achieve. In the Pacific War, one side or the other (or sometimes both) violated these principles repeatedly, not just in isolated instances, but as a matter of policy.

What made the Pacific War arguably more brutal and cruel than even the war against Nazi Germany was a powerful and pervasive racism on both sides: the Anglo-American and the Japanese. As the MIT historian John Dower has demonstrated, "the end results of racial thinking on both sides were virtually identical . . . arrogance, viciousness, atrocity, and death."[3] The Japanese had stereotyped Americans as decadent and ineffectual, a "race" of "soft" unworthy cowards, thus unlikely to fight back (after the attack on Pearl Harbor), a people worthy only of contempt. The American stereotype of the Japanese adversary is illustrated by the comments of a woman named Peggy Terry, whose interview by Studs Terkel appears in his book, "The Good War." Peggy Terry told Terkel that whereas the Germans "were good lookin' and they looked like us . . . with the Japanese, that was a whole different thing. We were just ready to wipe them out. They sure as heck didn't look like us. They were yellow little creatures that smiled when they bombed our boys."[4] In other words, the Japanese were generally viewed not just as an enemy with interests irreconcilable with our own, but as wantonly cruel, almost inhumanly so. They were often portrayed throughout the war by American cartoonists as various species of animals, often monkeys or even insects.

Robert McNamara tells Errol Morris in "The Fog of War" that in the Pacific War, he "analyzed bombing operations, and how to make them more efficient—i.e., not more efficient in the sense of killing more, but more efficient in weakening the adversary." In fact, soon after McNamara was reassigned to the Pacific, from the European theater, there would no longer exist in Allied planning any meaning-ful distinction between "killing more" Japanese, and "weakening" the Japanese capacity for making war against the U.S. and its allies. What had previously been widely regarded as indiscriminant, im-moral, unacceptable bombing of civilian targets—it was often called "terror bombing" by those who opposed it—was rechristened "area bombing," and "strategic bombing." Its ostensible objective: to break the will of the adversary to carry on the fight—to destroy the enemy's morale, and by this means shorten the war.

It happened this way: beginning in 1940, the Nazis began bomb-ing London and other British cities indiscriminantly. The British re-taliated by bombing German cities indiscriminantly, once they ac-quired the capacity to do so.[5] For example, in July and August 1942, the British Royal Air Force (RAF), in collaboration with the U.S. Army Air Force, bombed Hamburg with incendiaries (or "firebombs"), which created a wholesale conflagration that burnt much of the city to the ground, creating firestorms of flame at temperatures of 1,000 degrees centigrade, with winds of 100–150 miles per hour, incinerat-ing people above and below ground. Dresden was similarly destroyed in a firebombing in February, 1945.[6] By late 1944, the defeat of the Nazis was apparently imminent, while the Pacific War was becoming more brutal by the day (as the Japanese refused to surrender in battle after battle to numerically superior American forces, taking horren-dous casualties, but also inflicting terrible losses on the Americans).

Thus it was that, near the end of 1944, the thirty-eight-year-old U.S. Air Force General Curtis LeMay, along with key people on his staff, including McNamara, arrived in the Mariana Islands, newly captured from the Japanese. The Marianas had been captured specif-ically so that they could be used as bases for the B-29 "superfortresses" with which the air war against Japan would be waged. LeMay defined his task this way: to "weaken the adversary," via burning up Japanese cities with incendiary bombs (a controversial idea, conceived by LeMay) and everything in them, including the Japanese themselves. McNamara, working as a planning officer in LeMay's command, was "part of a mechanism," as he says in "The Fog of War," that would burn up Japan until the government in Tokyo surrendered, or until Japan was completely destroyed, whichever came first.

In the film, McNamara cites the American theologian and moral philosopher Reinhold Neibuhr, who asked in 1946: "how much evil must we do in order to do good?"[7] There are, alas, no hard and fast rules for adjudicating such a question in specific cases. But who can doubt that McNamara is sympathetic to the assessment in a major British history of the Second World War, regarding the firebombing of Tokyo on March 9–10, 1945, and the massive bombing that followed, including the two atomic bombings in August of 1945? The air campaign against Japan, write these historians, was "sheer, unadulterated murder."[8] Was it justified? Possibly. But mass murder by the "good guys" was nonetheless required to subdue the "bad guys" in order to bring "the good war" to an end. One of the virtues of "The Fog of War" is that it forces its audience to grapple with these uncomfortable truths about the Pacific War.

Documents

The following excerpt from the record of LeMay's force, the XXI Bomber Command, gets us closer to the "reality" of the Pacific War, seen through the prism of planners and analysts like LeMay and McNamara. Note the experimentation with various bombing methods. Immediately after LeMay's arrival in the Marianas, the missions remained the traditional ones associated with so-called "precision bombing": industries were targeted, relatively small numbers of bombers were involved, and the weapons were conventional bombs. But the bombing was imprecise and ineffective. By February 1945, LeMay had decided to try something new: massive firebombing of Japanese cities with bomber forces of unprecedented size. Between February 24th and March 18th, the XXI Bomber Command attacked some of Japan's largest cities, using incendiaries, and with forces for each mission three to four times the size of those deployed before February 24th. The strategy worked. In Tokyo alone, sixteen square miles were totally destroyed. Approximately eighty to one hundred thousand people were killed outright, and a million were left homeless. Canals boiled. People burst spontaneously into flames. The Sumida River overflowed with human corpses. LeMay's assessment was typically coarse, but accurate: the citizens of Tokyo, he said, had been "scorched and boiled and baked to death."[9]

[U.S. Army Air Force XXI Bomber Command Missions Over Japan, March–April, 1945.][10]

XXI BOMBER COMMAND MISSIONS, 1944–45 [EXCERPTS]

Date	B-29s	Target	Target Type	Bomb Type
1944				
Dec 18	89	Nagoya	Factories	HE, I
Dec 22	78	Nagoya	Factories	I
Dec 24	29	Iwo Jima	Airfields	HE
Dec 27	72	Tokyo	Factories	HE
1945				
Jan 3	97	Nagoya	Urban Areas	HE
Jan 9	72	Tokyo	Urban Areas	HE

(Jan 14–Feb 19, 15 missions were carried out against targets in Japan, almost exclusively with HE, each with an average of fewer than 100 B-29s.)

Date	B-29s	Target	Target Type	Bomb Type
Feb 24	229	Tokyo	Urban Areas	I
Mar 4	192	Tokyo	Urban Areas	I
Mar 9	325	Tokyo	Urban Areas	I
Mar 11	310	Nagoya	Urban Areas	I
Mar 13	301	Osaka	Urban Areas	I
Mar 16	330	Kobe	Urban Areas	I
Mar 18	310	Nagoya	Urban Areas	I

(Mar 24–Apr 12, 14 missions were carried out, using either HE or M, against industrial targets throughout Japan. The XXI Bomber Command had depleted its supply of incendiary bombs in the raids of Feb 24–Mar 18. Massive incendiary bombing was resumed on Apr 13, after the Command was resupplied with sufficient incendiary bombs.)

HE=High Explosives; I=Incendiaries (Firebombs); M=Mines

We now enter the universe of the probability and statistics of bombing that was the daily bread of Robert McNamara during the war. These grim numbers show that LeMay's campaign to burn up Japan, while "working" (in the sense that the missions have hurt both industrial production and morale), has also created manpower

"In that single night, we burned to death 100,000 Japanese civilians in Tokyo: men, women, and children."

problems. What McNamara demonstrates is that even at relatively low loss rates, LeMay may be forced to cut back his campaign by the early fall, due to a shortage of crews (assuming, of course, that Japan has not yet capitulated). A shortage may or may not occur, according to McNamara's memorandum, depending on the assumptions one brings to the analysis. For example, what will be the loss rate; and will B-29 crews from Europe arrive in the Pacific in time to bolster U.S. manpower? Note that this memorandum is dated 22 May, and is concerned with the situation that might develop by October or November. McNamara, a lieutenant colonel, knows nothing of the existence of the atomic bomb, or the plans to use it against Japan. General LeMay has been informed, however, about The Bomb. It will be his command that ultimately drops one atomic bomb each on Hiroshima (on August 6) and Nagasaki (on August 9), producing results so horrible that the Japanese, despite having vowed a fight to the death, capitulated. In addition, note the stark reality described by McNamara's analysis: at the standard thirty-five sorties for completion of tour, between 30 and 51 percent of those flying the B-29s can expect to die before the end of their tour. And toward the end of the memorandum is a chilling index of the difference in the brutality of the European and Pacific wars: in Europe, 57 percent of the crews shot down and captured by the enemy are expected to survive as POWs, while only 10 percent are expected to survive imprisonment by the Japanese.

[Memorandum from Lt. Col. R. S. McNamara to Twentieth Air Force Chief of Staff, Gen. Lauris Norstad, 22 May 1945, regarding XXI Bomber Command combat crews.][11]

MEMORANDUM TO: C/S, Twentieth Air Force [classified "SECRET"]
FROM: Lt. Col. R. S. McNamara
SUBJECT: Summary of 22 May Conversation in re
                           XXI B.C. Combat Crews

It is clear . . . that to continue to operate all crews at a maximum is the equivalent of maximizing present combat effort at the cost of future effort. By flying available crews 6 sorties [or 100 hours per crew] per month in June and July, the Command can exceed programmed effort in those two months by 2000 sorties, or by 23%. The cost of this increased effort would not be felt until late October or early November when crew strength would be sufficiently depleted to force activity below the programmed level. At that time crews would be 6% less than authorized and the monthly sortie effort would be reduced by approximately 6% or 400 sorties a month. However, if, during the next 6 months, actual crew flow to the theater exceeds that programmed, or if the actual crew loss rate is less than the programmed rate of 1.6% per sortie, the actual crew inventory on hand in late October may be equal to, or in excess of, plan. As a result, programmed effort during these later months could be maintained even though maximum effort were achieved in June and July.

· · ·

Part IV—Chance for Survival of XXI B.C. Crews:

The tables below indicate that at the 1.1% crew loss rate sustained by the XXI B.C. during the period 1 March through 15 May, the average crew had a 70% chance of completing the prescribed tour. This compares to a similar figure for the 8th A.F. of 68%. If the chance for completing the tour is adjusted to allow for those crew members who will not complete the tour but who will survive as prisoners, etc., the 1.1% loss rate of the XXI B.C. gives the XXI B.C. crews an estimated chance of survival of approximately 73% compared to an estimated chance for survival of 88% for 8th A.F. crews.

. . .

TABLE I: EFFECT OF LENGTH OF TOUR AND LOSS RATE PER SORTIE ON CHANCES FOR COMPLETING TOUR.

SORTIES IN TOUR	CHANCE FOR COMPLETING TOUR			
	1% loss/ Sortie	1.25% loss/ Sortie	1.50% loss/ Sortie	2.0% loss/ Sortie
20	82%	78%	74%	67%
25	78%	75%	69%	60%
30	74%	69%	64%	55%
35	70%	64%	59%	49%
40	67%	60%	55%	45%

TABLE II.-COMPARISON OF XXI B.C. AND 8TH A.F. COMBAT CREW CHANCE FOR SURVIVAL.

TX:Chance for completion of XXI B.C. 35-mission tour,
    —at planned loss rate of 1.5% 63%**
    —at 1 Mar–15 May loss rate of 1.1%..................73%**

TX:Chance for completion of prescribed tour
    —1 July '44 to 1 Jan '45
    actual loss rate of 1.0% 68%

Chance for survival with life
    —1 July '44 to 1 Jan '45
    actual loss rate of 1.0% 88%***

*Assumes that official AAF planning rate of 1.6% includes 1.5% for casualties and .1% for reclassifications, etc.

**Assumes that 10% of crew members lost on missions against Japan survive.

***Based on AAF reports, approximately 57% of crews listed as losses on missions against Europe survived as prisoners, escapees, etc.

Little need be said by way of introduction to the three recollections which follow, except to point out the obvious: those on the receiving end of LeMay's campaign to burn up Japan saw the situation differently than American bomber crews, or their commanding generals and their subordinates. The stories are wrenching, heartbreaking.

Errol Morris has said on numerous occasions that a particularly disturbing aspect of "The Fog of War" is not a revelation that Robert McNamara (or anybody else dealt within the film, for that matter) is an evil man who was involved in evil deeds. Instead, according to Morris, McNamara is a good man who found himself, during the Second World War (and the Vietnam War), involved in evil deeds. We agree with Morris that a world in which good people produce evil outcomes is much more troubling that a world in which evil derives simply and exclusively from the likes of a Hitler or a Stalin—certifiably perverse and enthusiastic killers of large numbers of human beings. The key question is: what permitted good people to kill innocent civilians in the way, and on the scale, that occurred in the Pacific War?

Here we believe the political theorist Hannah Arendt may be able to help us understand what happened. In Eichmann in Jerusalem, *her account of the 1960 trial of former Nazi Lieutenant Colonel Adolf Eichmann, Arendt offers two criteria for how "crimes against humanity" occur in our era: first, the existence of what she called "the death factory," in which "all the forces of calculation are coolly directed at . . . a process of sustained and unmitigated terror"; and second, that Eichmann's role in the Nazi effort to exterminate the Jews is an example of "the banality of evil," the principal characteristic of which is not that evil deeds derive from people who are inherently evil, but rather from their "remoteness from reality"—their "inability ever to look at anything from the other fellow's point of view."[12] These are Arendt's criteria: cold-blooded calculation that makes killing efficient, and the absence of empathy for the human reality that lay behind the numbers denoting the enemy.*

LeMay told McNamara that "if we'd lost the war, we'd all have been prosecuted as war criminals." It is worth pondering whether, in light of the criteria provided by Hannah Arendt, one agrees with LeMay's assessment. Whether or not we agree with LeMay, we are left staring into the abyss of McNamara's query in the film: "what makes it immoral if you lose and not immoral if you win?"

[Japanese eyewitness accounts of the firebombings.][13]

"10 March, Capital in Flames."[14]

We were among those surrounded by flames on 10 March 1945. My mother, older sister, and I tried to make our escape. Wherever I went, a wave of fire rushed toward me. Finally I made it to Oshiage station. There were thousands of people there. It was so hot and suffocating that I pressed my cheek to the ground. The air was cool and clean down there. I saw the legs of all sorts of people in front of me. Occasionally on my way a man I didn't know would splash ditch water from a bucket on us and urge us on, saying it was just a little further. Behind me a man sat covered with a large quilt. My back pressed against his, I waited for day to break, fearful and worried about the heat.

With the coming of the pale dawn, people started heading for home. Several military trucks came by around that time. Thinking they had come to help us, I stood up, and the man behind me toppled over. I shook him, but he was dead. They said he died from the smoke and the heat of the flames.

On the way home, I thought I saw some black work gloves. When I took a closer look, they were hands that had been torn off. Many red fire trucks were burned out on the major road next to the streetcar tracks, with firemen dead on their vehicles. The dead were blackened and had shrunk to the size of children. It was impossible to tell if they were men or women.

I finally made it back to the charred remains of our house. My mother and sister were there. We hugged each other, weeping . . .

Shinoda Tomoko, fifty-seven (f),
housewife, Yaita

"Hand Like a Maple Leaf."[15]

This is the first time for me to write about a sad wartime memory.

When I was in the fourth year of girls' school, I left Tokyo and went to

Fukui Prefecture to produce aircraft parts in a war plant as a member of the volunteer corps. This had once been an impressive silk-weaving factory, but with the worsening of war conditions it had been converted to a war plant. It took grim resolution for us young maidens to toil through our lives full of hunger and smeared with grease. Having just arrived, I wasn't familiar with the area, and I felt forlorn hearing the sound of explosions, shrieks, and wails.

A four- or five-year-old girl must have gotten separated from her parents, and she clutched my hand, saying "Take me with you." Feeling a bit relieved, I told her, "Let's get away from here together." Holding hands tightly, we ran for our lives. Flames rose everywhere. The little girl's face was black from sweat and dirt, and her eyes shone bright with relief.

Just then I saw a firebomb dropping toward us, spewing flames and making a shrill noise. In that instant, I dropped the little girl's hand and ducked into a nearby vacant house. Then, "Oh no, the girl!" I cried. I turned around to see behind me several people engulfed in a ball of flame, their screams rising up with the flames. A fragment of the little girl's padded hood drifted high into the sky.

The little girl died because I had let go of her hand for just an instant. I didn't even know the name of the cute little girl. I have never been able to forget the feeling of her soft, little hand, like a maple leaf, in mine. My heart still aches after the passage of forty years.

Okubo Michiko, fifty-eight (f)
housewife, Iwaki

*"A Keepsake of My Daughter Amid the Wasteland."*16

The massive air raid on Tsuruga on 12 July, close to the War's end, made an unforgettably powerful impression on me. The enemy's large formation of aircraft dropped incendiary bombs as if they were dumping water on the city. The shore breeze fanned the flames rising from various places in the blacked-out, silent city, turning it instantly into a living hell.

I was then stationed as a communications officer in the Central Area Detachment (136th unit). I set out before dawn the following morning on a scouting mission to assess the damage to the demolished communication lines and prepare for recovery. Amid the stench of death emanating from the still burning bodies of many victims, I urged my reluctant horse forward and rushed about the city. I was shocked to see a firebomb sitting like a

"What makes it immoral if you lose and not immoral if you win?"

porcupine on the white gravel on the grounds of Kibi Shrine.

As day broke, I saw a burned-out wasteland almost devoid of people. In the distance a lone elderly woman in a kimono and wooden clogs repeatedly leaned over to pick up pieces of something with chopsticks. She put the pieces on a plate. I approached her and asked her what she was doing. With a stately and unflinching demeanor, she replied, "I've lost everything, and now my daughter has turned into this. I want to have a keepsake of my daughter so that I can pray for her soul." So saying she continued to pick up and place on the dish pieces of brain from her daughter's burnt skull.

I had seen many scenes of the wretchedness of war, but this scene of a mother's love for her child impressed on me the cruelty of war, which causes such pain for innocent citizens. The scene was so brutal that I have kept it to myself, but I decided to send this in after reading the column.

Otsubo Hiroaki, sixty-four (m),

retired, Kamio

Dialogues

In the following selection, we get the war in the Pacific according to Gen. Curtis LeMay, largely in his own words, via interviews with his authorized biographer, Thomas M. Coffey. LeMay, like his (then) subordinate Robert McNamara, became a significant player on the world's stage without some of the advantages enjoyed by others. He came from modest circumstances in southeastern Ohio, and had gone to Ohio State University, rather than West Point, then the traditional preparatory school for Army Air Corps officers. He quickly established himself as an officer obsessed with the operational details of missions under his command. He was also known as a commander of considerable physical courage, shown, for example, in his insistence on leading many of the missions against targets in Germany. But LeMay would gain worldwide fame (or infamy, depending on one's point of view) at the age of thirty-eight for his single-minded and ruthless pursuit of the air war against Japan. The effort to burn up Japan was due to a remarkable extent to LeMay, and LeMay alone. He conceived it, he pushed hard to obtain the resources he needed for it, he designed it and he risked his career on its success. Without LeMay's leadership, the war in the Pacific might have been a very different war.

In what follows, we are allowed a glimpse behind the famous taciturnity, scowl and chewed cigar of LeMay—traits McNamara emphasizes in "The Fog of War." LeMay tells us, in his own words, what he believed he was up to. His mission was to shorten the war and prevent the necessity of a U.S.-led invasion of the main islands of Japan. This was indeed crucial, given examples of Japanese ferocity such as they displayed during the battle for Okinawa in April–June 1945. On this tiny island, about 50,000 Japanese troops had been killed, and fewer than 300 prisoners taken, indicating that the Japanese fully intended to follow through on their famous pledge to give the Americans a bloody battle to the death, in which hundreds of thousands, even millions might be killed.[17] But we also we encounter a LeMay far less sure of himself than the man described in "The Fog of War" by McNamara as "totally intolerant of criticism." He knew if the massive raid on Tokyo failed, his career would likely be over, and he could imagine it failing in many ways.

LeMay's interlocutor, Thomas Coffey, notes the irony in LeMay's expression of compassion (on the night of the Tokyo raid) for the suffering of the people of India, where he was once stationed. It is ironic, as Coffey notes, "considering the way the people of Tokyo would be in an hour or so." We leave it to readers to decide for themselves whether LeMay intended his comment to be ironical, or not.

"In order to win a war should you kill 100,000 people in one night, by firebombing or any other way? LeMay's answer would be clearly 'Yes.'"

[Comments by General Curtis LeMay, ed. by Thomas M. Coffey.][18]

None of LeMay's associates during the war suggested that he was one of those strange soldiers who actually enjoyed it. He was as anxious as anyone to win it and go home, which provides perhaps the primary explanation for the firmness of his decision to launch what was destined to be the most destructive series of attacks in the history of mankind. In reconstructing his thoughts at the time, he later wrote: "No matter how you slice it, you're going to kill an awful lot of civilians. Thousands and thousands. But, if you don't destroy the Japanese industry, we're going to have to invade Japan. And how many Americans will be killed in an invasion of Japan? Some say a million.

We're at war with Japan. We were attacked by Japan. Do you want to kill Japanese, or would you rather have Americans killed?"

. . . [T]he field order for the first mission [the Tokyo firebombing] didn't go out to the wings until March 8, just after lunch, about thirty hours before the planes would take off. The target: ten square miles in the center of Tokyo. The assignment: not just to raise havoc in the area but to obliterate it. . . .

Glen W. Martin, then a colonel in command of the 504th Bomb Group, has described the reaction of the Tinian-based crews at the briefing for this historic mission: "The preamble . . . included some rather SOP [standard operating procedure] items such as standard air-sea rescue arrangements. Gradually the briefing schedule approached the operational phase and the target was announced: Tokyo. And then the map was uncovered and the route was shown and then finally, bearing in mind that we had been bombing [at] around 30,000 feet, the bombing altitude was given, 5,000 feet. The tension and the interest on the part of those hundreds of people in the briefing room were truly remarkable. There was visible excitement and interest and eagerness."

The drama took a surprising turn when the announcement came that the guns and gunners were to be left at home: "That was not entirely a satisfactory situation as far as the crews were concerned. It wasn't so much because of defense—they were quite prepared to rely on the command channel—they knew LeMay went over every mission in detail. They had a lot of confidence in LeMay and his staff and right down through the wing and right on through the group and into the squadron. So there was no real concern about someone having made an error in what the enemy defenses would look like. But they wanted their crew integrity, and the gunners wanted to go with their crews.

. . .

In [LeMay's memoir], *Mission With LeMay*, there was a mention of his fears about all the things that could go wrong, the calculations that might prove false, the defensive surprises the Japanese might have ready, the American mothers who might one day blame him for the stupid, needless loss of their sons.[19] Many years after the book was published, he recalled again his feelings at that time.

"I'll admit I walked the floor [during that mission]," he said, "because I couldn't go on it. I would have gone on it. I went on the mission [in Europe] when I said we'd go straight in [with no evasive action]. That's the time when the commander goes with his troops. A lot of people didn't like this five-thousand-feet-over-the-target. But I couldn't go. I might have argued for a few more missions if it weren't for [the expected arrival of the atomic bomb], but with that it was out of the question. So I picked [Gen. Thomas S.] "Tommy" Power to lead the mission. Not only lead it but get up there first, stay there until the last plane came through, and draw me pictures of the outline of the fire at intervals. I'll admit I was nervous about it.

I made the decision. I had weighed the odds. I knew the odds were in my favor. But still, it was something new. I could have lost a lot of people and appeared to be an idiot."[20]

. . .

"If this raid works the way I think it will," LeMay said [to his press officer, Col. St. Clair ("Mac") McKelway, at 2:00 AM, 10 March 1945], "we can shorten this war. In a war, you've got to keep at least one punch ahead of the other guy all the time. A war is a very tough kind of proposition. If you don't get the enemy, he gets you. I think we've figured out a punch he's not expecting this time. I don't think he's got the right flak to combat this kind of raid and I don't think he can keep his cities from being burned down—wiped right off the map. He hasn't moved his industries to Manchuria yet, although he's starting to move them, and if we can destroy them before he can move them, we've got him. I never think anything is going to work until I've seen the pictures after the raid, but if this one works, we will shorten this damned war out here."

After looking at his watch, he said, "We won't get a bombs-away for another half-hour. Would you like a Coca-Cola? I can sneak in my quarters without waking up the other guys and get two Coca-Colas and we can drink them in my car. That'll kill most of the half-hour."

They sat in his staff car at the edge of the jungle that surrounded his headquarters and drank their Cokes while they talked about India, where both had been stationed. "The way all those people are in India gets you down," LeMay remarked with some irony, considering the way the people of Tokyo would be in an hour or so. "It makes you feel rotten."

A few minutes after they returned to the operations control room, the first bombs-away message arrived from the sky above Tokyo. It was quickly decoded and handed to LeMay.

"Bombing the primary target visually," it said. "Large fires observed. Flak moderate. Fighter opposition nil."

. . .

About nine o'clock the next morning, LeMay was at North Field to meet Tommy Power's returning plane. Though General Power was extremely tired, with dark circles under his eyes, he was also well-satisfied.

"It was a hell of a good mission," he shouted to LeMay from his cockpit seat. After releasing his own bombs, he had climbed to ten thousand feet, as LeMay had instructed, and circled the city for an hour, watching the other planes drop their deadly loads. At first, there was a sprinkling of fires throughout the target area. Then these fires grew until they merged into one great conflagration. By the time Power returned home, the center of Tokyo was an inferno.

Though all the other eye-witness reports confirmed Power's observations, LeMay didn't have the conclusive results of the raid until about midnight of the 10th, when the first reconnaissance photos, taken that afternoon, were developed. These pictures were overwhelming. They showed that at least fifteen square miles of Tokyo had been obliterated.

The official Japanese figures, which took a month to compile, would eventually show that the catastrophe was even worse than the first aerial photos indicated. Actually, 16.8 square miles of Tokyo had been destroyed. There were 83,793 fatalities and 40,918 were injured. (More than half the fatalities resulted from suffocation when the fire used up the oxygen in the air.) A million people were left homeless as 267,171 buildings were destroyed. But most important to the Allied war effort, 18 percent of Tokyo's industry was gone. The fire that engulfed Tokyo that night of March 9–10, 1945, was surpassed only by the 1923 earthquake, also in Tokyo, as the most horrendous disaster ever visited upon any city in the history of mankind. The great fires of San Francisco, Chicago, London and ancient Rome were small by comparison. At the cost of only fourteen B-29s, LeMay had found out how to destroy Japan's capacity to make war.

. . .

A few minutes after his planes returned home from Tokyo the morning of March 10, . . . [LeMay] ordered his three wing commanders to get them ready for another mission that very evening, against Japan's largest aircraft center and third largest city—Nagoya.[21]

Three days after Gen. Curtis LeMay's XXI Bomber Command had dropped the second of two atomic bombs on Nagasaki, President Harry Truman delivered a radio address to the American people, explaining what had happened and why:

We have used [the bomb] against those who have attacked us without warning at Pearl Harbor, against those who have starved and beaten and executed American prisoners of war, against those who have abandoned all pretense of obeying international laws of warfare. We have used it in order to shorten the agony of war. . . . [22]

Truman's statement contains in a nutshell the two-pronged rationale of the U.S. for the campaign to burn up Japan and ultimately, to drop atomic bombs on two of their major cities. First, the normal rules of warfare don't apply in the Japanese case; in essence, they have gotten what they deserve, having behaved despicably toward their Western foes and even toward those they presumed to "liberate" in east Asia, such as the citizens of Singapore, the Philippines, Thailand, Burma, China and Vietnam—locales in which the Japanese committed some of the war's worst atrocities. Second, the Japanese have refused all opportunities given them to surrender, and instead seem insistent on fighting until, quite literally, Japan is totally in ruins and most of its people are dead.

There is no point in dwelling here on the grotesque details of the methods used by the Japanese to torture and execute civilians, prisoners, enemies, and even ostensible allies. Nor is it necessary to recount the damage done in this manner, in actuarial tables and other "body counts." Suffice it to say that it is difficult to decide which puts a greater strain on belief: the pervasiveness of the culture of cruelty and torture which existed wherever the Japanese empire spread in the 1930s and 1940s, or the apparent pleasure the Japanese took in flaunting their abuses before the world.[23] Some of the most grotesque acts were carried out against prisoners of war—defenseless, starving, dying men and women. If the Japanese had their Tokyo and their Hiroshima, POWs among their adversaries had their "Bataan Death March" through the Philippines in 1942, and the construction of the "Railroad of Death" in Thailand and Burma in 1943–44.

In the dialogue which follows, a British victim of Japanese torture as a prisoner of war encounters a Japanese victim of the atomic bombing of Hiroshima. Each is a survivor of the horror of the Pacific War as it was typically meted out by the respective sides: Japanese torture and abuse of individuals on a massive scale; and U.S. bombing of Japanese civilians, also on a massive scale. Their encounter exemplifies the suffering endured by each side during the Pacific War, and it does so by providing figurative snapshots of two individual lives, forever marked by what they endured. It is told in the voice of the former POW, who is a man evidently full of empathy for his Japanese interlocutor.

[An encounter between a Japanese survivor of the atomic bombing of Hiroshima, and a British former prisoner of Japanese forces in Indonesia.][24]

I had forgotten the date until the moment I walked into that television studio in America at about six o'clock in the evening of Wednesday, August 6th.

I was due to be interviewed about Africa in some current affairs program.[25] All day long my mind had been trying to concern itself with my native continent. It is a concern which normally comes to me easily. Yet, on this occasion I had been aware of some unusual resistance in my mind to directing itself to the problems of Africa, no matter how urgent they appeared on the surface. The meaning of this resistance only became clear when I arrived at the studio and saw the man who was already in the process of being interviewed on the same program for the ten minutes before I myself had to appear. He was Japanese, a man I guessed to be about seventy years of age, with close cropped gray hair.

. . .

It was, of course, the anniversary of the dropping of the first atom bomb on Hiroshima, and the young American interviewer was extracting, with skill and delicacy, from the little old Japanese gentleman his experience of that great and terrible day.

He was, he said, a doctor. Both he and his wife were Christians. He was at work in his surgery and his wife was in the Japanese equivalent of a drawing-room, sitting at her harmonium [organ]. He could hear her playing a Christian hymn—no, he no longer remembered which particular hymn it was because his mind was on medical things and he heard it only in snatches. In any case, the shock of the horror that followed had been so great that to this day he found it difficult if not impossible to remember what had happened immediately before. Besides she had not been at the harmonium long when the bomb fell. She and his four children in other parts of their house were killed instantly; he, miraculously, was spared. . . .

I stood there then for some seven more minutes while he was made to tell in great detail his experience, from the moment the bomb fell to what he finally saw when he crawled out of the ruins of his own house to look for help in the shattered city outside. The detail needs no repetition here because it has all been minutely recorded, is well-known, and is the one part of the story told over and over again, to such an extent that it presents itself on the scene of the contemporary mind as it would have been presented on millions of television screens in America that evening as being the full story of that great and terrible day.

. . . As a result, we accept, like this young American interviewer—he could have been no more than five at the time of Hiroshima—that this tragic Japanese version is an authentic microcosm of the macrocosm of the whole truth. This aspect suddenly seemed of such overwhelming importance to me that there in the studio I was compelled to immediate action.

All this while the producer of the program, who had brought me into the studio, had been standing silent at my side, caught up in the horror of the story as had been everyone else, from cameramen and their assistants to interviewer. I took him by the arm and drew him with me out of the studio. He followed like someone coming out of a trance. I closed the door silently behind us and begged him to forget all about Africa. I told him that I too had been involved in the tragedy of Hiroshima. No, I had not been in Hiroshima itself. I had been thousands of miles away in Java, but what had happened to me in Java was as much a part of the story of Hiroshima and Nagasaki as what had happened to the people in the doomed cities themselves. . . . [W]e had worked together before, and in the end my argument that it would be wrong to let only this one Japanese voice, authentic as it was, speak for the day, won him over. He agreed to allow me, at the end of the prescribed moment, to take over from his interviewer and to put to the little Japanese doctor my own version of the day.

So it happened that when the official interview ended, the voice of the producer announced a change of plan, saying that instead of speaking on Africa I, who had been a Japanese prisoner of war for three and a half years, would have a discussion about Hiroshima with the Japanese doctor. I had only ten minutes for a long and complex story but I remember I began by trying to reassure the Japanese doctor, more tense than ever at this unexpected elaboration of his interview, that I wanted to tell him something which I hoped would help him to make peace with the tragedy of Hiroshima even more effectively than with his obvious magnanimity he had already done. If I remember rightly I began saying all this very badly in Japanese, not only to reassure him but as the only means available to me of showing him how involved I felt with him and his people in what happened on that day. I went on then as quickly as I could, in English, to tell him my part of the story. . . .

. . .

I began by trying to describe to the Japanese doctor what life had been like in a Japanese prisoner-of-war camp . . . I skimmed over the grimmest of my own experiences. For instance, I said little of how before I was brought into a so-called "regular" prisoner-of-war camp I had been made to watch Japanese soldiers having bayonet practice on live prisoners-of-war tied between bamboo posts; had been taken to witness executions of persons of all races and nationalities, for obscure reasons like "showing a spirit of willfulness," or not bowing with sufficient alacrity in the direction of the rising sun.

I could have digressed on this one facet of my experiences for hours, because I would never have thought it possible that in our time there could still have been so many ways of killing people—from cutting off their heads with swords, bayonetting them in the many variations of the ways I have mentioned, to strangling them and burying them alive; but, most significantly, never by just shooting them.

I say "significantly" because the omission of this contemporary form of killing . . . made us realize how the Japanese were themselves the puppets of immense impersonal forces to such an extent that they truly did not know what they were doing.[26]

. . .

I tried to compress the quintessence of all this into the ten minutes I had with the . . . Japanese doctor in the television studio in America that evening. I tried to stress how certain I was that if the atom bombs had not been dropped on Hiroshima and Nagasaki, the war would have dragged on, the Japanese would have fought as they had fought everywhere else to the bitter end, from island to island, and so on to the last, in the islands of Japan proper. . . . [A]nd apart from many many more Japanese dead, hundreds of thousands of Americans and their allies would have died as well. Above all for me, selfish as it may sound, there was the certain knowledge that if the bomb had not been dropped, and the Emperor had not been able to intervene, Field-Marshal Terauchi would have fought on and hundreds of thousands of prisoners in his power would have been killed. . . .[27]

[A] deliberate massacre was to be coordinated with the day on which the Allied invasion began in the Southeast Asian theater of war that was under Terauchi's command. We knew now that this invasion, by forces under the command of Lord Mountbatten, was planned and ready to begin on September 6th, that is to say, within three weeks of Japanese capitulation [on August 15].[28]

. . .

. . . [A]mong the staff records captured at Terauchi's headquarters, evidence was found of plans to kill all prisoners and internees when the invasion of Southeast Asia began in earnest. I begged the doctor, therefore, to accept that, terrible as the dropping of the two atom bombs had been, his wife and the many thousands who died with her had died in order to save the lives of many hundreds of thousands more. I had tried to speak to him in this way not only for myself but for thousands thus saved, and would like him to know how we would be forever in his wife's debt as well as that of her fellow-victims.

Those of us who had survived like him and myself could only discharge our debt by looking as deeply and as honestly as we could into the various contributions we had made to this disaster. The war and the bomb, after all, had started in ourselves before they struck in the world without, and we had to look as never before into our own small individual lives and the context of our various nations. . . . Could I through him thus presume to acknowledge my debt of life to his wife and beg him to believe she had not died in vain?

Whether I helped him by my story, and whether he agreed with my conclusions, I could not tell for certain. All I know is that at the end of our television discussion, before we left on our separate ways, he bowed to me as the Japanese general and his officers on that fateful August day had done [when word of the Japanese surrender reached the prison camp].

Hissing between his teeth as the old-fashioned Japanese used to do when moved, he came out of his bow to say: "Would you please be so kind as to allow me to thank you for a remarkable thought."

He added to that, after a pause, the traditional farewell of the Japanese, which in itself reflects much of their spirit charged so heavily with provision of fate: the Sayonara that just means: "If it must be."[29]

The Dilemma: "How Much Evil Must We Do in Order to Do Good?"

Americans instinctually resist the question posed by this conundrum. We think there is something wrong with the question, at least when applied to ourselves. Why, we wonder, did Reinhold

Niebuhr, an American from Missouri (despite his German name), put the issue in these terms, in which any nation seeking to do good in the world, including the United States, is seemingly convicted of wrongdoing *a priori*, before even setting forth to do what it believes is the right thing? Niebuhr asked the question in 1946. It was an appropriate time for the question to be asked by an American liberal like Niebuhr. Yes, the Second World War was over. And yes, the war was just, at least in the sense that the twin evils of German Nazism and Japanese imperialism absolutely had to be defeated, as they had. But no, according to Niebuhr, winning does not imply the absence of moral culpability—that everything done in the service of winning the war is somehow "good," or "moral."

The most far-reaching effect of the Second World War on the U.S., Niebuhr believed, was that America as a nation must at last learn to deal with *guilt*: with the knowledge that as a major player in a world order devoid of morality or, often, even law and order, Americans had better jettison their traditional notion of American "exceptionalism." We are *not* exceptionally "good," and many of our actions in World War II proved it, according to Niebuhr. In fact, because of our military might, we had become capable of perpetrating evil on a heretofore unprecedented scale, and we'd better get used to living with that responsibility. We too, he and others argued at the time, have committed acts so awful that "evil" is really the only term that adequately describes them. And no class of acts illustrated this more conclusively than the firebombing of German and Japanese cities, and the atomic bombing of Hiroshima and Nagasaki. In these attacks men, women and children were, as General Curtis LeMay is quoted in the chapter as saying, "scorched and boiled and baked to death." The only way to escape the conclusion that such acts are anything other than evil (whether "justified" or not; whether viable alternatives existed or not), is to withhold empathy utterly and totally from the victims. It is to deny the humanity of those we victimize. It is to claim that the defenseless men, women and even the children somehow *deserved* to be "scorched and boiled and baked to death."

Now, at the beginning of a new century, and nearly sixty years after the conclusion of World War II, we see a new sprouting of American self-righteousness—a reversion to our traditional tendency to see the world in terms of black and white, evil and virtue. Stimulated in large part by the terrorist attacks on New York and Washington, many Americans appear to approve of their government's "circling of the wagons"—of dividing the world into friend and foe, terrorist or civilized, and the like. Public discourse in the U.S., for example, has recently become suffused with terms like "axis of evil"; nations and groups are said to oppose the U.S. because they inexplicably "hate our freedom." The U.S., in addition, continues to refuse to allow its citizens to be prosecuted by the new International Criminal Court (ICC). Presumably, those who favor continued exclusion of U.S. citizens from jurisdiction by the ICC feel we have nothing to feel guilty about, a position difficult to maintain, one might suppose, in the wake of the spring, 2004 scandal over maltreatment of Iraqi prisoners in Baghdad's, Abu Ghraib prison.

Does any of this matter? We believe it does, because it appears to demonstrate to the rest of the world that Americans are incapable, or perhaps unwilling, to extend empathy to those they/we victimize in our pursuit of what we take to be doing good, whether in Afghanistan or Iraq, or elsewhere; or in the September 2002 U.S. declaration that it has the right to preemptively attack anywhere, any time it perceives a threat to itself, with whatever degree of military force it chooses. In our insistence on our own moral purity, however, we demonstrate to most of the rest of the world that we are still in denial, still believe ourselves to be "exceptional" and thus guilt-free, still unwilling to come to grips with the implications our actions have for others. Thus, much of the world continues to resist American self-righteousness as fiercely as Americans resist the claim that in order to do good, doing evil is also often involved.

See Appendix B, Lesson Four, for further discussion of this dilemma.

"I am inclined to believe that if Kennedy had lived, he would have made a difference. I don't think we would have had 500,000 men there."

CHAPTER 5

Lesson Five: "Be Prepared to Reexamine Your Reasoning"

ROBERT McNAMARA: *What makes us omniscient? Have we a record of omniscience? We are the strongest nation in the world today. I do not believe we should ever apply that economic, political, and military power unilaterally. If we had followed that rule in Vietnam, we wouldn't have been there. None of our allies supported us. Not Japan, not Germany, not Britain or France. If we can't persuade nations with comparable values of the merit of our cause, we'd better reexamine our reasoning.*

. . .

ERROL MORRIS: *When you talk about responsibility for something like the Vietnam War, whose responsibility is it?*

ROBERT McNAMARA: *It's the president's responsibility. I don't want to fail to recognize the tremendous contribution I think Johnson made to the country. I don't want to put the responsibility for Vietnam on his shoulders alone. But I do—I am inclined to believe that if Kennedy had lived, he would have made a difference. I don't think we would have had 500,000 men there.*

ROBERT McNAMARA and ERROL MORRIS in "The Fog of War."

At the very beginning of *"The Fog of War," Robert McNamara says, "the conventional wisdom is: don't make the same mistake twice, learn from your mistakes. And we all do." This seems uncontroversial as applied to individuals; it is generally consistent with our common sense and our day-to-day experience. We learn, as the saying goes, in the "school of hard knocks." We get "knocked," we try to understand why, we reassess our strategy and tactics, and try something else. If it works, we stick with it. If it doesn't, we go through the reassessment process again. And so on, until we succeed or give up. Yet if the admonition to "learn from your mistakes" is such a commonplace, why did McNamara even mention it, and why did Errol Morris include the comment in his film?*

One reason must be that the principle scarcely seems to apply at all to the episode most closely associated with McNamara, the Vietnam War. America's involvement in Vietnam began in earnest in 1954, when French colonial rule in Southeast Asia ended, with Vietnam being split in two by the terms of the July 1954 Geneva Accords. After Geneva, a communist government in Hanoi, allied with Moscow and Beijing, ruled North Vietnam, while a pro-Western, anticommunist government in Saigon took over in South Vietnam.[1] From 1954 onward, the U.S. became ever more deeply involved, and its leaders appear in retrospect to have been mostly oblivious to the lessons of the French defeat, or even to the lessons that should have seemed obvious from the Americans' own evolving, and increasingly frustrating and bloody experience in Vietnam. Historian Barbara Tuchman, looking back on the history of the U.S. in Vietnam, famously called it "the march of folly," from beginning to end an example of the "pursuit of policy contrary to self-interest." The reason? Tuchman, a plain-speaking historian of the old school, called it simply "wooden-headedness, the source of self-deception."[2] The tragedy in Vietnam, according to Tuchman, derived principally from the inability of leaders in the Eisenhower, Kennedy, Johnson and Nixon administrations to learn: from French mistakes, from their U.S. predecessors' mistakes, or from their own mistakes.[3]

Between 1954, when the U.S. replaced the French as the dominant Western power in Vietnam until 1973, when the Paris Peace Accords were signed, ending U.S. military involvement in the war—during those nearly twenty years, the U.S. neither succeeded, nor gave up, its "folly" in southeast Asia, which ultimately cost more than three million Vietnamese lives, more than 58,000 American lives, and hundreds of billions of dollars. In the terms of another key phrase used by McNamara in the film: the tragedy occurred because successive U.S. administrations, incapable of defeating the Vietnamese communists militarily, were unable (or unwilling) to "reexamine . . . [their] reasoning." As a consequence, the U.S. was finally forced to withdraw in defeat.

Evidence that has only recently become available—some of it having surfaced only in 2003—suggests that there may have been at least one important exception in this multigenerational "march of folly" of U.S. presidents who failed to reexamine their reasoning on Vietnam: John F. Kennedy. Here is the punch line: it appears now as if Kennedy did reexamine his reasoning with regard to Vietnam in a fundamental way. In fact, he seems to have decided by (not later than) mid-1963 to begin the process of withdrawing U.S. military personnel from Vietnam. We believe this conclusion is strongly suggested in the documents and dialogues excerpted below.

We hasten to add that we take no position here on what have become the two most frequently debated Kennedy "counterfactuals," or what-ifs: first, what would Kennedy have done regarding Vietnam if he had lived and served out a second term as president; and second, in what way, if any, might Kennedy's inclination to withdraw from Vietnam have motivated whichever groups and/or individuals who were responsible for his assassination? Those interested in these controversies should consult the last dialogue, below, between Noam Chomsky and James K. Galbraith, and the works referred to in the endnotes to that dialogue.

Our purpose here is a more modest one than resolving these essentially irresolvable controversies over the Kennedy counterfactuals. It is also more closely connected with the historical data. We want simply to introduce this new evidence regarding what Kennedy actually decided, and what his decisions reveal about the conditions under which it is possible to respond positively to Robert McNamara's admonition in "The Fog of War" to "be prepared to reexamine your reasoning." "Reasoning" is McNamara's compact term for one's way of thinking about the international system and America's place in it.

The mode of "reasoning" that John F. Kennedy brought with him to the White House may appear, from our vantage point early in this 21st century, so counterintuitive, so refuted by what we now know, that some may be tempted to question Kennedy's qualifications for the presidency. What leaders of Kennedy's generation took to be the reality of the international system may seem stranger than fiction to those with little or no memory of the Cold War, let alone the Second World War. We now know that communism collapsed because it didn't work; it was a collosal, worldwide failure. So some may wonder whether Kennedy and his cohorts—a group sometimes dubbed "the best and the brightest"—could actually have believed what we are about to attribute to them.[4] We assure you that they could—and they did. To keep incredulity among the younger generations to a minimum, it may help to keep in mind that Kennedy was born in 1917—not quite a year later than Robert McNamara—just as the U.S. was entering the First World War.[5] If Kennedy were alive in the fall of 2004, when this book is being finished, he would be eighty-seven years old.

The worldview of Kennedy and his generation was shaped almost entirely by the two epochal events of their adult lives: fighting and winning the Second World War, and the onset of the Cold War. Kennedy's "reasoning" about the world that shaped him—and every member of his administration—was therefore firmly anchored in the following fundamental unquestioned beliefs:

- *Munich. Beware of another "Munich." Do not make the mistake with totalitarian regimes that the British made at the September 1938 meeting with Adolf Hitler near Munich, in which British Prime Minister Neville Chamberlain attempted to "appease" Hitler by assuring the Nazi leader that Britain would not oppose Germany's attempt to annex part of Czechoslovakia. Hitler was not appeased. Germany kept gobbling up Europe. Conclusion: totalitarian regimes are never appeased.*
- *Military Force. Totalitarian regimes must be opposed with overwhelming military force on the part of the Western democracies. Such regimes cannot be bluffed, nor is compromise an option.*
- *Dominoes. Some areas of the world are especially vulnerable to a communist takeover, such that if one country is allowed to fall, the rest will tip over like a row of dominoes.*

- *Vietnam.* South Vietnam is the most significant such "domino" in southeast Asia, perhaps in the world. If it is allowed to "go communist," the entire region, not excluding Japan, is at risk of a communist takeover.
- *America's Mission.* The U.S., for a variety of reasons, has the primary responsibility to lead the fight against communism, regardless of the cost to America in blood and treasure.

One can argue, of course, about whether the Kennedy-era mindset is best organized in exactly this way—whether there are four or six principal beliefs or some other number instead of five, for example; or whether or not Kennedy, McNamara and their colleagues "should have" held such beliefs, and so on. Yet there is no doubt that these assumptions were among the most deeply held by Kennedy and his generation of American political and military leaders. More to the point we wish to make: it is hardly surprising to discover that a leader who believed what Kennedy believed when he came to office would also be committed to the preservation of South Vietnam as an anticommunist bastion, no matter what the cost, no matter how great the sacrifice.

But what is surprising—startling, in fact—is that Kennedy's experience after taking office on January 20, 1961 should lead him very soon to begin to doubt the validity of this cluster of deeply held beliefs he brought to the evolving situation in Vietnam. But in light of the new evidence, this appears to be exactly what happened: Kennedy began not just to follow McNamara's admonition to "be prepared to reexamine your reasoning," but he radically reexamined his reasoning about America's role in Southeast Asia. The data strongly suggest that he actually ordered what now seems almost unbelievable, given the beliefs he brought to office. By the spring of 1963, he had set in motion plans for a complete withdrawal of all U.S. military personnel from South Vietnam, to be completed by December 1965. Moreover, it appears that this decision was not contingent on successfully preserving South Vietnam as independent and anticommunist.

The potential, but unrealized, significance of Kennedy's decision is immense. By the spring of 1963, the U.S. had taken fewer than 500 casualties in Vietnam—killed or wounded in action. This was less than one one-thousandth (.001) of the 58,159 Americans ultimately killed in action in Vietnam, and the 304,000 wounded in the fighting.[6] Kennedy was murdered on November 22, 1963, and thus did not live long enough to try to implement his decision—to grapple with the many difficulties he would have faced in trying to fashion a politically feasible withdrawal from Vietnam. Why Kennedy's successor, Lyndon Johnson, did not even try to implement that decision is discussed briefly below, in our remarks introducing the dialogues. The impact of the presidential transition in November 1963 is passionately debated in the exchange in that section between Noam Chomsky and James K. Galbraith.

The following documents highlight some of the events that led Kennedy to reexamine his reasoning about Vietnam. The archival materials are clustered in four groups: (1) Prior Assumptions; (2) Debacle at the Bay of Pigs; (3) The November 1961 Showdown; and (4) The Decision to Begin the Withdrawal. The dialogues that follow offer just a tantalizing sample of the fierce debate that continues to rage about how to interpret the information now available regarding Kennedy's Vietnam decisions.

Documents

PRIOR ASSUMPTIONS

The origins and evolution of Kennedy's worldview is sampled in this section via three excerpts from sources that appeared over a period of more than twenty years: the book-length version of his senior thesis at Harvard, published in July of 1940, when he was twenty-three; a speech given in 1956 on America's responsibilities to South Vietnam, when he was a thirty-nine-year-old U. S. Senator; and his inaugural address as President, given on January 20, 1961, when he was forty-three. In substance there is little about them that is unique to Kennedy. Rhetorically, however, what is easily recognizable as the mellifluous Kennedy style of argument seems to have been there from the outset: the use of historical examples, the economy of phrasing, the sometimes soaring imagery. The message of the inaugural is: communism is on the offensive; America must lead the fight against it.

And the commitment to a country like South Vietnam must be total and unwavering. America under Kennedy must be prepared to "pay any price, bear any burden," on its behalf.

[John F. Kennedy, *Why England Slept*, July 1940.][7]

England made many mistakes; she is paying heavily for them now. In studying the reasons why England slept, let us try to profit by them and save ourselves her anguish.

. . .

What does it signify for our country? We must be prepared to recognize democracy's weaknesses in competition with a totalitarian form of government. We must realize that one is a system geared for peace, the other for war. We must recognize that while one may have greater endurance, it is not immune to swift destruction by the other.

. . .

We must keep our armaments equal to our commitments. Munich should teach us that; we must realize that any bluff will be called. We cannot tell anyone to keep out of our hemisphere unless our armaments *and the people behind these armaments* are prepared to back up the command, even to the ultimate point of going to war. There must be no doubt in anyone's mind, the decision must be automatic: if we debate, if we hesitate, if we question, it will be too late.[8]

[Senator John F. Kennedy, "America's Stake in Vietnam," June 1956.][9]

(1) *First,* Vietnam represents the cornerstone of the Free World in Southeast Asia, the keystone to the arch, the finger in the dike. Burma, Thailand, India, Japan, the Philippines and obviously Laos and Cambodia are among those whose security would be threatened if the red tide of Communism overflowed into Vietnam. . . .

(2) *Second,* Vietnam represents a proving ground of democracy in Asia. However we may choose to ignore it or deprecate it, the rising prestige and influence of Communist China in Asia are unchallengeable facts. Vietnam represents the alternative to Communist dictatorship. If this democratic experiment fails, if some one million refugees have fled the totalitarianism of the North only to find neither freedom nor security in the South, then weakness, not strength, will characterize the meaning of democracy in the

minds of still more Asians. The United States is directly responsible for this experiment—it is playing an important role in the laboratory where it is being conducted. We cannot afford to permit that experiment to fail.

(3) *Third* . . . Vietnam represents a test of American responsibility and determination in Asia. If we are not the parents of little Vietnam, then surely we are the godparents. We presided at its birth, we gave assistance to its life, we have helped to shape its future. As French influence in the political, economic and military spheres has declined in Vietnam, American influence has steadily grown. This is our offspring—we cannot abandon it, we cannot ignore its needs. And if it falls victim to any of the perils that threaten its existence—Communism, political anarchy, poverty and the rest—then the United States, with some justification, will be held responsible; and our prestige in Asia will sink to a new low. . . .

[President John F. Kennedy, excerpts from his "Inaugural Address," January 20, 1961.][10]

Let every nation know, whether it wishes us well or ill, that we shall pay any price, bear any burden, meet any hardship, support any friend, oppose any foe to assure the survival and success of liberty. . . .

In the long history of the world, only a few generations have been

"We saw Vietnam as an element of the Cold War"

granted the role of defending freedom in its hour of maximum danger. I do not shrink from this responsibility; I welcome it. . . .

To those new states whom we welcome to the ranks of the free, we pledge our word that one form of colonial control shall not have passed away merely to be replaced by a far more iron tyranny.

DEBACLE AT THE BAY OF PIGS

Shortly after midnight on April 17, 1961, approximately 1,200 Cuban exiles began to arrive at the Bay of Pigs, on the south coast of Cuba. Trained by the CIA, their goal was to establish a beachhead and hold it against counterattack by the army and militia of Cuban government forces led by Fidel Castro, whose movement had come to power in Cuba in January 1959. The invaders, like their U.S. sponsors, believed the Cuban people would rally to their side. They did not. The invaders were defeated in fierce fighting within seventy-two hours by Cuban government forces. U.S. forces did not intervene. The new administration of President John F. Kennedy was humiliated. The invaders who survived were imprisoned and subjected to a public "show-trial" in Havana that represented the beginning of a virulent anti-Americanism on the part of the Cuban government. The regime of Fidel Castro was consolidated and became instantly pro-Soviet. The Kennedy administration was left in disarray and confusion.

The Bay of Pigs debacle remains arguably the single most humiliating event in the recent history of U.S. foreign policy—not the biggest disaster or the most costly, but the most ridiculous or absurd, the most psychologically incomprehensible to most Americans as well as the rest of the world. It was the "perfect failure," as one journalist wrote at the time.[11] As the world saw it, the greatest power on earth was defeated in three days by one of the poorest and weakest of nations. Upon hearing the news of the disaster, the new president said to his aide, Theodore Sorensen: "How could I have been so far off base. . . . How could I have been so stupid to let them go ahead?"[12] Kennedy would never make that mistake again.

We have included three excerpts from documents that were not written for public consumption, documents which contain a brutal honesty seldom, if ever, seen in public pronouncements or published memoirs of government officials. Note especially the eyewitness account of how shattered Kennedy appears to have been by the events, from the diary entry of Chester Bowles, of the Kennedy State Department. But note, too, in the excerpts from McGeorge Bundy and Arthur Schlesinger, Jr., that Kennedy has pointedly asked each of these aides to be as critical as possible of those responsible, beginning with Kennedy himself. They are to pull no punches. Bundy gives it to him straight: never delegate to the military decisions of any magnitude; never get involved if you can't succeed. And Schlesinger reports to Kennedy with brutal honesty that, in effect, the NATO Allies worry that, contrary to what they thought prior to the Bay of Pigs fiasco, Kennedy may well be an incompetent fool with a penchant for military adventures. It is an unusually curious and confident president who asks for, and receives, that kind of blunt feedback. All of Kennedy's decisions on Vietnam would be deeply affected by this chastening experience. Other events of course also played a role in Kennedy's ongoing "reexamination" of his "reasoning." But none compared in impact to the Bay of Pigs debacle.

[Chester Bowles, "Notes on Cuban Crisis," April 20, 1961.][13]

Cabinet meeting on Thursday, April 20th, the first day immediately after the collapse of the Cuban expedition became known.

I attended the Cabinet meeting in Rusk's absence and it was about as grim as any meeting I can remember in all my experience in government, which is saying a good deal.

The President was really quite shattered, and understandably so. Almost without exception, his public career had been a long series of successes, without any noteworthy setbacks. Those disappointments which did come his way, such as his failure to get the nomination for Vice President in 1956 were clearly attributable to religion.

Here for the first time he faced a situation where his judgment had been mistaken, in spite of the fact that week after week of conferences had taken place before he gave the green light.

. . .

The discussion simply rambled in circles with no real coherent thought. Finally after three-quarters of an hour the President got up and walked toward his office. . . .

When a newcomer enters the field and finds himself confronted by the nuances of international questions, he becomes an easy target for the military-CIA-paramilitary type answers which are often in specific logistical terms which can be added, subtracted, multiplied or divided.

This kind of thinking was almost dominant in the conference and I found it most alarming. The President appeared the most calm, yet it was clear . . . that he had been suffering an acute shock and it was an open question in my mind as to what his reaction would be.

[McGeorge Bundy, "Some Preliminary Lessons of the Cuban Expedition," April 24, 1961.][14]

First, the President's advisers must speak up in council. Second, secrecy must never take precedence over careful thought and study. Third, the President and his advisers must second-guess even military plans. Fourth, we must estimate the enemy without hope or fear. Fifth, those who are to offer serious advice on major issues must themselves do the necessary work. Sixth, the President's desires must be fully acted on, and he must know the full state of mind of friends whose lives his decisions affect. Seventh, forced choices are seldom as necessary as they seem, and the fire can be much hotter than the frying pan. Eighth, what is and is not implied in any specific partial decision must always be thought through. Ninth: What is large in scale must always be open, with all the consequences of openness. Tenth: Success is what succeeds.

[Arthur Schlesinger, Jr., "Memorandum for the President: Reactions to Cuba in Western Europe," May 3, 1961.][15]

The first reactions to Cuba were, of course, acute shock and disillusion. . . . After Cuba, the American government seemed as self-righteous, trigger-happy and incompetent as it had ever been. . . . "Kennedy has lost his magic," one person said to me. "It will take years before we can accept the leadership of the Kennedy Administration again," said another. Friends of America warned me not to underestimate the gravity of the damage: "Make sure that our people in Washington understand how much ground we have lost" (Drew Middleton); "It was a terrible blow, and it will take a long, long time for us to recover from it" (Lord Boothby).[16]

I should add that nearly all the reactions I encountered expressed sorrow over the decision to invade rather than the failure of the invasion. "Why was Cuba such a threat to you? Why couldn't you live with Cuba, as the USSR lives with Turkey and Finland?"

. . .

A number of people seriously believe, on the basis of newspaper stories from Washington, that an American invasion of Cuba is a distinct and imminent possibility. A [London] *Observer* editor said to me, "If Cuba were just an accident, alright. But everything since Cuba suggests that the Kennedy who launched that invasion was the *real* Kennedy—that all his talk about "new methods" of warfare and countering guerrillas represents his *real* approach to the problems of the Cold War—that he thinks the West will beat communism by adopting communist methods and transforming itself into a regimented paramilitary society on the model of the Soviet Union." Several people said, "It's not Cuba that worries me; it's the aftermath."

THE NOVEMBER 1961 SHOWDOWN

By the fall of 1961, it is a different President Kennedy who responds to the pleas of his advisers to become militarily involved in an effort to thwart communism—this time in South Vietnam. A team led by General Maxwell Taylor has just returned from Saigon, on November 2, and their report—the "Taylor Report"—recommends that the President authorize the immediate deployment of between eight and ten thousand American combat troops to Vietnam, with more to follow. Kennedy is not enthusiastic, and he delays a decision. To impress upon his commander-in-chief the gravity of the situation, including the need for immediate action, Secretary of Defense Robert McNamara, writing on behalf of himself, his deputy Roswell Gilpatric, and the Joint Chiefs of Staff, sends the President a memorandum on November 8, laying out what is at stake, and recommending that Kennedy begin thinking in terms of an ultimate commitment of up to 205,000 U.S. combat troops. Still, Kennedy defers a decision, and asks for other opinions.[17]

The minutes of the November 15 meeting are highly illuminating. All his senior advisers are in favor of committing combat troops to Vietnam. In response to their various arguments for the urgency of sending U.S. combat troops, Kennedy argues the following: clarity is lacking regarding the rationale for a military intervention—it's not as clear as Korea in 1950, or Berlin in 1961; the most important U.S.

allies do not support an intervention; many millions of dollars have already been spent, with little or no effect; you can't bluff (or deter) guerrillas, you have to fight them, and no invading army is likely to win such a fight; and U.S. forces would be vulnerable, leading to attacks on them, followed by U.S. retaliation and escalation to a wider war. In other words, "no." Kennedy somewhat assuaged his hawkish cabinet by authorizing the dispatch of more U.S. advisers and equipment to be put at the disposal of the South Vietnamese army. Advisers, yes; but no combat troops.[18] It seems likely that this showdown with his advisers galvanized Kennedy's resistance to sending U.S. combat troops to Vietnam. Certainly it was educational for his advisers, who could hardly have missed the point: this president is not enthusiastic about sending the U.S. Army to fight a war on South Vietnam's behalf.

[Robert S. McNamara, "Memorandum for the President," November 8, 1961.][19]

MEMORANDUM FOR THE PRESIDENT

The basic issue framed by the Taylor Report is whether the U.S. shall:

a. Commit itself to the clear objective of preventing the fall of South Vietnam to Communism, and

b. Support this commitment by necessary immediate military actions and preparations for possible later actions.

The Joint Chiefs, Mr. [Roswell] Gilpatric [Deputy Secretary of Defense] and I have reached the following conclusions:

1. The fall of South Vietnam to Communism would lead to the fairly rapid extension of Communist control, or complete accommodation to Communism, in the rest of mainland Southeast Asia and in Indonesia. The strategic implications worldwide, particularly in the Orient, would be extremely serious.

2. The chances are against, probably sharply against, preventing that fall by any measures short of the introduction of U.S. forces on a substantial scale. We accept General Taylor's judgment that the various measures proposed by him short of this are useful but will not in themselves do the job of restoring confidence and setting [South Vietnamese President Ngo Dinh] Diem on the way to winning his fight.

3. The introduction of a U.S. force of the magnitude of an initial 8,000

men in a flood relief context will be of great help to Diem. However, it will not convince the other side (whether the shots are called from Moscow, Peiping, or Hanoi) that we mean business. Moreover, it probably will not tip the scales decisively. We would be almost certain to get mired down in an inconclusive struggle.

4. The other side can be convinced we mean business only if we accompany the initial force introduction by a clear commitment to the full objective stated above, accompanied by a warning through some channel to Hanoi that continued support of the Viet Cong will lead to punitive retaliation against North Vietnam.

5. If we act in this way, the ultimate possible extent of our military commitment must be faced. The struggle may be prolonged and Hanoi and Peiping may intervene overtly. In view of the logistic difficulties faced by the other side, I believe we can assume that the maximum U.S. forces required on the ground in Southeast Asia will not exceed six divisions, or about 205,000 men . . . Our military posture is, or with the addition of more National Guard or regular Army divisions can be made, adequate to furnish these forces without serious interference with our present Berlin plans. . . .

["Notes on National Security Council Meeting, 15 November 1961."][20]

Mr. Rusk explained the Draft of Memorandum on South Vietnam. He added the hope that, in spite of the magnitude of the proposal, any U.S. actions would not be hampered by lack of funds nor failure to pursue the program vigorously.

The President expressed the fear of becoming involved simultaneously on two fronts on opposite sides of the world. He questioned the wisdom of involvement in Vietnam since the basis thereof is not completely clear. By comparison he noted that Korea was a case of clear aggression which was opposed by the United States and other members of the UN. The conflict in Vietnam is more obscure and less flagrant. The President then expressed his strong feeling that in such a situation the United States needs even more the support of its allies in such an endeavor as Vietnam in order to avoid sharp domestic partisan criticism as well as strong objections from other nations of the world. The President said that he could even make a rather strong case against intervening in an area 10,000 miles away against 16,000 guerrillas with a native army of 200,000, where millions have been spent for years with no success. The President repeated his apprehension concerning support, adding that none could be expected from the French. (Mr. Rusk interrupted to say that the British were tending more and more to take the French point of view.) The President compared the obscurity of the issues in Vietnam to the clarity of the positions in Berlin, in contrast of which could even make leading Democrats wary of proposed activities in the Far East.

Mr. Rusk suggested that firmness in Vietnam in the manner and form of that in Berlin might achieve desired results in Vietnam without resort to combat. The President disagreed with the suggestion on the basis that the issue was clearly defined in Berlin and opposing forces identified, whereas in Vietnam the issue is vague and action is by guerrillas, sometimes in a phantom-like fashion. Mr. McNamara expressed an opinion that action would become clear if U.S. forces were involved since this power would be applied against sources of Vietcong power including those in North Vietnam. The President observed that it was not clear to him just where these U.S. forces would base their operations other than from aircraft carriers which seemed to him to be quite vulnerable. General Lemnitzer confirmed that carriers would be involved to a considerable degree and stated that Taiwan and the Philippines would also become principal bases of action.

With regard to sources of power in North Vietnam, Mr. Rusk cited Hanoi as the most important center in North Vietnam and it would be hit. However, he considered it more a political target than a military one and under these circumstances such an attack would "raise serious question[s]." He expressed the hope that any plan of action in North Vietnam would strike first of all any Vietcong airlift into South Vietnam in order to avoid the establishment of a procedure of supply similar to that which the Soviets have conducted for so long with impunity in Laos.

Mr. [McGeorge] Bundy raised the question as to whether or not U.S. action in Vietnam would not render the Laotian settlement more difficult. Mr. Rusk said that it would to a certain degree but qualified his statement with the caveat that the difficulties could be controlled somewhat by the manner in which actions in Vietnam are initiated.

The President returned the discussion to the point of what will be done next in Vietnam rather than whether or not the U.S. would become involved.

THE DECISION TO BEGIN THE WITHDRAWAL

President Kennedy has sent Robert McNamara and Gen. Maxwell Taylor to South Vietnam in late September 1963, to gather information on what seems to be a rapidly deteriorating situation in Saigon, and in the countryside. The regime, led by President Ngo Dinh Diem, and his brother, internal security chief Ngo Dinh Nhu, has over the past year become increasingly brutal and incompetent in its efforts to suppress the communist insurgency. In addition, Diem and Nhu have undertaken to repress any public expression of unhappiness with their conduct. Thousands have been arrested, jailed and/or executed. The most dramatic challenge yet to Diem and Nhu has come during the late spring and summer of 1963, during an uprising of Buddhists, whom the militantly Roman Catholic Ngo brothers have crushed with wanton brutality, so much so that Buddhist monks began to set fire to themselves in public places in protest—events which shocked the world.[21]

Thus the report delivered to Kennedy on October 2, 1963, by McNamara and Taylor has somehow to address this conundrum: the situation in Saigon and in the countryside is deteriorating, which would seem to increase the need for U.S. troops, if South Vietnam is to be saved from a communist takeover, on the one hand; while on the other hand, McNamara and Taylor know that Kennedy manifestly opposes turning the struggle into a U.S. war, which it would become if American combat troops were sent to Vietnam in substantial numbers. They can be absolutely certain of this because Kennedy has already, in the spring of 1963, ordered McNamara and the Joint Chiefs to set the bureaucratic wheels in motion to withdraw most, if not all, U.S. advisers by the end of 1965.[22]

What to do? This time, there will be no showdown between a president and at least these two advisers—McNamara and Taylor—as there was in November 1961. By the fall of 1963, these two leaders of the fact-finding mission to Saigon have locked onto the wavelength of the President. They split the issue into two parts: militarily, they say that the anticommunist effort is succeeding and will continue to succeed. Thus the withdrawal of U.S. advisers can begin by pulling out 1,000 by the end of the calendar year (1963). The political situation, however, is worse than ever and, while Diem and Nhu are the worst kind of authoritarians—both brutal and incompetent at the same time—McNamara and Taylor do not recommend, at least for the time being, throwing U.S. support behind a group of South Vietnamese military officials seeking to overthrow the Diem government via a coup d'etat, because they believe it unlikely that any subsequent regime will be better.

In the excerpt from the McNamara-Taylor Report, note that there is no mention of eventually putting in 205,000 combat troops, as there was in McNamara's memorandum of two years before. Instead, the emphasis is on the mechanics of taking people out. Also absent from the McNamara-Taylor Report are any illusions about the eventual success of the Diem government, or even any conceivable government that might replace it. It is difficult to avoid the conclusion that McNamara and Taylor are of one mind with President Kennedy, who has decided to get out of Vietnam—quietly, gradually, with no dramatic moves, at least until after the 1964 presidential election—but emphatically out, not more deeply in.

At this point, it seems that President Kennedy has, in McNamara's terms, more or less fully reexamined his reasoning, as have McNamara and Taylor. It has been decided that the American people should not, after all, have to "pay any price, bear any burden," in pursuit of an independent, anticommunist South Vietnam. This conclusion is reinforced by the recently declassified transcripts of audiotaped discussions between Kennedy and McNamara on October 2 and 5, 1963, which follow the report, below.

["McNamara-Taylor Report to the President, October 2, 1963."][23]

CONCLUSIONS

- The military campaign has made great progress and continues to progress.
- There are serious political tensions in Saigon (and perhaps elsewhere in South Vietnam) where the Diem-Nhu government is becoming increasingly unpopular.
- Further repressive actions by Diem and Nhu could change the present favorable military trends. On the other hand, a return to more moderate methods of control and administration, unlikely though it may be, would substantially mitigate the political crisis.

- It is not clear that pressures exerted by the U.S. will move Diem and Nhu toward moderation. Indeed, pressures may increase their obduracy. But unless such pressures are exerted, they are almost certain to continue their past patterns of behavior.
- The prospects that a replacement regime would be an improvement appear to be about 50–50. Initially, only a strong authoritarian regime would be able to pull the government together and maintain order. In view of the preeminent role of the military in Vietnam today, it is probable that this role would be filled by a military officer, perhaps taking power after the selective process of a junta dispute. Such an authoritarian military regime, perhaps after an initial period of euphoria at the departure of Diem and Nhu, would be apt to entail a resumption of the repression at least of Diem, the corruption of the Vietnamese Establishment before Diem, and an emphasis on conventional military rather than social, economic and political considerations, with at least an equivalent degree of xenophobic nationalism.

RECOMMENDATIONS

We recommend that:

- General [Paul] Harkins review with Diem the military changes necessary to complete the military campaign in the Northern and Central areas by the end of 1964, and in the Delta by the end of 1965.
- A program be established to train Vietnamese so that essential functions now performed by U.S. military personnel can be carried out by Vietnamese by the end of 1965. It should be possible to withdraw the bulk of U.S. personnel by that time.
- In accordance with the program to train progressively Vietnamese to take over military functions, the Defense Department should announce in the very near future presently prepared plans to withdraw 1000 U.S. military personnel by the end of 1963.
- To impress upon Diem our disapproval of his political program we:
- Withhold important financial support of his development programs.
- Maintain the present purely "correct" relations with the top of the South Vietnamese government.
- Monitor the situation closely to see what steps Diem takes to re-

duce repressive practices and to improve the effectiveness of the military effort. We should recognize we may have to decide in two to four months to move to more drastic action.

- We not take any initiative to encourage actively a change in government.

[Transcripts of audiotape recordings of White House meetings regarding Vietnam on October 2 and October 5, 1963.][24]

October 2, 1963, 11:00 AM.

President Kennedy: That's going to be an assumption, that it's going well, that if it does go well—

Robert McNamara: Yes, sir. One of the major premises—two major premises we have—first, I believe we can complete the military campaign in . . . the fourth quarter of '65.[25] Secondly, if it extends beyond that period, we believe we can train the Vietnamese to take over the essential functions and withdraw the bulk of our forces. And this thousand is in conjunction with that, and I have a list of the units here that are represented by that number—

President Kennedy: Can't they . . .

McGeorge Bundy: What's the point of doing that?[26]

Robert McNamara: We need a way to get out of Vietnam. This is a way of doing it. And to leave forces there when they're not needed, I think, is wasteful and complicates both their problem and ours.

. . .

I think, Mr. President, we must have a means of disengaging from this area. We must show our country that means . . . I am sure that . . . we can withdraw the bulk of our U.S. forces according to the schedule we've laid out, worked out, because we can train the Vietnamese to do the job.

October 2, 1963, 6:05 PM.

President Kennedy: My only reservation about it is, if it commits us to a kind of a, if the war doesn't continue to go well, it will

look like we were overly optimistic. And I'm not sure what benefit we get out [of it] at this time by announcing a thousand.

Robert McNamara: Mr. President, we have the thousand split by
units. So that if the war doesn't go well, we can say that these
thousand would not have influenced the course of action.

President Kennedy: And the advantage?

Robert McNamara: And the advantage of taking them out is that
we can say to the Congress and the people that we do have a
plan for reducing the exposure of U.S. combat personnel to the
guerrilla actions in South Vietnam. Actions that the people of
South Vietnam should gradually develop a capability to suppress
themselves. And I think this will be of great value to us in meeting the very strong views of [Sen. J. William] Fulbright and others that we're bogged down in Asia and we'll be there for
decades.

October 5, 1963, 9:30 AM.

Robert McNamara: . . . [T]he thousand people are just not
needed out there, in terms of carrying out certain functions.
There's no reason . . . [unclear]

President Kennedy: Well, I think the only thing is, is hardly, from
a public point of view, a withdrawal just would seem illogical.
It's going to have to be pulling them out rather than just doing
it by attrition. I think we're doing it to have some impact, then I
think we can't do it unless . . . otherwise to we ought to just do
it by rotation.

Robert McNamara: That's the way we've proposed to do it.

President Kennedy: Rather than any formal announcement in the
near future.

Robert McNamara: Or we can do it just through normal attrition,
normal rotation.

[people talking over each other]

President Kennedy: Let's just go ahead and do it, without making
a public statement about it.[27]

Dialogues

The fortieth anniversary of President John F. Kennedy's assassination, in the fall of 2003, elicited a good deal of commentary on Kennedy and Vietnam. After all this time, the question still haunts: did Kennedy intend to pull out of Vietnam and, if he did, would he have been able to do so, given the political complications that would follow from what many would have perceived as a president's passive acceptance of an American defeat? Would Kennedy have done what his successor Lyndon Johnson did not do: refuse to "Americanize" the war? The new documentation suggests that Kennedy had made up his mind to withdraw. Why, then, did not Johnson follow suit?

This is not the place for an in-depth inquiry into the many profound differences between Kennedy and Johnson, and the way these may have led them to decide differently on Vietnam.[28] *Our purpose here is rather to focus on Kennedy's capacity to "reexamine his reasoning" on Vietnam, which we believe was impressive. But something must also be said about Johnson's unenviable situation as he took the oath of office on November 22–23, 1963, aboard Air Force One, on the flight back to Washington from Dallas.*

For all his prescience on Vietnam, Kennedy made three critical errors—or what seem in retrospect clearly to be errors—knowing as we do about Kennedy's murder in Dallas. Together, these errors made it difficult, perhaps impossible, for Johnson to pick up where Kennedy left off. First, Kennedy seems never to have explained his motives in any detail to his senior advisers regarding his opposition to sending combat troops to Vietnam. Second, as Robert McNamara says in "The Fog of War," Kennedy and some of his advisers had, in effect, authorized a coup in Saigon that resulted in the November 1, 1963, murder of Diem and Nhu, followed by chaos and a succession of South Vietnamese leaders whose incompetence made some U.S. advisers yearn for the days of Diem. It would be Johnson, not Kennedy, however, who would have to deal with this progressively deteriorating situation.

Third, and perhaps most important, Kennedy's public statements about U.S. policy in Vietnam were masterpieces of equivocation. It was from such statements as the following (taken from dozens of such statements by Kennedy) that Johnson doubtless derived the belief that he was actually carrying out Kennedy's policies. On September 9,

1963, Kennedy was asked by David Brinkley of NBC-TV whether he believed the so-called "domino theory" applied to Vietnam. Kennedy responded: ". . . I believe it. I believe it . . . if South Vietnam went . . . it would give the impression that the wave of the future in Southeast Asia was China and the Communists. So I believe it."[29] On September 25, 1963, Kennedy appeared to retreat from the absolute commitment he expressed to David Brinkley, when he told newsman Walter Cronkite of CBS-TV: "[I]n the final analysis it is the people and government [of South Vietnam] itself who have to win or lose this struggle. All we can do is help. . . . " Yet Kennedy still concluded by saying: "But I don't agree with those who say we should withdraw. That would be a great mistake."[30] So what was Johnson supposed to think? More to the point, what had the American people been led to think by the suddenly deceased president? The message was profoundly contradictory: the U.S. had to do whatever was necessary to prevent the dominoes from falling in Vietnam, by guaranteeing an independent, anticommunist South Vietnam. However, only the South Vietnamese themselves could actually produce such a result in the long run— something that few U.S. officials believed was possible.

We now know from historical documentation, some of it only recently made available, that a wide gap existed between Kennedy's private decisions and his public stance on Vietnam. How do we account for this? It seems clear that Kennedy felt that it was politically unwise to reveal his true position on Vietnam until after he had been reelected in the November 1964 election. Was his position justified? As Barbara Tuchman has written, "Kennedy was no wooden-head. . . . His position was realistic, if not a profile in courage."[31]

The two dialogues that follow were stimulated by the 40th anniversary of the Kennedy assassination, and by the recent release of documents and transcripts of tape recordings revealing more clearly than ever before Kennedy's decision to withdraw from Vietnam. In the first, Robert McNamara explains how Kennedy could have believed in the domino theory but still have planned to withdraw. In the second, one can witness the passion that is still evoked merely by arguing that Kennedy did, or did not, plan to withdraw from Vietnam. For those too young to have much memory of that war, or who have none at all, it should be kept in mind that this debate is about far

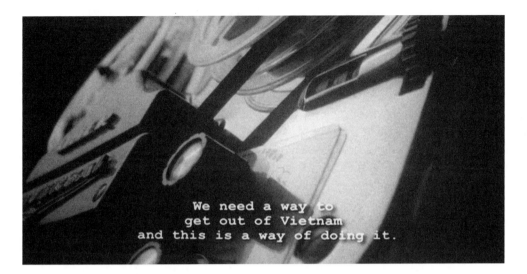

more than which debater wins the argument. It is about the proposition that more than three million people need not have died; that an entire country and region of the world need not have been turned into a desecrated killing field; and that the United States, the world's most powerful country, need not have been brought to its knees by a poor but supremely dedicated people, and then torn asunder by issues associated with the war.[32]

[Anthony Lewis, Robert S. McNamara and Theodore C. Sorensen, discussion of Kennedy and Vietnam, October 22, 2003.][33]

Anthony Lewis: There's a . . . (inaudible) in the current issue of the *Boston Review* by James Galbraith . . . the thrust of this one—and it refers to the very meeting [of October 2, 1963] you've just mentioned, Bob. The headline of the piece is "Exit Strategy in 1963: JFK Ordered a Complete Withdrawal From Vietnam." It refers to the joint report of yourself and Maxwell Taylor. And it says that recommendation—it gives the number, so I'll say it, Section I-B of the McNamara-Taylor Report—recommendations read that a (inaudible)—complete withdrawal be completed by the end of 1965, and that the Defense Department should announce in the very near future, presently prepared plans to withdraw 1,000 of 17,000 military personnel.

Theodore C. Sorensen: That's absolutely correct.

Robert McNamara: But there was much controversy—this is the point I want to make—[this was] not by any means [the] unanimous view of his advisers. Many, many were opposed to approving a plan to remove all advisers and all military support within two years—by the end of '65.

Many, many were opposed to withdrawing 1,000 within 90 days. And then after that decision was made, many, many were opposed to announcing it. And the proposal was made to announce it because those who favored the action knew enough about government to understand those who lost would live to fight another day, unless the . . . [decisions to withdraw the 1,000, and to announce the withdrawal] were put in concrete. The way they were put in concrete was to announce it.

And he [President Kennedy] went through those controversies. And the tape is very clear on this. First, the controversy over whether to establish the plan and have it as an official government policy. And second, the controversy over whether to put it in concrete by announcing it. He did both. And as I say, believing as I do now—and I think I understand it better now than I understood it then—that he believed the primary responsibility of a president was to keep the nation out of war if at all possible. I [therefore] do not believe that he would have had 500,000 men in Vietnam.

He [President Kennedy] believed in the domino theory. With hindsight, I think it was wrong. He believed that we would lose. If we were to lose South Vietnam, as Eisenhower said, we'd weaken the security of the West across the world. Eisenhower believed it, Kennedy believed it, I believed it, we all believed it. I think we were wrong.

But despite that he would have withdrawn, because I think he felt—and on this he was wiser than many others—that even if the domino theory was correct [and] the security of the West would be weakened across the world if we lost Vietnam, he believed it was unlikely that we could retain it by the application of external military power. And he was absolutely correct in that.

[Noam Chomsky and James K. Galbraith, an exchange on Kennedy and Vietnam.]

Noam Chomsky: [There has been] renewed fascination with the Kennedy era, even adulation for the fallen leader who had escalated the attack against Vietnam from terror to aggression . . . based upon the claim, prominently advanced, that Kennedy intended to withdraw from Vietnam; and was assassinated for that reason, some alleged. The revival was spurred by Oliver Stone's [1991] film *JFK*, which reached a mass audience at that time with its message that Kennedy was secretly planning to end the Vietnam War, a plan aborted by the assassination.

. . . [T]he picture of Kennedy as the leader who was about to lead us to a bright future of peace and justice was carefully nurtured during the Camelot years, with no little success, and has been regularly revived. . . .

This line of argument has been at the core of the [Kennedy] revival of the past few years. Currently available evidence indicates that it is entirely without foundation, indeed in conflict with substantial evidence. Advocates of this thesis will have to look elsewhere, so it appears.[34]

James K. Galbraith: [Noam] Chomsky despises the Kennedy apologists: equally the old insiders and the antiwar nostalgics—Arthur Schlesinger and Oliver Stone—and the historical memory of "the fallen leader who had escalated the attack against Vietnam from terror to aggression." He reviles efforts to portray Kennedy's foreign policy views as different from Johnson's.

. . .

[Yet] John F. Kennedy had formally decided to withdraw from Vietnam, whether we were winning or not. Robert McNamara, who did not believe we were winning, supported this decision. The first stage of withdrawal had been ordered. The final date, two years later, had been specified. These decisions were taken, and even placed, in an oblique and carefully limited way, before the public.

. . .

It is not difficult to understand why [President Lyndon]

Johnson felt obliged to assert his commitment to Vietnam in November 1963. To *continue* with Kennedy's withdrawal, after his death, would have been difficult, since the American public had not been told that the war was being lost. Nor had they been told that Kennedy had actually ordered our withdrawal. To maintain our commitment, therefore, was to maintain the illusion of continuity, and this—in the moment of trauma that followed the assassination—was Johnson's paramount political objective. . . . [35]

Left in charge, Lyndon Johnson temporized, agonized, and cursed the fates. But ultimately he committed us to [a] war that he knew in advance would be practically impossible to win. Nothing can erase this. And yet meanwhile, alongside McNamara, he too prevented any steps that might lead to an invasion of the North, direct conflict with China, and nuclear confrontation. . . .[36]

Noam Chomsky: Having worked through the relevant documentation that James Galbraith cites, I was curious to see how he could reach his conclusions in his article "Exit Strategy" (October/November 2003), at variance with the mainstream of scholarship and other commentary, as he notes. The basic method turns out to be simple: deletion.

As for others, the centerpiece of Galbraith's discussion of the withdrawal plans is NSAM 263 [National Security Action Memorandum 263], in which JFK gave qualified approval to the recommendations of Robert McNamara and Maxwell Taylor, who were greatly encouraged by the military prospects in South Vietnam and were "convinced that the Viet Cong insurgency" could be sharply reduced by the end of 1965."[37] They therefore advised "An increase in the military tempo" of the war throughout South Vietnam and withdrawal of some troops in 1963 and all troops in 1965—if this could be done *"without impairment of the war effort"* and with assurances that *"the insurgency has been suppressed"* or at least sufficiently weakened so that the U.S. client regime (GVN [Government of South Vietnam]) is *"capable of suppressing it"* (my italics; the crucial condition throughout). Once again they stressed that the "overriding objective" is victory, a matter "vital to United States security." JFK approved their recommendations, while distancing himself from the withdrawal proposal and approving instructions to Ambassador Lodge in Saigon stressing "our fundamental objective of victory" and directing him to press for "GVN action to increase effectiveness of its military effort" so as to ensure the military victory on which withdrawal was explicitly conditioned.[38] The president, Lodge was informed, affirmed "his basic statement that what furthers the war effort we support, and what interferes with the war effort we oppose," the condition underlying NSAM 263, as consistently throughout the period and beyond.

JFK and his advisers were concerned with the "crisis of confidence among the Vietnamese people which is eroding popular support for GVN that is vital for victory," and the "crisis of confidence on the part of the American public and Government" who also do not see how "our actions are related to our fundamental objective of victory"—JFK's invariant condition. JFK (and his advisers) recognized that the war was unpopular at home, but regarded such lack of support—as well as GVN initiatives toward political settlement—not as an opportunity for withdrawal, but rather as a problem to be overcome, because it posed a threat to the military victory to which they were committed. The significance of these facts for the thesis under discussion is obvious.

Virtually all of this was deleted from Galbraith's account of NSAM 263, and the tidbits that remain he clearly misinterprets. Thus he does quote the qualification that troops can be withdrawn only "when they are no longer needed," but fails to recognize that this is simply another reiteration of the unwavering commitment to military victory.

By this method, Galbraith is able to draw the conclusions rejected by virtually everyone he cites, who use the same documentary record (in all relevant cases) but without crucial omissions and misreadings. His treatment of his own prime example [NSAM 263] is typical, as interested readers can readily discover.

Galbraith also deletes much else of crucial significance, including the shifting plans of Kennedy and his advisors that are closely correlated with changing perceptions of the military situation, clearly a critically important matter; the absence of any record by the memoirists of any thought about withdrawing without victory, e.g., in Arthur Schlesinger's virtual day-by-day account;[39] the fact that JFK's most dovish advisors (George Ball, Mike Mansfield, etc.) reiterated their firm commitment to victory after the assassination, and in the months that followed praised LBJ for carrying forward JFK's policies with "wise caution" (Ball), urging that LBJ's "policy toward Vietnam was the only one we could follow" and strongly opposing the withdrawal option and diplomatic moves advocated by Wayne Morse (Mansfield), as did Robert Kennedy, who, as late as May 1965, condemned withdrawal as "a repudiation of commitments undertaken and confirmed by three administrations"; and a great deal more of very considerable relevance to this thesis.[40]

There is no need to review these matters, which are covered in detail in literature that Galbraith claims to refute, including my *Rethinking Camelot*, which also documents the revisions of the record that were introduced after the war became unpopular, the basic reason why such material (including much on which Galbraith uncritically relies) is unreliable for any historian. Galbraith claims further that this book was immediately refuted by Peter Dale Scott, but here there is another rather significant omission.[41] Galbraith fails to point out that his claim is logically impossible: Scott does not even mention the book in the "epilogue" to which Galbraith refers, and was plainly unaware of its existence. Scott did mention an article of mine, which he apparently read so hurriedly that he seriously misunderstood its topic and was unaware of the documentation on which it was based, crucially, thousands of pages of recently released documents which, though I did not specifically refer to it, undermined Scott's speculations to which Galbraith refers, published 20 years earlier in a collection of essays on the Pentagon Papers that I edited.[42] Galbraith, like Scott, believes that I was relying on the Pentagon Papers; a look at the opening paragraphs suffices to correct this quite crucial error. But Scott's departure from his usually careful work is irrelevant here, so there is no need to pursue it.

Rather surprisingly, Galbraith relies heavily on John New-

man's deeply flawed account, which establishes its conclusions
by elaborate tales of "deception" of JFK by those around him,
through "in his heart [JFK] must have known" the truth so we
can ignore the documentary record which leaves no trace of
what JFK, alone, "had to notice."[43] This strange performance
too is reviewed elsewhere in detail, and need not be discussed
here.

No one—even JFK himself—could have known how he would
react to the radically changed assessments of the military/politi-
cal situation immediately after his assassination. It is conceivable that he might, for the first time, have made decisions
counter to those of his closest associates and advisers and cho-
sen to withdraw (or perhaps to escalate more sharply). There is,
however, no hint in the record that he contemplated withdrawal
without victory, as we discover when we fill in the crucial blanks
in Galbraith's account, as is done in the extensive literature to
which he refers, while evading its evidentiary base, and adding
nothing of particular relevance.

Kennedy-Johnson State Department official Lincoln Gordon,
later president of Johns Hopkins University, once warned
against "Camelot myth-making"—an observation that merits
some reflection.[44]

James K. Galbraith: Confusion over these matters could be reduced by a little more care in specifying what is and is not at issue.

In October 1963 there were 17,000 U.S. military "advisers" in
Vietnam. They were doing some fighting, and taking some
losses, but in the main their mission was to train and assist the
South Vietnamese army, which was more than ten times larger.
They faced an insurgency involving as yet few North Vietnamese
forces. U.S. withdrawal at that time would not have meant the
early collapse of South Vietnam. It would not have ended the
war—except from the point of view of direct involvement of
U.S. soldiers.

It is therefore reasonable that, into the early fall of 1963
when official military forecasts were still fairly optimistic, the
administration should simultaneously plan to "intensify the war
effort" and plan for withdrawal of our soldiers. Three key facts

that have since emerged are these. First, the official optimism was disbelieved at the very top of the Kennedy administration, notably by McNamara. Second, Kennedy set a course for a decision to withdraw, from which he was not deterred by what then became a deteriorating official military prospect. This explains Kennedy's concern, evident on the tapes, that the withdrawal be implemented in low key and not be tied to the perception of military progress. Third, the decision to withdraw was taken and then carefully, but not altogether completely, edited out of the record available to historians until the late 1990s.

I believe that the work of Peter Dale Scott, John Newman, and most recently Howard Jones will stand, when the dust settles, as the path toward truth in this matter.[45] My article mainly provides a synthesis of their work. Readers who want to check Noam Chomsky's claim that other historians "use the same documentary record" to reach opposite results can look for themselves at the materials cited. It isn't so.

Let me add that I am disturbed by the suggestion about "Camelot myth-making." An antiwar activist in my early life, I only became involved in this matter at the time of the Newman-Chomsky-Scott debates in 1993. My impression of Newman (a career military officer at the time) and of Scott (with whom I have only corresponded) is that neither can fairly be accused of Kennedy worship. Kennedy's October 1963 decision to withdraw happened. But Kennedy was nonetheless prepared to leave U.S. soldiers in harm's way for two more years, mainly (I believe) to reduce the political consequences of pulling them out before the 1964 election. This should have, as my essay states, an ambiguous effect on his reputation.

In 1993 Chomsky laid out key questions that had to be answered. Having said that, answers are available that were not available then. Chomsky is mistaken when he denies this. Readers may safely treat his latest intervention as being what it appears to be: hasty, heated, and insubstantial.[46]

The Dilemma: Leaders Must Learn from Their Mistakes.

Many who study President John F. Kennedy's decisionmaking in the Cuban missile crisis have become fascinated by the following counterfactual, or "what-if?": what if the Cuban missile crisis had occurred *before* the Bay of Pigs fiasco, rather than the other way around? Of course, in one sense, the question makes little sense. We now know that the Bay of Pigs invasion was the precipitating event that led the Cubans to approach the Russians in desperation for assistance, which in turn led Nikita Khrushchev to respond to the Cuban request with an offer of nuclear missiles. So without the Bay of Pigs debacle in April 1961, there may well have been no Soviet missiles shipped to Cuba, hence no Cuban missile crisis in October 1962.

But the counterfactual is more profound, in our view, than its historical improbability might suggest. The question it raises is this: if President Kennedy had not made a huge mistake in April 1961— a mistake for which he immediately and repeatedly accepted personal responsibility, both to his advisers and to the public—might Kennedy have made a mistake of incomparably greater significance in October 1962? Might he have done what most of his advisers were urging him to do: order an air strike against the Soviet missile sites in Cuba; and follow it up with an invasion of the island, inadvertently plunging the world into nuclear war? We believe his cautious, deliberate approach in October 1962 is traceable, in part, to his incautious, credulous acceptance of his advisers' recommendations in April 1961. Had Kennedy not learned from his mistake in April 1961, to treat military and intelligence advice skeptically, we think it less likely that he would have resisted attacking and invading Cuba.

After April 1961, Kennedy never again accepted unquestioningly the advice of his intelligence and military advisers. Kennedy's skepticism and caution was evident, and controversial even among his close advisers, with regard to Vietnam. From the moment Kennedy was inaugurated, the Joint Chiefs of Staff had pushed hard for what seemed to Kennedy to be a U.S. takeover of the effort to subdue the insurgency in South Vietnam. But as the documents and dialogues in this chapter demonstrate, Kennedy resisted the pressure. He died unconvinced that the problem of preserving the independence of an anticommunist South Vietnam had a military solution. He may well have believed it had no solution whatever, at least none that the U.S. alone could implement, in the absence of a viable South Vietnamese leadership.

We believe it is instructive to compare the Kennedy administration's trajectory on Vietnam with the G. W. Bush administration's plunge into war with Iraq. To justify the urgency and necessity of the invasion and occupation of Iraq, all senior U.S. officials, from the president on down claimed that Iraq posessed weapons of mass destruction (WMD) that were ready to be used, and that Saddam Hussein's government worked hand in glove with Osama bin Laden's al-Qaeda network. Senior officials also predicted confidently that after a brief occupation of Iraq, a peaceful handover to Iraqi "democrats" would occur, followed by a "democratization" of the Middle East.[47] We now know that throughout the U.S. preparations for invasion, there existed no convincing evidence that WMD were in Iraqi hands. We also know that there was no meaningful involvement by Iraq with those al-Qaeda operatives who planned and carried out the attacks of 9/11. Furthermore, the occupation of Iraq has been a violent, chaotic disaster for both Iraqis and Americans.[48] These are facts. We are not here accusing anyone of outright lies. It is enough simply to state the obvious: a lot of officials, at the highest levels, made a lot of mistakes. But, as far as we are aware, however, no senior U.S. official involved in the decision to invade Iraq has admitted making even a single consequential error either in deciding to go to war or in planning for postwar Iraq.[49]

Kennedy famously said that success has a thousand fathers, while failure is an orphan—a principle he fortunately violated with regard to the Bay of Pigs. We should ask ourselves: having refused to admit any mistakes (to say nothing of taking personal responsibility for such mistakes as were made) with regard to Iraq, how confident should we feel about such an administration's ability to handle peacefully and successfully some 21st-century equivalent of a "Cuban missile crisis"—a nuclear confrontation, should it occur, perhaps with North Korea or Iran? Our answer is "not very confident." Apparently firm in their belief that no significant mistakes were made regarding Iraq, U.S. officials can therefore have learned nothing significant from it that might be applied when all the chips are on the line, and the U.S. itself, and the world, is mortally threatened by a nuclear-armed menace.

See Appendix B, Lesson Five, for further discussion of this dilemma.

"The effect of *The Fog of War* is to impress upon us the frailty and uncertainty of our leaders."
Roger Ebert, *Chicago Sun-Times*

"The verdicts on [McNamara's] confessions range from mild praise . . . to utter rage . . .
Frank Rich, *The New York Times*

"Though the movie may not change many minds about McNamara, it richly humanizes him, a valuable feat atop all the fascinating reflection.
Mike Clark, *USA Today*

"For those of my generation, the true resonance in the film may be in the constant juxtaposition between the then and the now of the McNamara life."
Stephen Hunter, *Washington Post*

" . . . a profound examination of the troubling proposition that good or well-meaning people can help create horrible and evil events . . . "
Michael Wilmington, *Chicago Tribune*

" . . . spellbinding reality cinema about duplicity and, worse, ignorance at the highest level."
Richard Corliss, *Time Magazine*

"Morris fills [his film with] skewed and crooked angles on McNamara himself—as if even the camera couldn't get a grasp on the elusive nature of this topic."
Jeffrey M. Anderson, *San Francisco Examiner*

"Morris uses McNamara's long life and firsthand experience to indicate how technology has made the ethics of war much more difficult to tread."
Dan Lybarger, *Kansas City Star*

"Truly remarkable—a history lesson, a mea culpa and one last chance to discuss a pivotal era with someone who was actually there."
Larry Carroll, *Filmstew.com*

" . . . a riveting reminder for those who remember; a required history lesson for those who don't."
Jean Lowerison, *San Diego Metropolitan*

"What's genuinely suspenseful about the movie is its journey into the heart and mind of McNamara."
Jay Boyar, *Orlando Sentinel*

" . . . may be the scariest movie of 2003."
Josh Larsen, *Sun Publications (Chicago, IL)*

Critical Essays: "I'd Rather Be Damned If I Don't"

ROBERT S. MCNAMARA: *Let me hear your voice level to make sure it's the same.*

ERROL MORRIS: *Okay, how's my voice level?*

MCNAMARA: *That's fine.*

MORRIS: *Terrific.*

MCNAMARA: *Now, I remember exactly the sentence I left off on. I remember how it started, and I was cut off in the middle. But you can fix it up some way. I don't want to go back and introduce the sentence, because I know exactly what I wanted to say.*

MORRIS: *Go ahead!*

MCNAMARA: *Okay.*

. . .

MORRIS: *After you left the Johnson administration, why didn't you speak out against the Vietnam War?*

MCNAMARA: *I'm not going to say any more than I have. These are the kinds of questions that get me in trouble. You don't know what I know about how inflammatory my words can appear. A lot of people misunderstand the war, misunderstand me. A lot of people think I'm a son of a bitch.*

MORRIS: *Do you feel in any way responsible for the war?*

MCNAMARA: *I don't want to go any further with this discussion. . . .*

MORRIS: *Is it the feeling that you're damned if you do, and if you don't, no matter what?*

MCNAMARA: *Yeah, that's right. And I'd rather be damned if I don't.*

ROBERT S. MCNAMARA and ERROL MORRIS, in "The Fog of War."

From the beginning, *the uniqueness of "The Fog of War" is evident. In the customary introduction to a documentary, a mellow, disembodied voice of a narrator announces themes and principal characters, accompanied by brief visual images of the events to be covered. The beginning of "The Fog of War," however, is jarring. A forty-something Robert McNamara in the 1960s is setting up a chart for a briefing to the news media. After a brief interlude in which the lead credits roll, an eighty-something McNamara—who we know is the subject of the film—appears to be issuing orders to Errol Morris, who is off camera, whom we know to be the director and producer of the film. What kind of film is this, and who is in charge of its content? Is it Morris, well-known for his deeply probing interviews, or McNamara, who is equally notable for his penchant for personal control? We are drawn ever deeper into the unfolding drama and become aware that the answer is that neither man is fully in control. The film is a collaboration between them.*

It soon becomes evident, moreover, that this is a documentary film with but one "talking head"—McNamara's. Morris is reaching for a new kind of documentary, by weaving the entire film around on-camera interviews with an eighty-five year old man whom many older viewers may not have thought about for nearly forty years, and whom younger viewers may never have heard of at all. This minimalist cast of characters—McNamara's voice and physical presence, and Morris' occasional, disembodied voice—matches the minimalist, edgy score of Philip Glass. The creative tension in the collaboration between what the control-oriented McNamara wishes to reveal, and what the relentless interviewer Morris wants to discover, gives the film a pervasive edginess.

The collaboration between Morris and McNamara is one that has limits, as we discover in the film's "Epilogue." Morris wants McNamara to say what he thinks and feels about his personal role in the origin and evolution of the Vietnam War. But McNamara refuses to do so, a decision Morris respects. As Morris has said often in interviews about the film, it is relatively easy to admit guilt and culpability. People do this every weekday morning on television talk shows. An admission of misdeeds is made, perhaps followed by tears and reconciliation. Then the show is over. Morris emphasizes that what McNamara has done, in the film and in several recent books, is more diffi-

cult than issuing a mea culpa. McNamara has devoted years and a good deal of energy discovering what went wrong in Vietnam—beginning with his own mistakes, but not ending there—and then to state the lessons to be learned for future generations.[1]

The Morris-McNamara mix poses a challenge for reviewers. Morris is an innovative, award-winning filmmaker, a filmmaker with a nearly cult-like following. McNamara too has a following, but of a markedly different sort. Morris describes it this way: "McNamara got the hat trick. He's hated by the left, the right, and the center. Congratulations!"[2] Reviews of the film are intertwined with reviews of the man. Moreover, reviewers who came of age during the turbulent '60s often reveal something of their own personalities, attitudes, and beliefs. Reading reviews of "The Fog of War" is often therefore a disorienting experience, in which the film and its subject are viewed independently.

Rarely has a documentary film attracted so many reviews—from film critics, political journalists and activists.[3] While the reviews are varied, generall, they tend to emphasize four features of the film: first, astonishment at McNamara's "performance." He was eighty-five when he was interviewed by Morris, but he seems to most critics to have lost little or none of the sharp analytical intelligence, combined with a scary intensity, for which he first became widely known nearly a half century ago. McNamara is so animated at times that he appears poised to fly right out of his chair and into the viewers' laps. This comes as a surprise to many, who previously had viewed him as formal, brusque, and standoffish, which was more or less his public persona when he was secretary of defense.

Second, the critics by and large believe that the film is technically remarkable. Many mention the stunning archival footage (some of which had never been seen before outside of archives). Critics also express their admiration for what has become a staple of an Errol Morris documentary—reenactments, such as his replay of dropping human skulls down stairwells, as was done at Cornell in the 1950s, to assess the impact of the "packaging" of passengers in automobiles. And critics especially note the "revolutionary" aspect of the film—which is Morris' effort to convince the audience of the film's objectivity, and to retain the viewers' interest, even though McNamara is the only person interviewed. McNamara, in effect, narrates his own biography. Or does Morris, in effect, "narrate" McNamara's autobiography? Morris, with his taste for irony and complexity, might say "both."

Third, almost everyone who has commented on the film has noted the uncanny effect of the timing of the film's appearance. Literally everything in the film is historical, including all of McNamara's interventions, all the archival footage and all the reenactments and special effects. Not one word is said about the attacks of 9/11, or the war in Iraq, which began in March 2003, for example.[4] Yet most critics have found it impossible to watch the film without reflecting on its relevance for contemporary U.S. foreign and defense policy. Many have used the occasion of reviewing the film as an opportunity to explore the similarities and differences between that which came, during the 1960s, to be called "McNamara's war" in Vietnam, and the 2003 U.S. invasion and subsequent occupation of Iraq.

Fourth and finally, reviewers return to their views of McNamara, the man: Did he or did he not apologize? Is he sorry? Is he telling the truth? All have watched the "same" film, and yet their answers to these questions do not converge. Is this Morris' artistry? McNamara's personality? Reviewer bias? The complexity of the situations McNamara describes? All of the above?

With a character as provocative as Robert McNamara, with a director/producer as inquisitive as Errol Morris, and with the film's subject matter resonating to newspaper headlines about the war in Iraq, is it any wonder that "The Fog of War" has been reviewed by well over 100 people from extraordinarily varied backgrounds? In the sections that follow, we present a sample of these reviews, along with commentary.[5]

■

McNamara and Morris Face the Media

"MCNAMARA . . . PERHAPS HAS NEVER USED GOOGLE."

Three weeks before "The Fog of War" won the Academy Award® for best documentary feature film, Robert McNamara and Errol Morris returned to the University of California, Berkeley, where each had at one time been a student. The occasion was a public forum, moderated by UCB journalism professor and New Yorker magazine staff *writer Mark Danner. The resulting conversation was almost as surreal as certain aspects of the movie. Danner pressed McNamara over and over to connect the lessons he draws from the Vietnam experience to the American war in Iraq and its occupation of the country. In each case, McNamara forcefully reiterated what he said was his standing policy: as a former defense secretary, never to criticize the conduct of ongoing conflicts in which the U.S. is involved, in order to avoid putting U.S. troops at further risk.*

But then Danner confronted McNamara with a quote from an interview in a Canadian newspaper, in which McNamara had been scathing on the Bush administration's conduct of the Iraq War.[6] But McNamara wouldn't take the bait, saying that he never expected people in, say, Berkeley, to read a piece in an obscure foreign newspaper, a comment that prompted the author of this report to note that McNamara "perhaps has never used Google." At last, McNamara tired of Danner's pressure to enlarge on the comments he made to the Canadian interviewer. How, then should his lessons from Vietnam be applied to Iraq, or any other contemporary issue? "You apply them," McNamara told the Berkeley audience. "You don't need me to point out the target. You're smart enough."

THE REVIEW: Bonnie Azab Powell, "Robert McNamara, Errol Morris Return to Berkeley to Share Lessons Learned From 'Fog of War'." University of California, Berkeley NewsCenter article, Feb 5, 2004.

Near the end of "Fog of War," Errol Morris's documentary about Robert McNamara's examination of his role in the wars of the 20th century, McNamara shares his philosophy for dealing with the press. "Don't answer the question they asked," the former Secretary of Defense (1961–1968) advises with a smile. "Answer the question you wish they'd asked."

McNamara relied heavily on that strategy during a February 4 forum at UC Berkeley devoted to "The Fog of War." The question posed in various ways by Mark Danner, the UC Berkeley Graduate School of Journalism professor who moderated the discussion with Morris and McNamara, was whether the lessons McNamara has drawn from the Vietnam War should be applied to the United States' current war in Iraq. In hundreds of prior interviews, McNamara has steadfastly refused to do so, claiming this would pose a risk to American soldiers in the field. (There is, however, an exception to that refusal, which we'll get to later.)

One of the most admired and later, the most vilified, leaders of his generation, McNamara has spent the last 20 years and three memoirs trying to navigate his personal "fog of war," the complex miasma of national decisions that resulted in the deaths of more than a million civilians in Japan and 58,000 U.S. servicemen and women (plus untold numbers of civilians) in Vietnam.[7] In contrast to today's exhibitionist climate, where Presidential candidates, celebrities, and ordinary people seek absolution on talk shows, McNamara has never publicly apologized for either Japan or Vietnam. "At first I thought McNamara's failure to apologize was a weakness of the book [1995's "In Retrospect," which inspired "Fog of War"]; now I think that it is one of his strengths," writes Morris in his director's statement. "It is much more difficult to analyze the causes of error than apologize for it."[8]

McNamara's perspective on his past is hard-won. And although he nimbly deflected Danner's attempts to elicit his comments on the present, it was clear that he wanted the packed Zellerbach Hall audience to learn from his mistakes—not from him. At 87, he simply belongs to a generation that equated patriotism with unquestioning loyalty to one's President and government: an idea that for younger generations has been tarnished by the Vietnam War, Watergate, the Iran-Contra affair, Monicagate, and other scandals.

Wisps of fog

Presented by the Goldman Forum on Press & Foreign Affairs and the Journalism School, the evening began with 40 minutes' worth of clips from Morris's film, currently in the running for an Academy Award® for Best Documentary.[9] The excerpts were shown in a sequence different from the movie's and failed to convey the complexity of "Fog of War," which intersperses Morris's interviews with McNamara and historical footage, stills, and recently unearthed taped conversations between McNamara and Presidents John F. Kennedy and Lyndon B. Johnson. The film covers McNamara's early life, touching on the four years he spent at UC Berkeley studying economics during the Great Depression, his and his wife's bout with polio, and his considerable achievements as a Harvard professor, one of the

Ford Motors' Whiz Kids, and then the company's first president from outside the Ford family.

But the bulk of "Fog of War" is devoted to the parts McNamara played in the 1945 firebombing of Japan during World War II, when he was a Statistical Control Officer and a captain in the U.S. Air Force; as Kennedy's Secretary of Defense during the 1962 Cuban Missile Crisis; and the escalation of the Vietnam War from 1963 to 1968, when he either resigned or was fired—he maintains he doesn't know exactly which—from Johnson's Cabinet.

For the film, Morris interviewed the then-85-year-old McNamara using a device he calls the Interrotron, a two-camera and Teleprompter arrangement that forces the subject to maintain eye contact with the camera, and thus the audience, at all times. The result is an unnerving intimacy that resembles a confessional booth, and McNamara confesses much. The storm of criticism over the detached manner in which he lists his mistakes comes from those who persist in seeing McNamara as "a computer-like man, a technocrat, a hawk who, through his arrogance, blundered into Vietnam," Morris concludes in his director's statement. "However, the presidential recordings—the weight of the historical evidence itself—do not bear this out. Instead, a far more complex portrait of the man emerges—one who tried to serve two very different presidents."

The subtitle of "The Fog of War" is "Eleven Lessons From the Life of Robert McNamara," and the film is punctuated with short statements that Morris drew from his interviews with McNamara. For example, "Rule No. 1: Empathize with your enemy," refers to McNamara's belief that Kennedy averted nuclear war by understanding what kind of a deal would allow Soviet leader Nikita Krushchev to save face, while No. 7, "Belief and seeing are both often wrong," is illustrated by a North Vietnamese attack on a U.S. warship that never actually happened—but the military so believed in it that it led to the Gulf of Tonkin Resolution, in which Congress gave Johnson full power to wage war on Vietnam.

History is written by the winners

Another, "Proportionality should be a guideline in war," which was among the segments shown on Wednesday night, refers to McNamara's role, with General Curtis LeMay, in the 1945 firebombings of 67 Japanese cities—before the bombs were ever dropped on Hiroshima and Nagasaki. McNamara wrote the report on the inefficiency of conventional bombing campaigns that may have inspired LeMay to take his B-29 bombers down to under 5,000 feet and rain fire on cities built of wood, killing nearly 1 million Japanese. In the film, McNamara says, "In a single night we burned to death 100,000 civilians—men, women, and children—in Tokyo. I was part of a mechanism that in a sense recommended it." He goes on to recount how LeMay admitted, "'If we lost the war, we'd all be prosecuted as war criminals.' He—and I—were behaving as war criminals. . . . What makes it immoral if you lose but not if you win?"

Such hard questions and observations—about the importance of empathizing with the enemy, about governments seeing what they want to believe, the ethical justification for "preventive" war—fairly beg to be applied to current events, or so suggested the forum's participants. UC Berkeley Chancellor Robert M. Berdahl, in his introduction of the event, quoted Morris as saying "I don't think that Iraq is exactly like Vietnam; I don't think history exactly repeats itself. But I do think many of the mistakes we made in Vietnam are all too relevant to the mistakes we are making today." Journalism School Dean Orville Schell agreed: "I think what makes everybody so interested in the subject of Errol Morris's truly great film is the resonance that it has with the war that we are currently in now."

Morris is happy to acknowledge the echoes, but McNamara will not give them voice.

The question that McNamara wanted to answer—and returned to over and over—was not what he could do to shed insight on the U.S. war with Iraq, but what the audience and Americans citizens could do for their country's future. "We human beings killed 160 million other human beings in the 20th century," he fairly shouted, jabbing his finger at Danner as aggressively as he does at the camera in the film. "Is that what we want in this century? I don't think so!"

Preventive war—an oxymoron

Morris, who left most of the talking to McNamara and Danner, echoed that sentiment. Referring to McNamara's earliest memory—as a two-year-old watching San Francisco celebrate Armistice Day and the end of "the war to end all wars"—Morris said, "Ironic, yes, because the end of World War I ushered in a century of the worst carnage in human history. . . . I am constantly reminded that war doesn't end war. I think there are several examples of this in the past," he added dryly. "The 'preventive war' itself is an oxymoron, and we're starting out the 21st century much as we did the century before. This to me does not augur well."

McNamara cut him off, addressing the audience fervently: "But, but, don't give up! I mean it! Don't give up! You individuals can do something about it!" He enumerated the ways: by pushing for the U.S. to develop a judicial system that governs the behavior of war (an easy way: participate in the rest of the world's International Criminal Tribunal system), by forcing Congress to debate publicly the nation's nuclear policy ("you'd be shocked if you knew what it was," he warned), and by raising not only the country's standard of living through national health care and better education, but the state of California's.

The author of a book on Haiti's war and a staff writer for The New Yorker, Danner has reported recently from Iraq and has sharpened his talons in two public debates about the war with writer Christopher Hitchens. To McNamara, he compared the Johnson administration's secretive behavior during Vietnam—about the scale, length, and cost of the war—with Secretary of Defense Donald Rumsfeld's and the Bush administration's approach to the war with Iraq. Faced with this historical duplicate of duplicity, Danner pressed McNamara to answer his question, not the one that McNamara kept answering.

"What I'm pushing you on," said Danner, "is not simply 'We can do better, we have to work for a better world.'" If McNamara has devoted the last 20 years of his life to "the notion that things can change, that lessons can be learned," he asked, what happens when we appear to have "a world where lessons haven't been learned, where in fact we seem to be in precisely the same world all over again?"

In response—or rather, the opposite—McNamara told a long anecdote about Johnson. Danner sighed. Morris tried next, attempting to draw out a McNamara reluctant to criticize any president, past or present. "You've said that cabinet officers serve at the pleasure of the president, and that 'Johnson was elected, I was not.' Is this a problem, that Cabinet officers feel they have to toe the line?" he asked. "Most Cabinet officers, from the past until today, believe they're there to represent the interests of the department— Agriculture represents farmers, Defense represents the military. Not at all!" McNamara answered (sort of). "Each of those secretaries represents the president! The president was elected, he had a platform." Although he would not criticize the Bush administration directly, he took a veiled swipe at Secretary of State Colin Powell for Powell's recent admission that he might have felt differently about the war in Iraq had he known no weapons of mass destruction would be found. "I don't believe any secretary should continue beyond the point where he feels he's being effective in pursuing both the president's programs and [if they are] different from what he believes, is being effective in helping the president change his program to what he believes is right," McNamara said.

McNamara's tenure at Defense ended shortly after he hand-delivered a memo to Johnson outlining his serious doubts about the continued escalation of the Vietnam War. Asked why he refused to share those doubts with the American public, even after leaving the government, for the war's remaining duration, McNamara was unapologetic. "You have to ask yourself, if you have tens of thousands of American lives at risk, whether it's in Iraq or Vietnam, if a senior official of the government says the government's policies are wrong, are you endangering those individuals?" he emphasized. "And the answer is bound to be, Yes! You've got to be very careful. You have a responsibility to the people whose lives are at risk. And that's true today in Iraq, and it was true in Vietnam."

The *Globe* comes knocking

Danner said that up until that day, he had "grudgingly accepted" McNamara's refusal to weigh in on Iraq, even after beseeching calls from scores of reporters. Then he pounced, brandishing a printout of a January 24, 2004, interview with McNamara by the *Toronto Globe and Mail* in which McNamara directly criticized the Bush administration.[10] "If 171 [journalists] asked you, clearly one asked you in a way that brought forth a bounty of opinion," Danner scolded, reading quotations from McNamara such as "We're misusing our influence. . . . It's just wrong what we're doing. It's morally wrong, it's politically wrong, it's economically wrong" and "There have been times in the last year when I was just utterly disgusted by our position, the United States' position vis-à-vis the other nations of the world." After Danner finished reading, Morris turned to McNamara and said quietly, "I applaud you for saying those things."

McNamara, who perhaps has never used Google, sputtered that he didn't think that anyone would actually see the Canadian newspaper article, but he acknowledged that all of its quotations were accurate. While urging the audience to engage in public debate about the war with Iraq, he once again refused to lead it.

Danner tried his question again. Although Morris wrote the 11 lessons in "Fog of War," not McNamara (who doesn't like the phrasing of all of them)[11], the structure came from the 11 lessons about Vietnam that Mc-Namara draws in his 1995 book, "In Retrospect: The Tragedy and Lessons of Vietnam." After reciting the originals . . . , Danner then said, "They seemed so to reflect, with uncanny accuracy, what happened before the [Iraq] war, what happened now, and—I hope not—but perhaps what will happen in the future. It's for that that I try to push you so, in helping us understand a little bit more . . . how we reached the point we find ourselves in today."

McNamara seemed almost persuaded. After a few boasts about the book's popularity on the best-seller lists and in history classes, he said, "I'm not suggesting you buy it—but the lessons are in there. . . . I put them forward not because of Vietnam, I put them forward because of the future." Almost, that is. "Now what you want me to do is apply them to Bush. I'm not going to do it! *You* apply them to Bush!" he admonished.

There was time for only one written question from the audience: whether the events of September 11 had, as the Bush administration said, "changed everything." McNamara disagreed, arguing that 9/11 simply further highlighted the importance of empathizing with the enemy. "If you don't have any other weapon you're going to use terrorism," he argued. "9/11 should have taught us to be more sensitive to Muslim and Israel-Palestine problems."

Danner used the audience question as his springboard for a final tilt at McNamara, but the former Secretary of Defense had packed up his notes and books even before Danner finished talking.

"As I told you, I am not going to comment on President Bush," McNamara said, patting his briefcase. "I refer you again to the 11 principles. You apply them! . . . You don't need me to point out the target. You're smart enough!"

". . . there were two versions of me watching the movie."

When Errol Morris appeared on the National Public Radio program "Fresh Air," listeners were treated to the unusual experience of hearing an interview by a well-known radio interviewer (Terry Gross), of an equally famous documentary film interviewer (Errol Morris), about Morris' interview that provides the central narrative of "The Fog of War." The resulting dialogue was open and sophisticated regarding the craft of interviewing. In many ways, a person like Robert McNamara is a test case for anyone's theories about interviewing, for he is famously difficult, demanding, even intimidating, and always intent on controlling both the process and the product.

Morris mentioned to Terry Gross that, in watching the movie, he has the impression that an eighty-five-year-old man is, in some sense, in conversation with his forty-five-year-old former self. This fascinated Gross. She recalled the feeling that "there were two versions of me watching the movie." On the one hand, she had no trouble empathizing with McNamara when he alludes to the terrible toll taken on his family by the stress of the Vietnam War. At the same time, however, another part of her was saying, "Well, I should think so," because the war was killing so many Vietnamese and Americans. This is a dominant theme of viewers old enough to remember the Vietnam War—a strong ambivalence about whether to empathize with McNamara and the regret and remorse he seems to feel about his role in the war or simply to condemn him for his role in the disaster.

THE REVIEW: Terry Gross, "Interview with Errol Morris." National Public Radio, 12:00 Noon EST, Monday, January 5, 2004. Produced at WHYY, Philadelphia, PA.

> **Terry Gross:** This is FRESH AIR. . . . My guest, Errol Morris, directed the new film "The Fog of War," which has been appearing on many critics' 10 best lists. This documentary is edited from over 20 hours of interviews with Robert McNamara, who served as secretary of Defense under Presidents Kennedy and

Johnson. He was one of the architects of the war in Vietnam, but he said that by the time he left the Johnson administration in 1968, he had become increasingly skeptical about the war and worried that more and more people were being killed and we weren't accomplishing our goals.

McNamara has remained an enigmatic figure. For many years, he would not speak about his role in the war. That silence was broken by his 1995 memoir in which he discussed what led to his growing skepticism, but he disappointed his critics by not apologizing for his role in the war.

. . . You know, one of the things that really astonished me watching "The Fog of War" was that McNamara was really lively, anecdotal, interesting. And I always thought of him, among other things, as cold and kind of inaccessible. In other words, that you'd never get anything out of him. What surprised you about actually talking with him?

Errol Morris: One of the things I like about interviews—maybe you feel the same way—to me, interviews are investigative. I never know what I'm going to hear. In fact, to the extent that I know what I'm going to hear, I'm not terribly interested. I want to be surprised. I want something unexpected to happen. And that certainly was the case with my interviews with Robert Mc-Namara, a picture of a very different kind of man than I had been familiar with years ago seeing him on television, reading about him in the papers, a far more interesting, far more complex man.

Terry Gross: Give me an example of something he said that really surprised you.

Errol Morris: Well, the most surprising thing was discovering that his role in Vietnam was different than I had thought. Remember, the Vietnam War was known to many people as "McNamara's war." He became not only associated with the war, people thought of it as his war, as though he was the person primarily responsible for it. He was the hawk. He was the guy who pushed other people towards escalation, to bombing, to troops on the ground. You want an explanation for how we became mired in Vietnam? Look no further than Robert S.

McNamara. And yet, as I got deeper and deeper into the story, my view of him and his role in history changed.

Terry Gross: How did it change?

Errol Morris: . . . There's this very odd conversation. "The Fog of War" actually has these recently released presidential recordings. Everybody knows Nixon made recordings, but it's less well-known that Kennedy and Johnson recorded their conversations as well. Kennedy recorded Cabinet meetings; Johnson recorded phone calls. So you can actually hear the president of the United States talking with McNamara, a front-row seat in history, if you like.

And there's one powerful conversation, October 2nd, 1963. This is less than two months before Kennedy was assassinated. We hear McNamara and the president talking, and McNamara is urging Kennedy to set a timetable, a schedule for getting out of Vietnam. This is the man who we considered to be the worst hawk of all in the administration, the most bellicose adviser of all in the administration.

. . .

Terry Gross: Now in talking about his role in Vietnam, he certainly gives the impression that he tried to talk President Johnson out of the war, tried to start decreasing our presence in Vietnam. Do you believe that that was consistently his point of view with Johnson?

Errol Morris: It's a tortured story. I believe that, if Kennedy had lived, in all likelihood, there would not have been extensive bombing and half a million ground troops in Vietnam. It's one of those great mysteries that can't be really answered for certain, but the story leans in that direction. There is a considerable amount of evidence that suggests that's the case.

One thing that's really interesting—I sometimes say, well, this revised story about Vietnam that emerges in "The Fog of War," it's not necessarily a better story. It's just a different story because it raises a whole set of different questions. If McNamara was opposed to the war, why did he become a part of its escalation? Why did he continue to serve Johnson if he disagreed with his policies? Why did he stay on until 1968? And why, when he left the administration, did he remain silent? War went on in '69, '70, '71, '72, '73, '74, '75. Between two and three million Vietnamese died and 58,000 Americans.

Terry Gross: Now aren't these the questions that he still refuses to answer? The questions that you just raised?

Errol Morris: Yes and no. The movie has an epilogue where I return to some of the central mysteries of this story. I feel that there are partial answers, but this is not a movie where every "T" can be crossed and every "I" dotted. There are mysteries that remain for me, having made the movie.

Terry Gross: ... [McNamara] reaches several conclusions and has several lessons that he feels like he's learned from his involvement in World War II and the Vietnam War. And one of his conclusions is you need to empathize with your enemy, but he says about Vietnam, "We didn't know the Vietnamese well enough to empathize and put ourselves in their shoes. We saw the war in Vietnam as a cold war; they saw it as a civil war." And when I heard him say that, I thought, you know, what a true and interesting lesson to have learned and to impart to us. But then I thought for a second, "Isn't that what the anti-war movement was saying all along? That, you know, this isn't just the cold war, this is a civil war? Why are we involved there?" I mean, isn't that something that people were shouting at him for years?

Errol Morris: Yes. This is a movie with one interview, but sometimes I think there are actually two characters: the 85-year-old McNamara speaking to the 45-year-old McNamara. And one of the questions...

Terry Gross: Yeah, I know exactly what you mean. I mean, as a viewer, that was my impression, too, yeah.

Errol Morris: And one question that keeps coming up again and again: Is this the same man? Are these two different men? Well, in one sense, of course they're not. But are they the same? And in what way are they different, if they are different?

You're absolutely right. Many of the things that McNamara says could've come out of anti-war demonstrators. It could've been things that they said verbatim in 1965. People who really hate McNamara—and there are many—when they hear about the lessons, they say, "Why do we want to hear anything this man says? Shouldn't he remain silent?" My answer is an emphatic "no." He has been so much a part of history, and the stories that he tells about history are really interesting and important stories. And they're stories by a man who knows.

Terry Gross: You know, you were talking about him being like the 85-year-old McNamara talking to the 45-year-old McNamara. And I felt, as a viewer, that there were two versions of me watching the movie. . . . When I was watching the movie and he says things like during the war in Vietnam, his family was so stressed out, his family got ulcers. I can't remember if he got ulcers, too. And—and that, you know, his family was just, like, sickened by all of the stress. And one part of me thought, "Wow, that's really interesting that, you know, it was so stressful on your family," and that elicited a very sympathetic response from me. But then the other part of me was saying, "Well, I should think so. The whole country was divided by this war. The country was at war with itself. Americans were dying, Vietnamese were dying. So many lives of Americans were totally changed by the war and . . . "

Errol Morris: America was totally changed by the war.

Terry Gross: Right. So, in that sense, I was thinking, "Well, you know, sure, you'd have ulcers. I mean, jeez." So I just felt myself having this constant dialogue with myself about my reactions to him and what he was saying. . . .

Errol Morris: . . . [W]e think that people have to be one thing when, in fact, they're many things. You said that people look at the movie and they say, "Well, McNamara is not being forthcoming here. McNamara is being evasive. McNamara is lying. McNamara is making remark after remark which is self-serving in some way." My answer is, "Of course, he's human." It is all there. But what is also there is what I would call an honest attempt to grapple with the past, to grapple with his own history and the history that he was part of.

· · ·

Terry Gross: You know, I interviewed McNamara in '95 after his memoir was published. And, you know, as I've said, I've never seen him be as interesting and lively and anecdotal as in your movie. And when I interviewed him, I guess, you know, all my instincts were, "Ask him why he hasn't apologized if he knew all this in advance. Ask him if he thinks he owes America an apology or an explanation." And, you know, I haven't listened back to the interview, but I think that's where I kept heading. And I'm wondering if your instinct was ever to do that yourself because the movie isn't that. You're not saying, "Well, then apologize," you know. You're letting him speak, you're letting him tell his story, and a lot of interesting things emerge, and those things are very lively and attention-getting. I mean, you want to hear it. And whether you end up completely believing it or not, you want to hear it. But was there ever an instinct in you saying, "Get him to apologize," you know?

Errol Morris: Sure. Absolutely. But....

Terry Gross: But did you kind of suppress that and just, like, let him talk, or did you keep kind of getting back to that?

Errol Morris: Did I kind of suppress it? I like the idea of suppressing it. Maybe. It's interesting because when you say there's something missing—if people say, "Well, McNamara didn't go as far as I would like," or, "McNamara really didn't apologize," or, "McNamara didn't really confess," I would ask myself: "What is it that they want to hear? What exactly are they looking for?" And I ask myself: "Do I want to hear McNamara apologize for the war?" And here's my answer: Not really.

Terry Gross: Mm-hmm. Why not?

Errol Morris: Because I don't think there is any apology for the war in this sense: How do you apologize for the death of 58,000 Americans and two to three million Vietnamese? I think he's done something far more interesting. He has gone back over the history of the war—don't forget, this is the man who ordered the Pentagon Papers to be created.[12] If you like, it's that same instinct to go back over the past, to look at it, to try to understand it.

For the totally unsympathetic, the people who will hate McNamara no matter what, they will look at this attempt to go back over the past as excuse-making: "Oh, yeah, sure, he's going back over the past, but he's going over the past just to provide a gloss on the past, to make himself look better." My answer is no. When he suggests that he and LeMay were war criminals in World War II, and he tells a story that is so different from any other story I've heard about that period, I don't look at it as an attempt to whitewash the past but as a sincere attempt to go back over the past, to think about the past.[13]

Terry Gross: Mm-hmm. When you interviewed McNamara—and this was about 24 hours' worth of interviews we're talking about—do you think he ever expected that you were warming him up and just laying the trap and, in the end, there would be an ambush?

Errol Morris: Well, I mean, certainly....

Terry Gross: Because, you know, that is an interview technique.

Errol Morris: It's not my technique.

Terry Gross: But he wouldn't necessarily know that, I mean, 'cause you never know till it's over.

Errol Morris: I mean, I'm always surprised. You know, I said that for me, interviews are investigative. When I was making "The Thin Blue Line" years ago, a movie credited with getting an innocent man out of prison in Texas, I was surprised how if I left people alone, if I allowed them to talk without interrupting them, I could learn so much more than in an adversarial interview. Maybe it's a difference in philosophy because when you're playing the Mike Wallace game, a well-known game in interviewing, when you back the subject against the wall, try to get him to contradict himself, it's kind of the police idea of interviewing. You have a subject. Break him down, make him fess up. I'm interested in something different. I'm not really interested in backing my subjects into a corner. I'm interested in learning something about how they see the world.

Terry Gross: Your interview with McNamara, as it is in the movie "The Fog of War," starts with him having to pick up where he left off, I guess, because, like, the tape or the film had run out, and he has to, like, pick up in the middle of the sentence....

You know how I was talking about how I had two reactions to a lot of the movie? I had two reactions to seeing this part of the interview, especially at the very beginning. Part of me said, "Wow, he's being kind of manipulative here. He knows exactly what he's going to say. He's saying it. You know, he's so kind of conscious of himself as an interviewee." But then the other part of me said, "Yes, he should be. He has something really important to say here about, you know, lessons about nuclear weapons and being, you know, in a position of power in the nuclear era. This is really important. I'm glad he remembered what he wanted to say." Tell me why you wanted to lead with this, in a way, very self-conscious moment of him saying, "I'm going to pick up exactly where I left off. I know what I want to say"?

Errol Morris: Well, among other things, he's a control freak.

Terry Gross: Right (laughs).

Errol Morris: And it's interesting to be reminded of that fact at the very beginning of the movie.

Terry Gross: At the very beginning, yeah. Uh-huh.

Errol Morris: In fact, at the very beginning of the movie, we see him in 1964 doing pretty much the same thing that he's doing in 2001.

Terry Gross: Now at one point he says to you that he learned early on, "Never answer the question that is asked of you. Answer the question that you wish had been asked of you." And he says, "And, quite frankly, I follow that rule. It's a very good rule." Did he follow that rule with you? Did he, like, consistently answer what you wanted him—you know, what you had asked, or did he just answer the questions he wished you had asked? Do you know what I mean? How much did he kind of control what the answers and what the message was going to be?

Errol Morris: I had an argument with my editor, Karen Schmeer, because ... in the actual interview itself, after he says this, I ask him, "Are you doing this to me?" And he smiles and laughs. She wanted to put it in; I didn't because I felt it was already implied.

Terry Gross: Right. Right.

Errol Morris: But, of course, there's always an element of that. There's an element of that here and now talking to you. Everybody wants to answer the questions they wished they had been asked. McNamara is not alone in that respect.

■

Robert McNamara and World War II

"WE BURNED TO DEATH 100,000 JAPANESE CIVILIANS IN TOKYO"

The Second World War has usually been portrayed in the U.S. as "the good war," a conflict in which those on the side of light and goodness (led by the United States) defeated the forces of darkness and evil (the fascists of Nazi Germany and imperial Japan). In fact, the war was a horrible, destructive bloodbath of unprecedented magnitude, in which fifty million people were killed. The inhuman cruelty of the German and Japanese regimes is well documented. Yet there are also plenty of reasons for the remaining veterans of the winning side in that war to feel remorse at the way they and their governments waged war against the Germans and Japanese. Any honest accounting of the moral conduct of the Allies in that war must include a consideration of the incendiary air bombardment of the civilian populations—defenseless men, women and children—of those countries.

Robert McNamara played a role in the firebombing campaigns waged against the cities and civilians of both Germany and Japan. (See chapter 4 for details.) He and his colleagues in the Department of Statistical Control showed General Curtis LeMay efficient ways of delivering unprecedented quantities of incendiaries (or "firebombs") to Hamburg, Dresden and other German cities and, finally, to all major cities in Japan. Sydney Schanberg notes that when McNamara is recounting his role in the firebombing of Japan, he becomes emotional, barely able to speak. Schanberg also notes that, in an unprecedented disclosure, McNamara in effect confesses to war crimes against the Japanese people (though because the U.S. won the war, none of its civilian or military leaders were forced to face war crimes tribunals, such as were held in defeated Germany and Japan). And in another portion of his interview with Terry Gross, Errol Morris describes the pivotal impact McNamara's commentary on the firebombing of Japan had on his conception of the film that became "The Fog of War."

THE REVIEW: Sydney H. Schanberg, "Soul on Ice." *The American Prospect,* **Nov. 2003, pp. 61–63.**

. . .

One of the movie's most powerful passages covers McNamara's little-known service in World War II, when he was attached to Gen. Curtis LeMay's 21st Bomber Command stationed on the Pacific island of Guam. LeMay's B-29s showered 67 Japanese cities with incendiary bombs in 1945, softening up the country for the two atomic blasts to come. McNamara was a senior planning officer. He describes in particular the firebombing of Tokyo, then a city of wooden houses and shops. "In that single night," says McNamara, his eyes filling with tears, the first of his several emotional moments in the film, "we burned to death 100,000 Japanese civilians in Tokyo—men, women and children." Newly retrieved military film taken from the air pans across 50 square miles turned to ash.

At this point, Morris abruptly asks McNamara if he knew "this was going to happen." McNamara replies: "Well, I was part of a mechanism that in a sense recommended it. I analyzed bombing operations, and how to make them more efficient." McNamara then recalls a moment after the war ended when he was standing with LeMay and the controversial general said to him, "If we'd lost the war, we'd all have been prosecuted as war criminals." "And I think he's right," says McNamara. "He, and I'd say I, were behaving as war criminals."

And then he does one of his flip-flops. He starts talking about the fuzziness of "the rules of war," apparently referring to the Geneva Conventions. "Was there a rule then," he asks rhetorically, "that said you shouldn't bomb, shouldn't kill, shouldn't burn to death 100,000 civilians in one night? . . . LeMay recognized that what he was doing would be thought immoral if his side has lost. But what makes it immoral if you lose and not immoral if you win?"

THE REVIEW: Terry Gross, "Interview with Errol Morris." National Public Radio, 12:00 Noon EST, Monday, January 5, 2004. Produced at WHYY, Philadelphia, PA.

. . .

Terry Gross: . . . [O]ne of the very interesting points that McNamara makes in the movie] is in talking about World War II

where he served under General Curtis LeMay and he participated in the planning of the firebombing of Tokyo in which
100,000 civilians were killed. And he says something very interesting about war criminals. Why don't we hear this excerpt of
your movie? This is an excerpt of Robert McNamara speaking in
Errol Morris' documentary "The Fog of War."

[Soundbite of "The Fog of War"]

Robert McNamara: I don't fault Truman for dropping that nuclear
bomb. The US/Japanese war was one of the most brutal wars in
all of human history: kamikaze pilots, suicide. Unbelievable.
What one could criticize is that the human race, prior to that
time and today, has not really grappled with what are—I'll call
it—the rules of war. Was there a rule then that said you should-
n't bomb, shouldn't kill, shouldn't burn to death 100,000 civilians in a night? LeMay said if we'd lost the war, we'd all have
been prosecuted as war criminals. And I think he's right. He,
and I'd say I, were behaving as war criminals.

Terry Gross: . . . Errol Morris, when he said that to you, were you
surprised to hear his thoughts about what makes a war crime a
war crime?

Errol Morris: Yes, particularly because this part of the interview
happened very early on, probably within the first half-hour of
my first interview with Robert McNamara.

The movie doesn't tell you—there's no flashing light that goes
on and says, "This is really something new, this is really something extraordinary." So much has been written about the dropping of the two atomic bombs on Japan in 1945. Comparatively
little has been written about the firebombing of 67 cities in
Japan before we bombed Hiroshima and Nagasaki. And here we
have McNamara, who was involved in these firebombings, speak
of them as a war crime. Very powerful, because aren't we all
used to thinking of World War II as a just war? After all, good
and evil were well-defined. We were on the side of good; they
were on the side of evil. And, yet, here is Robert McNamara
telling us, "Yes, that was true, but there is conduct within a just
war which is criminal." Very, very powerful and very interesting.

. . .

Terry Gross: Can you talk a little bit about how you see the job of making what is basically an interview into a movie, into something that will be cinematic, that we will actually want to look at, you know, for a couple of hours, or nearly a couple of hours?

Errol Morris: . . . Whenever I hear a story, particularly if it's a good story, images immediately come to mind, and it becomes very hard to resist the temptation to shoot those images. In fact, usually I am unable to resist the temptation, and I go ahead and do it. Part of "The Fog of War" is a story of dropping things from the sky—bombing, if you like. And we have many instances of it in the story, from the firebombing of Tokyo to bombing in Vietnam.

There's another curious story among the many jobs that Robert McNamara has had over the years. He was also president of the Ford Motor Company. Not so well known, he pushed for safety at a time where safety was never really thought about. He argued for padded dashes, collapsible steering wheels and, first and foremost, seat belts. And he tells this remarkable story—this is the kind of thing you can't possibly make up—about how they dropped skulls down a stairwell at one of the dormitories at Cornell in order to determine the effect that automobile crashes had on the human body, an instance where dropping things actually produces good rather than evil. And, yes, I illustrated it.

I sometimes think of my movies like a dream, a dream about 20th century history, a series of questions, of puzzles, of mysteries. And the hope is that the visuals take you deeper and deeper into those mysteries, that is if I've done my job well.

■

Robert McNamara and the Cuban Missile Crisis

"LeMAY SAYS THIS IS WORSE THAN MUNICH."

Even for those of us who grew up during the Cold War, it is becoming increasingly difficult to remember what all the fuss was about. The principal enemy, the Soviet Union, ceased to exist in

December 1991. It has been succeeded by a Russian Federation that no longer considers the West an enemy and is, in any case, a demonstrably second- or third-rate power (except for its possession of a large arsenal of nuclear weapons). China, while ostensibly still communist, is a hotbed of capitalist development, and increasingly, a trading partner of supreme importance to the developed world, especially the U.S. So really, the Cold War wasn't really all that dangerous. Was it?

Yes, it was! And the scariest episode by far, in the long nightmare of the East-West Cold War, was the Cuban missile crisis of October 1962. One of the eerie, even frightening aspects of "The Fog of War," is the way it immerses the viewer in the words, images and dread of the missile crisis, the closest call ever to a major nuclear war. (See chapters 1 and 2 for details.) The film, according to David Talbot, invites all of us, no matter what our age, experience or knowledge, to understand the missile crisis in a new way, as if for the first time. As McNamara says in what is perhaps his most impassioned statement of the entire movie: rational individuals—President Kennedy, Soviet Chairman Nikita Khrushchev, and Cuban leader Fidel Castro—came "that close to the total destruction of their societies"—and by "that close," McNamara means very, very close.

Errol Morris tells Talbot that at least as remarkable as the closeness of the brush with nuclear war was the attitude of the Air Force Chief of Staff, General Curtis LeMay, who was only slightly more extreme than many other senior officers in the U.S. military at the time. Having just barely survived the crisis without going to war, Kennedy got from LeMay not applause or gratitude, but a sullen insult. Recalling a passage on the audio tapes made secretly by President Kennedy, Morris tells Talbot, "LeMay says this is worse than Munich"—worse than the British attempt to "appease" Adolf Hitler's Nazi Germany on the eve of World War II. As shocking as it seems, the Joint Chiefs of Staff were convinced that the U.S. should use the Cuban missile crisis as a pretext to launch an essentially unprovoked attack on the Soviet Union, communist China, and their allies in Central Europe, with the objective of destroying them completely, while the U.S. still had a commanding advantage in nuclear weapons. The alternative, according to those who held this view, would be to fight an inevitable global nuclear war later on, when the Soviets and Chinese had narrowed the nuclear gap between themselves and the U.S.

What makes the study of the Cuban missile crisis so valuable and necessary—what makes it more than a kind of Halloween tale with which to frighten people born after the early 1960s—is, as McNamara says in "The Fog of War": "that danger exists today." That is, today, just as in the long gone Cold War, thousands of nuclear weapons exist, ready to be launched at little more than a moment's notice. Does this make sense? Of course not. When some of our students discover that something like another Cuban missile crisis could actually happen—could actually result in the destruction of entire nations, including the United States—they report that they have trouble sleeping at night. So should anyone who knows the facts of the matter: what almost happened in October 1962, and what could happen today, or tomorrow.

THE REVIEW: David Talbot, "The Fog Around Robert McNamara." Salon.com, Feb. 28, 2004.

David Talbot: ... [A] riveting section of your film deals with the Cuban missile crisis in October 1962, when McNamara says we were a hair's breadth away from nuclear holocaust. It's startling for people today to realize how close we were, and how hard-pressed Kennedy and his inner circle, including McNamara, were by the military hard-liners to go to war.

Errol Morris: There's an amazing moment if you listen to the recordings when the Joint Chiefs confront Kennedy. And it's really, really, really frightening.

David Talbot: What do they say?

Errol Morris: They're basically saying that Kennedy should invade and bomb Cuba. And he should do it sooner rather than later. All he's doing through delay is giving the Soviets more time to get ready to launch an attack on the United States. That delay is unconscionable, and that anything other than a military response is unconscionable. There's a moment... when Curtis LeMay the famously zealous Air Force chief says to Kennedy, "This is worse than Munich."

David Talbot: And of course, he knew what a slap in the face that was to Kennedy, whose father, Joe, was considered a Nazi appeaser before World War II.

Errol Morris: Yes, indeed. That is part of that story. Thank you very much.

David Talbot: How does Kennedy respond?

Errol Morris: Kennedy does not respond. There's silence. Kennedy says very little to the generals.

One of the things that really fascinates me about that moment, where LeMay says this is worse than Munich, is that it goes right back to a question you ... about historical analogies. Iraq, Vietnam, Munich, the Cuban missile crisis, the danger of this sort of thing. But let's look at the reality here.

First of all, the Kennedy administration had been given faulty information by the CIA. They had been told there were no Soviet warheads on Cuba. OK, so what should the president conclude? Perhaps the Joint Chiefs are absolutely right. Act sooner rather than later. Take out the missiles, take out the missile launchers and the missile sites before the warheads arrive. Although in fact several of those Joint Chiefs wanted to go a little further than Cuba, they wanted to go take out the Soviet Union and China as well. They had big appetites. But we now know that if LeMay and the other Joint Chiefs had had their way, and there was bombing and an invasion, the local Soviet commanders who had autonomy would have used those missiles with warheads against the United States. Can I say this with certainty? No. But was there a good likelihood if we invaded and bombed that they would reply? Yep. So that in this instance, "appeasement" averted a catastrophe. The analogy to Munich isn't an analogy at all. People often make these analogies. What is Munich? It's a way of calling a leader like Kennedy a candy-ass. And because of your weakness, because of your policies, everyone will have to suffer. It will lead to an even worse catastrophe than you can imagine. In this instance—wrong! The diplomatic solution proved to be the correct one.

David Talbot: So during the Cuban missile crisis, "The Fog of War" makes clear that the Kennedys and McNamara acted heroically, and by defying the generals, saved the world.

Errol Morris: ... I believe that McNamara, throughout the Cuban missile crisis, was a restraining force on the military. And helped keep us out of war. ... [T]here's a reason why General LeMay is in this movie so prominently, because he represents a dark part of American history that was there, it was real. This was not a figment of McNamara's imagination. He knew all too well what he was dealing with.

■

Robert McNamara and the Vietnam War

"THE PAIN OF VIETNAM STILL HOVERS OVER THIS COUNTRY."

The title of this examination of "The Fog of War," "Soul on Ice," will be obscure to those born after the turbulent 1960s, when the war in Vietnam escalated to an American war. It refers to a book of the same title by the (then) Black Power radical, Eldridge Cleaver, who ran for vice-president on the Socialist Workers Party ticket in 1968, alongside Tom Hayden, a founder of the Students for a Democratic Society. Cleaver meant to convey the impression that he had plenty of "soul," that he was so "cool" that his soul was "soul on ice." The comparison between Cleaver and McNamara must therefore be entirely ironical: McNamara, believing the fate of his soul uncertain at best because of his actions with respect to Vietnam, still finds it impossible to warm to the deeply personal issues regarding his role in the war. He remains "on ice." Obviously, whomever gave this piece its ironical title is no youngster.

Sydney Schanberg approaches McNamara and the war in a Socratic manner, bearing many questions, but few sure answers. He notes what he calls McNamara's "ambidextrous explanations"— admitting mistakes, but refusing to be drawn into a discussion of his personal culpability and guilt. He sees in McNamara a man of considerable "neediness," who seems to him to implore the audience to forgive him for actions taken, and not taken, that contributed to the horror of the Vietnam War, a war whose trauma, as Schanberg notes, "still hovers over this country." And as the reviewer implies in his conclusion, the very recent history of U.S. foreign policy, including the 2003 U.S. invasion and subsequent occupation of Iraq, demonstrate what happens when the mistakes made by U.S. leaders with regard to Vietnam are forgotten or ignored.

THE REVIEW: Sydney H. Schanberg, "Soul on Ice." The American Prospect, Nov. 2003, pp. 61–63.

In *The Fog of War*, a revelatory new documentary about his life and times, a disquieted Robert McNamara implores us to understand why he did the things he did . . . as a secretary of defense and pivotal decision-maker during Vietnam, which some Americans came to call "McNamara's War."

In his 1995 memoir, *In Retrospect*, McNamara said of himself and the other architects of the Vietnam conflict, "[W]e were wrong, terribly wrong. We owe it to future generations to explain why." But he prefaced this nostra culpa by explaining that their intentions had always been honorable. "We of the Kennedy and Johnson administrations who participated in the decisions on Vietnam acted according to what we thought were the principles and traditions of this nation," he wrote.

He offers the same kind of ambidextrous explanations throughout *The Fog of War* documentary, which in a way functions as a sequel to the book. There are distinct differences, however. The book was McNamara's; the nearly two-hour film is the work of Errol Morris, a gifted documentarian who demonstrated against the war in his student days. While Morris seeks to show McNamara as a complicated man rather than the simplistic "monster" conjured by the anti-war movement, his movie is anything but a puff piece. . . . A key to the depth in Morris' film is his camera: This is one of those interview-based films (interlaced with previously unaired historical footage) in which the camera stares hard into the man. And the man, for the most part, does not look away. He stares back, ever straining to make his case to the audience, revealing, perhaps, more than he imagines.

Such a moment comes when, during some network television footage about American casualties in Vietnam, Morris' voice (he remains off-camera throughout the film) asks McNamara whether he felt he was "the author of stuff" or merely "an instrument of things outside your control."

"Well, I don't think I felt either," says the former defense secretary. "I just felt that I was serving at the request of the president, who had been elected by the American people. And it was my responsibility to try to help him to carry out the office as he believed was in the interest of our people." I wonder if McNamara realizes that many people will hear this response as just another version of "I was only following orders."

. . .

McNamara's detractors will likely say that . . . he could have saved a lot of lives when he was running the Pentagon . . . by going public with his knowledge that the Vietnam War was a lost cause. . . .

But it must also be said that it is McNamara alone, among the many planners of the war, who has come forward to say he was wrong. Henry Kissinger, in all his revisionist books and speeches, has never admitted to a single regret or mistake. McNamara's admissions may be incomplete, but they are nonetheless a contribution to history, and the act must have taken a certain kind of courage, for he knew that by coming forward at all he was offering himself up for the slaughter.

That exposure to vilification is clearly on McNamara's mind when Morris, at the end of the documentary, puts to him the two seminal questions the filmmaker has obviously been saving up. McNamara doesn't disappoint him, showing agitation as he evades both probes.

Errol Morris: After you left the Johnson administration, why didn't you speak out against the Vietnam War?

Robert McNamara: I'm not going to say any more than I have. These are the kinds of questions that get me in trouble. You don't know what I know about how inflammatory my words can appear. A lot of people misunderstand the war, misunderstand me. A lot of people think I'm a son of a bitch.

Errol Morris: Do you feel in any way responsible for the war? Do you feel guilty?

Robert McNamara: I don't want to go any further with this discussion, It just opens up more controversy. I don't want to add anything to Vietnam. It is so complex that anything I say will require additions and qualifications.

After such words, there can be no doubt in the viewer's mind that McNamara is a tormented being. . . .

After watching him under Morris' filmic microscope and listening to his guarded phrasing, my instincts tell me he is crying out for forgiveness but unable to get the words out. In his book and in this film, he has put himself on trial, seeking acquittal and absolution. Yet he cannot bring himself to say the ultimate words: that he bore personal responsibility. Maybe he hasn't taken the necessary first step, which is to forgive himself.

You can hear McNamara's neediness throughout this film. He compulsively says at every turn how smart he is, and how at every stage of his life he rose above the rest. . . . Perhaps these badges of success that McNamara clings to are the crutches that hold him up in a time of inner darkness. That's just a guess. All I can really say with certainty is that this is a film that needs seeing and is worth seeing because, no matter how often one of our politicians announces that we have put it behind us, the pain of Vietnam still hovers over this country. The new film footage and previously unheard tapes of Johnson's telephone conversations with McNamara make the movie a potent history lesson at a moment when the nation needs all the history reminders it can get.

"I HAD A LOT OF FEELING FOR HIM ON THAT BASIS."

A dramatic feature of "The Fog of War" is Robert McNamara's impassioned description of the day in 1965 when, to protest the war in Vietnam, Norman Morrison, a Quaker from Baltimore, burned himself to death beneath McNamara's office window at the Pentagon. In a controversial follow-up comment, McNamara states that he admired the courage of Morrison, and even felt kinship toward him because he and Morrison were both "sensitive human beings," struggling—each in his own way—with difficult moral issues associated with the war. As this reviewer notes, McNamara's comparison of himself with Norman Morrison angered many, including the MIT linguist and political commentator Noam Chomsky, who dismissed McNamara as a "small-time engineer who . . . didn't understand anything that was going on, including what he himself was doing."

Ironically, Morrison's widow, who is the principal subject of this article, feels differently. She says she admires McNamara for going as far as he does in expressing his responsibility for the killing in Vietnam. She resonates to the passages in which McNamara alludes to the pain he caused his family because of his role in the war, and the need he has felt for so long to keep his emotions bottled up inside. "I had a lot of feeling for him on that basis," she says, recalling how difficult it was for her to continue to support the Quaker opposition to the war after the death of her husband. Rather than anger toward McNamara, Anne Morrison Welsh, whose husband gave his life in an effort to end "McNamara's war," feels empathy toward him, even though many others become enraged with McNamara's efforts to de-

scribe his feelings of comradeship for both Norman Morrison and his widow.

THE REVIEW: Carl Schoettler, "'Fog of War' Recalls One Man's Ultimate Protest, and Gives His Widow Hope It Changed One Mind." *The Baltimore Sun,* **February 29, 2004.**

"Norman Morrison was a Quaker. He was opposed to war, the violence of war, the killing. He came to the Pentagon, doused himself with gasoline, burned himself to death, below my office. He held a child in his arms, his daughter. Passers-by shouted, 'Save the child.' He threw the child. The child lived and is alive today.

"His wife issued a very moving statement: 'Human beings must stop killing other human beings.' And that's a belief I shared. I shared it then. I believe it even more strongly today.

"How much evil must we do in order to do good? We have certain ideals, certain responsibilities, recognizing at times you must engage in evil [but try to] to minimize it."

Thus former U.S. Secretary of Defense Robert McNamara describes the immolation of Norman Morrison in the new documentary "The Fog of War."

The biographical film focuses on McNamara as a technician of war during the firebombing of Japanese cities during World War II and as a planner of war in Vietnam. He's 87 now, but forceful in defining his life. His face fills most of the screen during much of the film. He looks and sounds like a man who believes what he's saying.

In the brief moment when he mentions Morrison, the Baltimore man who took his own life in protest of the war on Nov. 2, 1965, he stares straight into the camera. His voice catches a bit. But not as much as it did when President Lyndon Johnson awarded him the Medal of Freedom for his seven years as secretary of defense during the Vietnam War. His eyes welled with tears on that occasion, and he could barely speak.

Norman Morrison's widow has not yet seen "The Fog of War." She's Mrs. Anne Morrison Welsh now, and lives in Black Mountain, N.C. She and Morrison were living in Govans on that day in 1965 when he drove to Washington in an old Cadillac, infant daughter Emily in tow, to burn himself to death beneath McNamara's window.

Morrison was a profoundly, almost mystically, religious man. He and Anne had been Quakers since early in their marriage. . . . Her voice often chokes with sorrow and she speaks with difficulty when she recounts memories of him. She recalls that time with great clarity, compassion and large-hearted forgiveness.

Welsh has read significant portions of McNamara's 1996 book, *In Retrospect: The Tragedy and Lessons of Vietnam*, notably the one page about her husband.

McNamara wrote: "Morrison's death was a tragedy not only for his family but also for me and the country. It was an outcry against the killing that was destroying the lives of so many Vietnamese and American youth. . . . I believe I understood and shared some of his thoughts."

. . .

Letter to McNamara

During the first of two hourlong interviews, Welsh notes that at the time the book came out, "no other public official connected with the war had made such a commitment or acknowledgement."

She was moved to write him.

"I was grateful that McNamara was able to do that to the extent that he did," she says. "I felt it was unusual and that it should be appreciated. So I sent him a letter of gratitude for going public with his conclusion that (the war) was a grave mistake. I know he didn't go as far as most of his critics felt he should, critics of the book, or responding to the book."

The semi-perpetual dissident, Noam Chomsky, for example, said the book had a kind of ring of honesty about it: "What it reads like is an extremely narrow technocrat, a small-time engineer who was given a particular job to do and just tried to do that job efficiently, didn't understand anything that was going on, including what he himself was doing."

McNamara called Welsh soon after he received her letter. They talked for 10 or 15 minutes.

"He expressed appreciation," she says, "and asked for permission to use it as he publicized the book. I said, sure. So he did exactly that. He and I actually had a very humane and cordial telephone conversation. It was a good talk. We shared how our families had been so deeply affected by the war.

"He admitted, personally, that his family had been deeply affected by Norman's death. But . . . he says in *In Retrospect*, he bottled up those emotions and really didn't deal with them himself as a person within the family."

Bottled-up emotions

In "The Fog of War," McNamara's voice cracks and he declines to talk about how Morrison's act affected his family. In the book, he says he knew that his wife, Margaret, and their three children shared many of Morrison's feelings about the war. Morrison's immolation "created tension that only deepened as dissent and criticism of the war continued to grow." He calls his tendency to turn inward and avoid talking with his family about his emotions "a grave mistake."

Welsh empathizes strongly

"As a mother of three children," she says, "and as a person, I myself felt that I sort of had to be brave and carry on in our Quaker efforts to help end the war. I held a lot inside, too. So I had a lot of feeling for him on that basis."

. . .

"I still feel that [McNamara's] a man who can almost say he's sorry and ask forgiveness. He's very close," she says. "Compared with most public officials, he's gone so far. I think he genuinely wants to prevent other Vietnams and he genuinely wants to work for world peace."

. . .

McNamara, Anne Welsh concludes, "must have a conscience. Somewhere there's a heavy load of guilt. There must be. There would have to be."

But in the film, McNamara refuses to discuss any feelings of guilt.

"I really don't want to go any further," he says. "It just opens more controversy."

"[THE] SOUTH VIETNAMESE . . . STORY: SPECTACULAR BETRAYAL."

An essential, often overlooked, chapter in the story of the U.S. war in Vietnam concerns the side that lost everything-the South Vietnamese, whom the Americans supported with much blood and treasure. The psychological trauma suffered by returning U.S. servicemen from this lost war was severe and often long-lasting. But for the South Vietnamese, the losers in Vietnam's civil war, the consequences were even more severe. Their choice was usually either to submit to what were called "re-education" camps, where they would be treated cruelly, and where thousands died of torture and privation; or risk their lives, and the lives of their families, by becoming "boat people," and leave the country illegally in the hope of somehow starting over in another country. Too often, however, the South Vietnamese would get stuck in refugee camps for years, often only to be sent back to Vietnam to be treated harshly. Even worse, for many, the boats and the refugees in them were never seen again after they left Vietnam.

This reviewer is the child of such "boat people," and he is bitter about the "spectacular betrayal" of his people by the Americans, who abandoned his people and their cause. Andrew Lam notes that the abandonment of his people continues in the way Americans understand the history of the war, in the lack of even a casual reference to the South Vietnamese in "The Fog of War." It is, according to Lam, as if "an entire people have conveniently ceased to exist." This is, he says, the most significant evidence that McNamara, while "a highly intelligent man," is nevertheless "living a kind of self-deception."

THE REVIEW: Andrew Lam, "A Remorseless Apology for the Horrors of Vietnam." *The San Francisco Chronicle,* **February 2, 2004.**

Living in Vietnam during the war as a child, I witnessed enough of American military power to know that no ideology or rationale can justify killing more than 3 million civilians. So it is gratifying to hear Robert S. McNamara, ex-secretary of defense under the Kennedy and Johnson administrations and one of the principal architects of that war, finally confess onscreen that he, too, thought it was a mistake for Americans to go into Vietnam.

Yet as I watched "The Fog of War," the documentary by Errol Morris about McNamara, I felt disappointed. McNamara is a highly intelligent man living a kind of self-deception. While readily confessing that the war was wrong, and that he knew it was wrong all along, he somehow absolves himself just as quickly. Arrogantly, the ex-secretary of defense suggests on camera that he did the best he could under the circumstances and that, if he hadn't been at the helm micromanaging the war's first half, things might have been far worse. Never mind that under his watch the war widened and escalated.

I had hoped for an honest, gut-wrenching mea culpa. Instead, McNamara's elaborate explanation sounds like an excuse. Not once did he say

"I'm sorry" to the victims. His well-argued confessions seemed rehearsed and disconnected from the emotional honesty one associates with remorse. It is as if the head acknowledged that mistakes were made, but the heart refused to feel the horrors that were unleashed.

Near the end of the film, McNamara talks about what he calls the fog of war. "What the fog of war means," he says, "is that war is so complex it's beyond the ability of the human mind to comprehend all the variables. Our judgment, our understanding are not adequate, and we kill people unnecessarily."

Errol Morris, known for his films "The Thin Blue Line" and "A Brief History of Time," uses that statement to give the movie its title. In a recent interview, Morris says, "I look at the McNamara story as 'the fog of war ate my homework' excuse." He adds: "After all, if war is so complex, then no one is responsible."

While the Vietnamese are not free of blame for killing each other in Vietnam's bloody civil war, McNamara and his bosses, Presidents Kennedy and Johnson, are clearly responsible for escalating it. McNamara kept sending American troops to Vietnam while knowing deep in his heart that the war was not winnable, and encouraged the South to continue fighting.

It is no wonder that South Vietnamese tell the story of their relationship with America as one of spectacular betrayal. The United States abandoned the South Vietnamese government in the middle of a war. Many South Vietnamese officials died in communist gulags after the war's end, and more than 2 million Vietnamese fled overseas as boat people, many ending up at the bottom of the sea. McNamara never made references to the suffering of the South Vietnamese people as a direct cause of his administration of the war, as if somehow an entire people have conveniently ceased to exist.

Survivors of the Vietnam War now waiting for an apology from McNamara or the U.S. government should not hold their breaths. McNamara left the Johnson administration in 1968. Despite what he knew about the war, he refused to speak out against it, and watched in silence as more body bags came home.

Foggy or not, someone as smart as McNamara should know right from wrong. If the secretary of defense knew it was wrong to continue the war, why did he keep his silence until now, more than three decades later? Morris asks him precisely that. "I'm not going to say any more than I have,"

McNamara responds. "These are the kinds of questions that get me in trouble. You don't know what I know about how inflammatory my words can appear."

The documentary has a subtitle: Eleven Lessons From the Life of Robert S. McNamara. One of them is "Believing and seeing are both often wrong." What that means to McNamara is that doing the right thing turned out to be an enormous error. To me, that means I can't trust the man's confessions. It seems the fog hasn't lifted at all for McNamara—it has only thickened with the years.

■

"The Fog of War" and the 21st Century

"HOW DO DECENT MEN COMMIT OR ABET EVIL ACTS?"

Samantha Power is an authority on the subjects of genocide and other "crimes against humanity," having won the Pulitzer Prize in 2003 for her book, "A Problem From Hell": America and the Age of Genocide. Thus she is especially interested in a film like "The Fog of War," in which one of the 20th century's major figures explicitly admits to "behaving as a war criminal" for his part in the firebombing of Japan in World War II; and who directed another war, in Vietnam, which killed millions of people, many of them innocent civilians. She notes that the admissions of Robert McNamara represent an anomaly in American history; there is little or no precedent for the highly visible self-reexamination to which McNamara has subjected himself with regard to his role in the Vietnam War. Power points out that "Americans [are] enthralled and repelled" by McNamara: enthralled, because of the novelty of his mission and the ongoing American obsession with the Vietnam War; and repelled, because his analysis has led him to question much of the received wisdom with which Americans define themselves and their relation to the world at large, with such loaded questions as "what makes us omniscient?"

"How do decent men commit or abet evil acts?" she asks. Robert McNamara has given the most authoritative answer provided so far with respect to the Vietnam War. The American leadership during the war described by McNamara was fraught with ignorance, arrogance,

lack of empathy toward both enemies and allies, and a belief that the goodness of their intentions justifies their actions. Moreover, she believes that, because of the relentless criticism to which McNamara's books, and this film, have been subjected, few "other officials will be eager to follow his example." This gives rise to the prospect of a 21st century dominated by an America that is militarily dominant, but whose attitude may again lead it (and the world) into disaster, because it has willfully refused to learn the lessons of Vietnam and its other failures.

THE REVIEW: Samantha Power, "War and Never Having to Say you're Sorry." *New York Times,* December 14, 2003, sect. 2, pp. 1, 33.

Sometime in the mid-1960's, the Vietnam War became known as "McNamara's War." In the seven years Robert S. McNamara served as Secretary of Defense for Presidents John F. Kennedy and Lyndon B. Johnson, the United States commitment in Vietnam soared—in a soothingly gradual fashion—from fewer than a thousand Americans to just under half a million. Mr. McNamara, in turn, went from being heralded as a whiz kid to being hounded as a war monger. In 1965, a Quaker protester set himself on fire below Mr. McNamara's Pentagon office window. In 1967, antiwar activists tried to burn down his vacation home in Aspen, Colo. And in 1972, an artist who spotted him on a ferry tried to heave him into the Atlantic Ocean.

A quarter of a century later, Mr. McNamara broke his silence, publishing "In Retrospect," his best-selling memoir. He asked how he and his fellow leaders could have pushed for a war he at last acknowledged was "wrong, terribly wrong." But after the deaths of three million Vietnamese and more than 58,000 Americans, many saw Mr. McNamara's public reckoning as, at best, incommensurate with the carnage and at worst, dishonest and self-serving. In a stinging editorial in 1995, The New York Times dismissed his "prime-time apology and stale tears, three decades late," contrasting the fates of the dead with that of Mr. McNamara, who, despite his torment, "got a sinecure at the World Bank and summers at the Vineyard."

The debate over Vietnam and the debate over Robert McNamara—debates that overlap, but that over the years have grown distinct—refuse to subside, partly because Mr. McNamara, now 87, refuses to go away. In

"The Fog of War: Eleven Lessons From the Life of Robert S. McNamara," opening Friday[14], Errol Morris, the ingenious Cambridge-based director of such documentaries as "The Thin Blue Line" and "Mr. Death," has given Mr. McNamara a big-screen chance to reflect upon a career of watching fallible human beings like himself make decisions that imperil or extinguish human lives.

While Mr. McNamara uses the film to propagate the "lessons" of his six decades in public life, Mr. Morris has another agenda: to raise questions that are moral, timeless and rarely broached with such subtlety. How do decent men commit or abet evil acts? And once they have done so, how should they interact with their victims, live with their consciences and pass along their insights? It is the indefatigable relevance of these questions that keep Americans at once enthralled and repelled by Robert S. McNamara. And it is the long-standing aversion of American decision-makers to address past mistakes that has helped undermine the American standing around the world and has hindered our ability to learn from history.

Mr. Morris is a first-class investigator, and he has hunted down fresh and provocative material, on subjects like the firebombing of the Japanese in World War II and Kennedy's intentions regarding Vietnam. He has elicited from Mr. McNamara a number of startling admissions. And he has released the film at a time when war and quagmire are very much on the mind of Americans. Revisiting Vietnam and the images of sprightly young G.I.'s so eager to serve, one is reminded how soldiers can be led astray by reckless ideology, shoddy intelligence and liberal hubris; how small, sequential decisions necessitate and compound one another; and how our faith in our own good intentions and our ignorance of local culture can undermine our objectives. (Among the 11 lessons Mr. Morris gleans from Mr. McNamara, Lesson No. 1 is "empathize with the enemy.")

But Mr. Morris is less interested in policy than in metaphysics. In a recent interview in New York, where he was promoting the film, he said he first became interested in Mr. McNamara because of an "endless fascination" with the extent to which "people who engage in evil believe in some real sense that they are doing good." Mr. Morris seems reflexively drawn to the gray zones of human morality. If "real Iagos" permeated the planet, the filmmaker rightly notes, life would be simpler, and in the end, probably safer. But the story gets more complicated when a man like Robert McNamara—who is not only debonair, but introspective and self-critical—comes along. "If evil is somewhat more ineluctable, it also becomes somewhat more problematic," Mr. Morris observes. "What is it? Where is it? Is it in some of us? Is it in all of us?"

And under what circumstances, he might have added, can we rationalize it? The most stirring scenes in "The Fog of War" surround America's fire-bombing of 67 Japanese cities in World War II, during which time Mr. Mc-Namara was working under Gen. Curtis LeMay of the Air Force. Mr. Morris unearthed spine-curdling government reports showing the raw calculus undertaken to speed America's victory. "In order to do good," Mr. McNa-mara says, articulating the film's ninth lesson, "recognize that at times you will have to engage in evil." In a single bombing raid, he recalls, "We burned to death 100,000 Japanese civilians in Tokyo—men, women and children." Some 900,000 Japanese civilians were killed overall. Was he aware this would happen? "Well, I was part of a mechanism that in a sense recom-mended it," Mr. McNamara tells Mr. Morris. "LeMay said, 'If we'd lost the war, we'd all have been prosecuted as war criminals.' And I think he's right. He—and I'd say I—were behaving as war criminals." He asks, "What makes it immoral if you lose and not immoral if you win?" The answer, of course, is that war's winners write the history books, and, if they can help it, they avoid legal accountability.

When it came to the Vietnam War, Mr. McNamara was an early advo-cate of escalation but came to realize the flaws in the American approach earlier than many of his colleagues. Yet in public, he continued to defend the war. And even after he was forced out by President Johnson in 1967, he refused to air his criticisms, though the war raged on for another eight long years.

Today he declines comment on Iraq out of the same sense of bureau-cratic loyalty. To the suggestion that dissent is often the highest form of loy-alty, he responds, "I think it's irresponsible for an ex-secretary of defense to comment, particularly if the comments are critical—about a president who is in the midst of a war with tens of thousands of American lives at risk, and is dealing with very, very delicate issues and relationships with other nations and with the U.N., and therefore I haven't and I'm not going to."[15]

But Mr. McNamara's views can be inferred from the film.[16] "What makes us omniscient," he asks, rhetorically. "Have we a record of omni-science?" He concludes, "If we can't persuade nations with comparable val-ues of the merits of our case, we better re-examine our reasoning."

Re-examining our reasoning is not something that has come naturally to American statesmen. In fact, Mr. McNamara is one of very few senior

American government officials ever to admit major error without being forced to do so. In an interview last month, I asked him why. "People don't want to admit they made mistakes," he said. "This is true of the Catholic Church, it's true of companies, it's true of nongovernmental organizations and it's certainly true of political bodies. My rule has been to surface the tough problems. It's very unpleasant to argue with people you admire and associate with. But you have to force debate."

By now, Mr. McNamara has learned how to speak about the trauma in his past in much the same way one learns to speak of the death of a loved one: by rote. In our conversation, he often repeated verbatim what he had said on camera. If a question probed tender territory, he pivoted, transitioning skillfully to one of his policy causes, like nuclear nonproliferation or the International Criminal Court. But despite all his best efforts, Mr. McNamara still broke down several times during the filming of "The Fog of War"—"a sign of weakness," he told me, embarrassed. On camera, he remains stoic as he says that his wife and son got ulcers when he was secretary of defense, and that his wife, who died in 1981, "may even ultimately have died from the stress." Mr. McNamara's emotions get the better of him when he goes on to say something he must know to be untrue. "But," he insists, waving his pen for emphasis, "they were some of the best years of our lives and"—here the tears start—"all members of my family benefited from it." He quickly masters the lump in his throat, and proclaims, unconvincingly: "It was terrific." In our interview, Mr. McNamara's eyes filled with tears at precisely the same moment. Though some politicians are known to muster tears as a ploy for sympathy, in the case of Mr. McNamara, who is famously controlling, they seemed anything but calculated; rather, they offered evidence that his public poise is outmatched by his personal demons.

Remarkably, what seems to grate at people most about Mr. McNamara these days is less his role in shaping a disastrous Vietnam policy than what many take to be his public martyrdom. While it is true that his reckoning is partial and unsatisfying, and while it is true that the book did help launch him back into the limelight, it is also true that he had a lot to lose by awakening the ghosts of Vietnam. By choosing to excavate the past, he has exposed himself to ridicule, resuscitated his lowest moments in public life and let an emotional genie out of the bottle. And since Mr. McNamara seems to have generated more scorn than those who never acknowledged error—e.g., Dean Rusk, Henry Kissinger, and three American presidents—it is unlikely that other officials will be eager to follow his example.

In the absence of full-fledged Congressional investigations, American policymakers rarely look back. They are bound by continuity and fealty across administrations and generations. With the proliferation of class-action suits and the advent of global courtrooms, American officials are now explicitly counseled to avoid public reckoning, for fear of creating legal liability (or constraining their ability to do it all over again, when it suits them). Whether regarding the Vietnam War, America's cold war assassinations or our misguided former alliance with Saddam Hussein, American officials keep their eyes fixed on the future. They rarely admit responsibility for failure, for costly meddling or for large-scale human suffering. They resist debate—internally or publicly—on how good intentions went astray. And they most certainly don't apologize to those harmed.

On those the rare occasions when American officials have expressed remorse for previous policies, they have tended to do so offhandedly. And while on these shores, such utterances were ignored or derided as insincere, in the countries grievously affected, many victims and survivors welcomed the gesture with surprising grace.

In keeping with tradition, Mr. McNamara has never apologized to the Vietnamese or the American people for the Vietnam War. But he has broken with house rules by expressing regret for mistaken policy choices. "I'm very proud of my accomplishments," he says in the film. "I'm very sorry that in the course of accomplishing something I made errors."

Errol Morris says Mr. McNamara's failure to apologize used to trouble him. But after taping 23 hours of interviews with him, and sharing many more meals and phone calls, the discomfort subsided. In truth, Mr. Morris says, he has come to like Robert McNamara, and to understand why so many of the tirades against him find fault with a "mea culpa" that he never issued. "An apology empowers us," Mr. Morris said, during our interview. "The person says, 'I'm very, very, very sorry,' and we can say, 'I accept your apology,' or we can say, 'Sorry, but saying sorry is not enough.' People so strongly wanted to say, 'I do not forgive you for what you've done' that they imagined an apology that didn't exist."

Of course, compiling the lessons of history hardly guarantees that they will be applied. Soon after Donald Rumsfeld assumed the job of secretary of defense in 2000, he actually took the unusual step of circulating a handout that distilled his 40 years of service. Mr. Rumsfeld's lessons were not dissimilar from those Mr. Morris elicited from Mr. McNamara. They include:

"It is easier to get into something than to get out of it."

"Don't divide the world into 'them' and 'us.'"

"Visit with your predecessors from previous administrations. . . . Try to make original mistakes, rather than needlessly repeating theirs."

The lessons, known as "Rumsfeld's Rules," were posted on the Pentagon Web site when Mr. Rumsfeld took office. They have since been removed.

The Dilemma: We Understand Backwards, but Must Live Forwards

The Danish philosopher and theologian Søren Kierkegaard wrote in a journal entry dated 1843: "It is perfectly true, as philosophers say, that life may be understood backwards. But they forget the other proposition, that it must be lived forwards." This epistemological dilemma has profound and disturbing implications for those who seek to learn the lessons of history to reduce the risk that the 21st century will be as violent and destructive as the 20th, or worse. Few dispute that history is our only reliable guide to the future. It is often said, moreover, that we must pay special attention to our mistakes, a position McNamara argues forcefully in "The Fog of War." We must, he says, "develop the lessons and pass them on."

Yet in fundamental respects, it is unclear how we can ever learn from such mistakes as we may make. Looking back, events seem to fall into recognizable patterns of cause and effect. We might convince ourselves that a more timely intervention here, or perhaps more patience there, would have resulted in a better outcome—a less violent outcome, for example. We call insights like these "learning from our mistakes." Yet Kierkegaard's point must be reckoned with. When we seek historical *insight*—beginning an inquiry when the outcome is known—we endeavor first, to explain that outcome; and second, to extrapolate what we believe we have learned to the future. But this is fundamentally different from engaging in *action*—trying to construct an acceptable outcome from the flimsy shards of available, often discrepant information, while coping with loss of control over events, shortage of time, high stakes, fatigue and other factors that reduce our ability to live our lives forwards as successfully as we typically believe we understand them backwards. The American philosopher William James put the distinction this way: there is knowledge *about*, which comes from books, and knowledge of *acquaintance*, which comes from experience.

A concrete instance demonstrates the dilemma of those who seek to link the dead past with the unborn future. Think of the difference, for example, between reading (or even writing) a history of the Cuban missile crisis, suffused with the knowledge that we escaped armageddon, on the one hand; and, on the other, actually experiencing the confusion and dread, maybe even panic and despair that such an outcome was even possible, let alone assured. As historians, whether amateur or professional, we see our task as explaining the many reasons why nuclear war did not occur. But as policymakers, our minds will have been filled with scenarios under which catastrophe is virtually inevitable, with no clear idea of whether or not it can be averted.

Notice that the difference between these two hypothetical exercises is *qualitative*, not merely quantitative. You might find the former (writing history) interesting. The latter (living what will become history) would, we conjecture, scare the daylights out of any sensible person. And yet we are told that we must study history in order to create, for example, a more peaceful world. In a sense, this is perhaps the most basic message of "The Fog of War"—from both Errol Morris and Robert McNamara. It is why they made the film. It is also why we have written this book. Learning from history may be difficult and the results uncertain, but that is no excuse for not trying. Those who refuse to try to learn from history are condemned to mere improvisation.

Reviewers' reactions to Robert McNamara exemplify Kierkegaard's dilemma acutely: we understand backwards, but must live forwards. Most reviews of "The Fog of War" contain two kinds of sub-reviews: a review of Errol Morris' film; and a "review" of the subject and narrator of the film, Robert S. McNamara. Reviews of Morris' film are almost uniformly glowing. "Reviews" of McNamara, however, tend to be more complex. These are typically sub-divided into two constituent clusters: reactions to the young McNamara's tenure as U.S. defense secretary from 1961 to 1968, and reactions to the elderly McNamara's performance in front of Morris' camera. Morris and Terry Gross discuss the matter in an excerpt in this chapter. Many viewers feel, as Gross did, that they have thus been exposed to a conversation of sorts between "two McNamaras." One is a confident, forty-something official who appears in archival footage, full of enthusiasm and confidence about the the war in southeast Asia. The other is a reflective, even regretful eighty-something retiree who admits mistakes and who has come to believe that the entire U.S. enterprise in Vietnam was mistaken. As Gross tells Morris, the rapid-fire, alternating appearance and reappearance of both of these radically different "McNamaras," led to "this constant dialogue within myself about my reactions to him and what he was saying." After all, the younger McNamara did not know the outcome of either the Cuban missile crisis or the war in Vietnam. The older McNamara knows all too well how much luck was involved in the escape of October 1962; and he knows the extent of his culpability for the tragedy in Vietnam.

In Robert McNamara, we have the rare instance of a former public official who has tried heroically (in our view) to bridge the chasm between understanding backwards and living forwards. The "two McNamaras" that appear in the film are, in reality, the same man trying to do two things simultaneously that are in many respects incompatible: to document his own experience as accurately as possible, including the misgivings, the false starts, and the deceptions (including self-deceptions), *and* to become a historian of that experience. As Sydney Schanberg notes in an excerpt in this chapter, this took "a kind of courage, for he knew that by coming forward at all he was offering himself up for the slaughter." In her fine essay in this chapter, Samantha Power makes the point this way: "Since Mr. McNamara seems to have generated more scorn than those who never acknowledged error—e.g., Dean Rusk, Henry Kissinger, and three American presidents—it is unlikely that other officials will be willing to follow his example."

McNamara's critics claim, by and large, that he did not go far enough in his self-criticism. But it should be asked: who has gone as far as he in fusing, within a single life, lived experience and historical understanding of that experience? Can we imagine, someday, witnessing "two Rumsfelds," or "two Cheneys," or "two Powells?" If not, our understanding is the poorer for it. And given the growth in the number and magnitude of ways the human race has developed to inflict violence on itself, we believe the world is also the more dangerous for there being few or no heirs of the "two Mc-Namaras" in "The Fog of War," and the research that led to this remarkable film. Then again, perhaps we are too pessimistic. For who in 1968 could have foreseen the phenomenon of the "two McNamaras?"

See Appendix B, Chapter Six, for further discussion of this dilemma.

"My earliest memory is of a city exploding with joy."

Wilson's Ghost

My earliest memory as a child is of a city exploding with joy. It was November 11, 1918. I was two years old. You may not believe that I have the memory, but I do. I remember the tops of the streetcars being crowded with human beings cheering and kissing and screaming. End of World War I—we'd won. But also celebrating the belief of many Americans- particularly Woodrow Wilson—[that] we'd fought a war to end all wars. His dream was that the world could avoid great wars in the future. Disputes among great nations would be resolved. How wrong he was.

. . .

I think the human race needs to think more about killing, about conflict. Is that what we want in this 21st century?

ROBERT S. McNAMARA, in "The Fog of War"[1]

Our aim in this Epilogue is to provide a context for Robert McNamara's message in "The Fog of War." It is our attempt to address various versions of the most frequently asked question at screenings of the film in which we have participated: "Why did Mc-Namara do this?" Why did he subject himself to this kind of scrutiny? Why did he, once again, turn himself into a lightning rod for critics from across the political spectrum? What kind of person is he? In short, *who is Robert S. McNamara?* The answer is that he is Woodrow Wilson's ghost. Explaining what we mean by this is our principal objective in this Epilogue.

Questions like "who is McNamara?" or "why did he do it?" reflect, more than anything else, Errol Morris' great success in conveying McNamara on screen as a complex, driven, immensely interesting and—as many have said, in one way or another—a scary guy. Especially on the big screen, it is a unique experience to find oneself almost ducking for cover, as this eighty-five-year-old man comes veritably leaping out of his chair at the audience, finger pointing, sometimes almost growling, other times fighting back tears, but always burning with an intensity that is, in fact, reasonably described as "scary."

Many want to know why, in his old age, he has opened himself up once again to charges of having committed war crimes—in the Pacific War in the 1940s, and in Vietnam in the 1960s? Why has he, yet again, revisited the nuclear horror of the near miss of the Cuban missile crisis—which he says in the movie we escaped by luck, rather than by the steely-eyed crisis management of McNamara and his colleagues in the Kennedy administration? What drives him to do this? Not only has he exposed himself yet again as a "sitting duck" to his critics, but he has even mustered the courage—or gall, depending on one's perspective—to put forward lessons he believes should be derived from his mistakes in these epochal events—lessons he presents as perhaps our best hope for avoiding another century of conflict, killing and catastrophe. In so doing, he has not only exposed himself to the possibility of criticism and condemnation, he almost seems to invite it. Again, it has been asked of us countless times by people who know we advised Robert McNamara and Errol Morris in the making of "The Fog of War": who is this guy?

McNamara himself has gone a considerable distance toward providing an answer—one kind of answer—to these probing questions, stimulated in many viewers of the movie by the virtual—but nonetheless intense—experience of going one-on-one with Robert McNamara. He has done so in *Wilson's Ghost: Reducing the Risk of Conflict, Killing and Catastrophe in the 21st Century* (written with James Blight, and published in 2001).[2] *Wilson's Ghost* does not contain the kind of deeply personal revelations some look for, when seeking explanations of McNamara's relentless activity as both a prophet of doom, and as an avowedly idealistic advocate of institutional reforms—in the United Nations, the U.S. government, regional security arrangements and much more—that he believes would, if enacted, lower the odds of the kind of doomsday disasters and near disasters in which he participated, and with which he remains concerned. He is uncomfortable with public confessions, of the type one can find daily on countless radio and television programs, on the Internet, and in a seemingly infinite array of popular magazines. In "The Fog of War," for example, he refuses to discuss in any detail the impact of the war in Vietnam on his immediate family. He is an anomaly in our tell-all era: a very public person who is also, paradoxically, a very private person as well.[3]

Wilson's Ghost, however, provides considerable insight into what makes Bob McNamara tick. It displays McNamara at his most expansive. It reveals the depths of his passionate concern for the human future, as well as his belief that it is actually possible to affect that future in ways that promote human survival and more: an enhanced quality of life for all human beings. These are ambitious, lofty, somewhat fuzzy objectives, especially for a man who is famous (or infamous) for his insistence on precision. Yet in an exercise of compression and conciseness, McNamara has been able to convey a good deal of the essence of what he is about in less than two pages: the "Manifesto" that leads off *Wilson's Ghost*.[4] We include it here, immediately below, as a kind of quasi-"document"—something to refer to, while proceeding through this concluding chapter, especially when questions arise along the lines of: "why did McNamara agree to be interviewed for 'The Fog of War'?" To put it another way, one that is a favorite personal locution of McNamara's: what is McNamara's "bottom line?" Here it is, what he is all about, in as concise a rendering from McNamara himself as we are ever likely to get.

A 21st-Century Manifesto: Choose Life over Death

The 20th century was, in important respects, a century of tremendous advancement for the human race. In developed countries, life expectancy increased dramatically; literacy became virtually universal; productivity—both industrial and agricultural—reached levels undreamed of previously; and income per capita grew to similarly stunning and unprecedented levels. Even in underdeveloped countries, people's lives began to improve, as potable drinking water, improved sanitation, better housing and other infrastructure improvements were introduced in many relatively poor areas. Although much remains to be done to advance the poorest of the poor, in these and other ways, the human race advanced dramatically during the 20th century in its capacity for dealing with many of the causes that brought untold suffering, impairment and early death to human beings throughout all of recorded history.

Yet the 20th century also produced a bloodbath of war and destruction that dwarfed earlier periods, as approximately 160 million human beings were killed in violent conflict. We enter the 21st century, moreover, with the capability of destroying all the gains of the 20th. We are demonstrating radically increased efficiency in killing our fellow human beings in cross-border wars, and in civil and communal conflicts. And there continues to hang over us the risk that whole nations will be destroyed in wars in which weapons of mass destruction are used.

This paradox of the 20th century—our success at saving, lengthening and improving lives, coexisting with our incapacity to prevent massive killing—is epitomized in the life of one of the century's most admired figures, Albert Schweitzer, winner of the 1952 Nobel Peace Prize, physician in rural Africa, musician, scholar and crusader for saving and improving the lives of his fellow human beings. His philosophy of "reverence for life," which he practiced in Africa, stood in stark contrast to the catastrophic events in Schweitzer's native Alsace, on the French-German border. Twice in his lifetime, in the world wars, it became a killing field in which human beings slaughtered one another by the tens of thousands with weapons whose development derived from the same scientific method as the medicine which allowed Schweitzer to save and improve lives in west Africa.

Woodrow Wilson, whose presidency encompassed the whole of the First World War and its immediate aftermath, was one of the first leaders of the 20th century to sense that without radical political changes, the human race might destroy itself in ever greater numbers in what he called metaphorically the "typhoon"—catastrophic wars of ever greater destructiveness. The key requirements to avoid the catastrophe, he believed, were to make a moral priority of reducing the killing, and to take a thoroughly multilateral approach to issues of international security. He failed utterly, however, to implement these objectives. Thereafter, Wilson's ghost haunted the 20th century: in the Second World War, in which fifty million people were killed; in the Cold War, with its nuclear fear and destructive "proxy" wars; and in the seemingly countless post–Cold War conflicts that threaten anarchy, death and destruction in many parts of the world today.

Why this anomaly? Why has the killing of human beings by other human beings been immune from the overall trend toward achieving longer, more fulfilling lives that characterized so much of the 20th century? We argue that fundamentally, the human race—in particular foreign and defense policymakers of the Great Powers—has not made the prevention of human carnage a central priority. In *Wilson's Ghost*, we describe the basis and implications of making a reduction in carnage a central priority—not the only priority, and at times perhaps not even the most important one—but a central priority nonetheless.

In the Old Testament book of Deuteronomy we are told, "I set before you life or death, a blessing or a curse. Choose life then." It has never been more important to reduce the curse of human killing, so that the blessings of life can be enjoyed now, and in succeeding generations.[5]

"McNamara Is a Very Scary Man"

Just as the ghost of Jacob Marley haunted Ebenezer Scrooge in Charles Dickens' *A Christmas Carol*, the ghost of Woodrow Wilson (the U.S. president from 1912 to 1921) has haunted world leaders from his day to ours. The message of Wilson's ghost is this: Beware of the kind of blindness and folly that led Europe's leaders into the First World War, a disaster theretofore without compare in world history; and beware of the temptation to believe that sustainable peace will be maintained simply by plotting to achieve an alleged "balance of power," without a strong international organization to enforce it.

That message has gone unheeded. The 20th century became the bloodiest century by far in all of human history. Now, half way through the first decade of the 21st century, conflicts have broken out anew around the globe, within states—in many countries of sub-Saharan Africa, the former Soviet Union, and of course the Islamic world; and between sovereign states—such as the U.S.-Afghanistan war, the U.S.-Iraq war and the seemingly never-ending struggle between Israel and the would-be state of Palestine. In addition, the 9/11 terrorist attacks on New York and Washington raised the specter, for the first time, that highly organized and well-financed nonstate actors, such as the al-Qaeda organization of Osama bin Laden, can threaten the basic security of the major industrial states. And hovering like a foreboding dark cloud over all these conflicts is the realization that we have, alas, retained the capacity utterly to destroy ourselves in a nuclear holocaust. This is the international context in which "The Fog of War" appeared, in 2003.

The North American premiere of "The Fog of War" occurred on August 30, 2003, at the Telluride (Colorado) Film Festival. In a discussion following the screening, a member of the audience got Robert McNamara's point just about right, in our view, regarding the relevance of Wilson's failure for us, nearly a century later. Here is what she said:

> That old man McNamara just kind of dumps Woodrow Wilson's failure—his tragedy—right in our faces. Do you remember that old folk song, "MTA," about that guy "Charlie" who has to ride the subway forever in Boston because he doesn't have the fare to get off? It starts off with the line: "Citizens hear me out. This could happen to you." I think that's what the old man is saying. Except this time it will be the total end, finis, because of nuclear

weapons. This movie—McNamara's message—is one of the scariest things I have ever experienced. McNamara is a very scary man, even at his age.[6]

For McNamara, Wilson is a kind of historical "mirror" with which to illuminate our own security risks, and a stimulus to finding ways to lower those risks. Wilson's ghost hounds us, according to McNamara, just as the ghost of Jacob Marley clanked in his shackles after Ebenezer Scrooge, admonishing his former colleague not to continue making the mistakes he made, or else he too would join him in perdition! The post–Cold War era, which began with optimism and hope, has already, in the space of a decade and a half, given way to apocalyptic predictions of "a clash of civilizations."[7]

McNamara's message, rooted in his remarkably varied experience and buttressed by his recent study of Wilson, is indeed frightening. Once before, he notes, the people of the U.S. and much of the world thought—though he emphasizes that it was more wishful thinking than carefully reasoning—that they were home free, that serious international conflict was a thing of the past. The Great War of 1914–1918 was supposed to be "the war to end all war." Instead, it was the merely the opening disaster in a century of increasingly brutal and lethal wars. This may not only happen again, in the 21st century; it may already be happening now, as in the U.S. "war on terror," and the declaration of President George W. Bush in his January 2002 State of the Union Address that the U.S. intends to seek "regime change" in the states he characterized as the "axis of evil"—Iraq, where the regime has already been removed, Iran, and North Korea.

Like Wilson of old, McNamara burns with intensity. He veritably leaps off the screen at us in "The Fog of War," as he exhorts us to get our collective act together, lest we yet live to experience a man-made, global tragedy of unprecedented proportions. We could, and we might, he warns in "The Fog of War," literally destroy whole nations, even large and powerful nations like the United States. We could, and we might, destroy human civilization.

This is not a feel-good message, to say the least. It is deeply unsettling, especially when delivered with the dilated passion of McNamara. Harvard scholar Samantha Power has noted that this seemingly omnipresent octogenarian, McNamara, "refuses to go away"—refuses, in other words, to let up, to take it easy, to relent, to stop issuing warnings, and to stop providing solutions which, in his view, might prevent the worst from happening. Power is far from alone, however, in noticing that his darkly prophetic, relentlessly propagated message can also be annoying to those who either hope he is wrong, or who worry that he may be right, but in any case conclude that they have heard enough of McNamara.[8] McNamara is unmoved by such criticism. In fact, he may well be the oldest really scary, really annoying person now living. Certainly, he must be the oldest, scariest, most annoying person ever to have "starred" in an Academy Award®–winning movie.

Woodrow Wilson and Robert McNamara's "Earliest Memory"

Robert McNamara returns repeatedly, as he does in "The Fog of War," to his earliest memory—to San Francisco, to "a city exploding with joy" on November 11, 1918.[9] As symbolized by this memory of McNamara's (and illustrated in the movie with dramatic archival footage), the post–First World War era began for Americans with a feeling of triumph, supreme optimism, moral conviction and idealism. It was also an occasion when a precocious, impressionable Robert McNamara experienced some portion of the emotion of the moment. The two-and-a-half-year old boy, standing on the streets of San Francisco, recalls adults on the tops of streetcars, acting oddly and wonderfully like the children he played with, for such was the ecstasy of the moment. On November 11, 1918—Armistice Day—the combatants in the First World War agreed to lay down their arms and go to Paris to work out a peace treaty. As McNamara emphasizes in "The Fog of War," many were celebrating simply because loved ones could now return home at war's end.

But not all were merely relieved by the prospect of a return to "normalcy," as the postwar was soon to be called by Wilson's successor as president, Warren G. Harding. McNamara is right to assert that at least some of the celebrations across America were about more than the prospect of family reunions and the return to normal life. President Woodrow Wilson had convinced himself, and

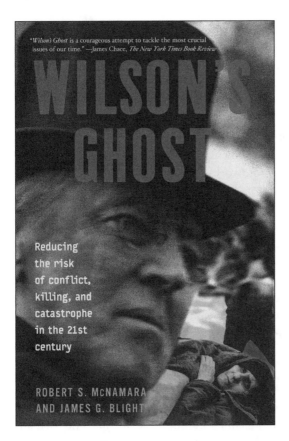

"His dream was that the world could avoid great wars in the future."

a good many of his constituents, that Armistice Day represented not merely the end of the most devastating war in world history, but also, in the phrase Wilson made famous, "the war to end all war." One can only try to imagine how this memory resonates now with McNamara, a man whose life, in common with everyone of his generation, was marked by the suffering, anxiety, and trauma of the Second World War, in which fifty million people died. In fact, at age eighty-five when "The Fog of War" was filmed, McNamara had borne witness to nearly an entire century virtually soaked in human blood.

What gives McNamara's earliest memory of Armistice Day its poignancy in the film is the fact that the memory is more than eighty years old, and in those intervening decades, *absolutely nothing* that seemed possible in that celebratory moment long ago actually occurred. Wilson's "war to end all war" was, instead, the war that begot a much bloodier, even more catastrophic war, a global society fractured seemingly beyond repair, and a civilization that may be doomed to self-destruction, if not diverted from its present nihilistic course.

How did this happen? Here is the rough chronology. In the peace conference in Paris following the Armistice, Wilson sought to lay the institutional groundwork for accomplishing what he believed were the two principal prerequisites for enduring peace in the 20th century: first, "peace without victory," a nonpunitive peace treaty devoted to reconciliation between Germany and its principal European adversaries in the war just concluded—England, France and Italy; and second, a League of Nations which would have the power to enforce the peace thereafter. Leadership of the League of Nations, he believed, would fall naturally to the Americans because they were relatively disinterested and lacked the cynicism the war engendered in many Europeans. "America," said Wilson during a speech praising the League, "is the only idealistic nation in the world."[10]

Wilson was right, alas. The greed, vindictiveness, bitterness and pettiness of the victorious Europeans toward Germany proved more than a match for Wilson's eloquent idealism. The British, French and Italian Allies considered Wilson to be intellectually brilliant, but almost childishly idealistic—and supremely arrogant and annoying. Here, for example, is how Wilson was viewed in Paris by David Lloyd George, the British Prime Minister and head of the British delegation to the Paris conference: "I really think that at first the idealistic president regarded himself as a missionary whose function was to rescue the poor European heathen from their age-long worship of false and fiery gods. He was apt to address us in that vein."[11] As Lloyd George and other Europeans saw it, Wilson came to Paris to preach, to inspire, obsessed as he was by the ludicrous objective of creating institutions which would thereafter forbid and prevent war. Lloyd George and the other European Allies, on the other hand, came to Paris unapologetically to claim the spoils due the victors of a war from the dreaded and hated Germans—to bleed the Germans dry, if they could get away with it.

Despite an almost superhuman effort that ultimately destroyed his health, Wilson failed to accomplish any of his major objectives. In the end, Germany was humiliated and embittered by the terms of the Treaty of Versailles, which required not only the ceding of vast tracts of land, but also the payment of exorbitant reparations to Germany's European enemies. Wilson's League of Nations, moreover, was rendered nearly irrelevant by America's absence from it, due to Wilson's failure to persuade the U.S. Senate to ratify the treaty creating it. During a cross-country speaking tour in the summer of 1919 on behalf of the treaty, Wilson suffered a stroke, from which he never fully recovered. The Senate voted down the League shortly thereafter. Much of Adolf Hitler's appeal to the Germans, during his rise to prominence in the 1920s, derived from his demagogic skill in characterizing the Germans as the victims of the Paris Peace conference and the Treaty of Versailles.

Thus did Wilson's personal tragedy reflect that of his country and the world. Almost before the ink was dry on the Treaty of Versailles, the nations of Europe began to sleepwalk ever more closely toward the abyss of human destructiveness known to history as the Second World War. Wilson died a broken and largely forgotten man in 1924, still unable to resolve the paradoxical premises of his presidency, and indeed of his vision for America and the world. He was a devout Presbyterian, and therefore a Calvinist with unbounded respect for the power of "original sin"—human frailty—to render human life an unmitigated horror from beginning to end, on the one hand; and yet, on the other hand, he seemed to many—not only to cynical Europeans like David Lloyd George—to be a starry-eyed idealist who felt with utter sincerity that he, and perhaps just he alone, had discovered, in the tragedy of the Great War (as the First World War was called, prior to the Second World War), the way "to end all wars."[12]

There is an unusually strong affinity between Wilson and McNamara. This is why our understanding of McNamara and his mission is enhanced by a consideration of some of Wilson's central concerns, along with Wilson's all-too-accurate prediction of the horror of the Second World War. The "voice" of McNamara in "The Fog of War" is very similar to Wilson's, on his rail tour of America in 1919, aimed at persuading Americans to embrace the Treaty of Versailles. He warned during that last-ditch effort to save the League of Nations that solutions to problems of war and peace must be *radical, if civilization is to avoid the typhoon*" of total destruction.[13] We now know that "typhoon" as the Second World War, and it very nearly did destroy civilization as Wilson conceived it. Wilson was, especially during his barnstorming tour in 1919, also "a very scary man." Historian Frank Ninkovich has captured the essence of this scary side of Wilson:

> Wilsonianism's . . . image of the world was utterly terrifying . . . Wilson was . . . the first statesman to understand the self-destructive side of modern international relations and to formulate a comprehensive new approach that promised to salvage society's progressive machinery. According to his grim diagnosis, only a radical experimental treatment promised any hope at all for a cure.[14]

And Wilson was right. The "experimental treatment"—a League of Nations with the power to prevent war and punish wrongdoers—was not invoked, unleashing a war so catastrophic that even Wilson, as grim as he could be, could scarcely have imagined its scale and ferocity. The Robert McNamara who recounts his earliest memory in "The Fog of War" knows all this, of course, knows it from experience, and knows it from study. It is the "earliest memory," therefore, of one whose hopes and dreams have been shattered. It is the memory of an old man who believes he may have one last shot at getting his fellow human beings to try the "experimental treatment" before the promise of his "earliest memory" is shattered once again, possibly for the last time.

A Street Saint or Wilson's Ghost?

McNamara says at the outset of "The Fog of War," that "my rule has been try to learn, try to understand what happened. Develop the lessons and pass them on." On the face of it this objective

seems laudable, but hardly exceptional. Yet, as was true for Wilson, when the lessons are propounded with the insistence and intensity that McNamara brings to the task, he seems scary; he makes people uneasy. Why is this?

In reviewing "The Fog of War," Roger Angell, the longtime fiction editor of *The New Yorker*, used an image that may help explain McNamara's (and Wilson's) scariness, and the reactions to it. Angell is almost (but not quite) as old as McNamara and, like McNamara, is a veteran of the Pacific Theater in the Second World War. He writes that he was deeply moved by the segment in "The Fog of War" on World War II, the war in which he and McNamara participated as young men. He was moved, but he was also made uneasy. His personal unease calls to mind, he says, an image of "old Robert McNamara . . . stand[ing] in our path with the bony finger and crazy agenda of a street saint."[15] Anyone who has ever been accosted on the street by a person full of doomsday predictions, and with "the solution" to whatever problem is his or her obsession, knows how this feels. McNamara accosts us on screen, bony finger pointing directly at everyone in the audience, full of admonitions to change or the end may well be at hand. One has the impression that, if he were physically present, he would not let you proceed out of the theater until you come to grips with both the problem he has identified, and his radical solution to it. This makes almost everyone uncomfortable, to one degree or another.

One need not believe simplistically that history is bound to repeat itself more or less exactly—in this case post–World War I history, which led to World War II, being repeated in a leadup to a hypothetical World War III—to give some credence, as does Angell, to both McNamara and his message. For while the "bony finger" is certainly in our faces, the agenda of this "street saint" is anything but "crazy." He participated firsthand in much of the history he recounts: the brutality in the Pacific in the Second World War; the close call to global doomsday during the Cuban missile crisis; and the uninformed and flawed decisionmaking that resulted in the Vietnam tragedy. This is what makes him *really* scary: he appears to know what he is talking about. In fact: *he may well be right, just as Wilson was right!*

For all these reasons, as was noted by the member of the audience in Telluride, "McNamara is a very scary man, even at his age." Given the length and trajectory of his life, we would say *especially* at his age. For Robert McNamara, Angell's "street saint," was *there* when Wilson proclaimed that the human race had a choice: to usher in a peaceful and harmonious world, by permitting his League of Nations to become the equivalent of a world government; or to let the sovereign nations lead the world into progressively more catastrophic wars. He was *there*, participating in many of the very events that, alas, proved Wilson to be prophetic. And now, he is still *here* in "The Fog of War," right in front of us, figuratively blocking our path, asking audiences of "The Fog of War" to act to prevent a repetition, or worse, of the tragedy he and his generation endured. He may give us the willies, as "street saints" often do. But if McNamara is right, if his agenda is not "crazy," then he is Wilson's ghost, a man clanking in his metaphorical chains, having returned from the hell on earth that was much of the 20th century, offering the human race one last chance to save itself.

The Tragic Reality of "McNamara's Century"

So what does "Wilson's ghost," this "very scary man" think we should be afraid of? What fuels McNamara's intensity and concerns? First, he would have us appreciate what happened in the 20th century—"McNamara's century," we may call it.[16] What was it, McNamara asks, that made the 20th century the bloodiest in all of human history?[17] How did war change during McNamara's life in ways that made it more deadly?

The rates at which civilians were victimized illustrate the changing nature of war in the 20th century. One source breaks down an estimated 105 million killed in 20th-century wars into 43 million military dead and 62 million civilian dead.[18] Another estimates that whereas at the end of the 19th century, approximately 10% of war deaths were civilians, 50% were civilians in the Second World War, and 75% were civilians in the wars fought in the 1990s.[19] From these estimates, it is clear that in the 20th century, war was a common occurrence, it was increasingly lethal, and its toll fell primarily on civilians—noncombatants, the elderly, women and children.

The 20th century was not just history's bloodiest century, therefore, but it was also the century in which noncombatant immunity—long held in the West to be a requirement of a "just" war—virtually ceased to operate. German journalist and scholar Josef Joffe recently gave this epitaph to the 20th century:

> How will we remember the 20th century? First and foremost, it was the century of the Three T's: total war, totalitarianism and terror . . . In the 18th and 19th centuries, enemies were defeated; in the 20th, they were exterminated in [places like] Auschwitz or in the killing fields of Cambodia."[20]

This applies equally to the roughly 80–100,000 people killed in the firebombing of Tokyo, the 140,000 people who died instantly at Hiroshima on August 6, 1945, and to the victims of the systematic terror inflicted over decades by Stalin and Mao on their own people.[21] No one knows how many died in the Stalinist purges and forced removals of the 1920s and 1930s, or how many died due to famines associated with Mao's "Great Leap Forward" initiatives and from the chaos of the Cultural Revolution. (The number usually cited is 20 million in each case.) Suffice it to say that millions died due to Stalinist and Maoist cruelty and mistakes.

It is obvious that whatever one fixes as the number killed in war and domestic conflict in the 20th century, the number must be understood as indicating only the approximate level of magnitude of the tragedy. No matter how the total is broken down, there can be nothing approaching numerical precision regarding any of the constituent numbers.

But if approximately 110 million died in war from 1900 through 1995; and if 20 million each died due to the brutal policies of Stalin and Mao; and if approximately 10 million died in war, or for reasons related to war, between 1995 and 2000 (a figure commonly used), we arrive at the figure of 160 million killed in conflict—including interstate and intrastate conflict. This figure is a useful approximation that illustrates the level of violence in the century just ended.

Most of these 160 million or so would have been civilians. How many? If we add the 60 million civilians we calculate were killed in war, to the estimated 40 million who died due to Stalin's and Mao's ideologically driven internal violence, something like 100 million of the 160 million killed due to violence and war in the 20th century were innocent civilians—an appalling statistic. Whatever the actual numbers may have been, there can be no dissent from the assessment of the 1997 report of the Carnegie Commission on Preventing Deadly Conflict: those numbers we can derive, however imperfectly, tell a tale of "mass violence on a scale that dwarfs all previous centuries."[22]

New Dangers in the 21st Century

Robert McNamara believes that the Carnegie Commission report is realistic. Consider, for example, the following calculations which, while speculative, are probably fairly conservative:

- What appears to be the most reliable estimate of the number of wars fought in the 20th century gives the number as 218.[23]
- Assume no increase in the number of wars in this century versus the last and no increase in their intensity.
- But recognize that the average population of the globe will nearly double.[24]

Under these circumstances fatalities from war would likely be substantially higher, at least 300 million. Further, let us assume that the rate of civilian casualties remains constant at approximately 75% (which is judged to be the approximate post–Cold War rate in the 1990s). In this case, 75% of 300 million yields a projected 225 million civilian war deaths.

We reiterate—as is done in *Wilson's Ghost*, where this argument is presented in greater detail—that these numbers are speculative. The estimation of *past* war deaths is just that—estimation, based on "data" of often unknown reliability. To the uncertainty attached to estimates of the pattern and number of war deaths in the 20th century we must, in dealing with projections into the 21st century, add additional uncertainties: the rate of technological advance and dissemination; political leadership or its lack; and a host of other essentially unknowable factors. So neither we, nor the Carnegie Commission, nor anyone else can say with any degree of precision how many people will have died in war by December 31, 2100. But our projections—300 million war deaths, 225 million of them civilians—may well be *underestimates*!

Is it any wonder, therefore, that McNamara believes the urgency of the Carnegie Commission's call to war-prevention in the 21st century is entirely warranted? It is, in fact, difficult to believe that our increasingly interdependent global village—civilization as we know it—can, in this century, withstand the killing of anything like 225 million innocent civilians without leading to political, economic and social instability that would severely penalize most, if not all, nations and all peoples.

And what if—as seems entirely possible—nuclear weapons were to be used in one or more of these conflicts? In that case, the estimates for war deaths would have to be revised significantly upward. For example, just a few nuclear detonations in a border war between India and Pakistan would likely kill millions—perhaps tens of millions—in densely populated South Asia. The same applies to a nuclear conflict in the Middle East between Israel and one or more Arab adversaries. And it is highly probable that the U.S. would be drawn inexorably into any conflict of this magnitude. Then what of the Russians and Chinese? What form would their probable involvement take? Alas, this worst-case scenario may not be as unlikely as we all hope it is.

Or is this possibility, disastrous though it would be, even the worst-case scenario, as it applies to the security of the U.S. and other Western states? In the wake of the 9/11 attacks on New York and Washington, along with documented efforts by al-Qaeda-linked groups to obtain and use nuclear weapons in their attacks, vulnerability to a direct nuclear attack on a major U.S. city can no longer be ruled out as wildly improbable. In an important new book, *Nuclear Terrorism*, Harvard's Graham Allison describes what he calls the problem of "the second shoe" in the U.S. intelligence community following 9/11: the anticipated followup terrorist attack from al-Qaeda operatives. What would they do to up the ante—to create as big an impression as had been created by the 9/11 attacks? The answer was and remains obvious: attack with a stolen or clandestinely constructed nuclear weapon.[25] The technical difficulties involved in either stealing or making a nuclear weapon are far from unsurmountable. Is al-Qaeda interested in this possibility? Lest there be any doubt, here is bin Laden's deputy Suleiman Abu Gheith in 2002: "We have the right to kill 4 million Americans—2 million of them children—and to exile twice as many and wound and cripple hundreds of thousands."[26] There is only one way to achieve this grisly objective: by detonating one or more nuclear weapons in a densely populated city.

Most of the filming of Errol Morris' interviews with Robert Mc-Namara occurred well before the attacks of 9/11.[27] If a "second edition" of "The Fog of War" should ever be contemplated, we believe its message, and the bearer of the message, might be even scarier then they were, to many, in the "first edition." Such is the world we now face, halfway through the first decade of the 21st century.

Three Imperatives for the 21st Century

What can we do? McNamara's response—and our response—is that solutions to the current predicament must be *radically* different from what is currently being proposed and implemented. McNamara formalized the core of his position by June 2001 in two imperatives, each of which runs radically counter to the received political wisdom of our own day, just as it did in Woodrow Wilson's era. The imperatives are:

- *The Moral Imperative.* Establish as a major goal of U.S. foreign policy, and indeed of foreign policies across the globe, the avoidance in the 21st century of the carnage—160 million dead—caused by war in the 20th century.
- *The Multilateral Imperative.* Recognize that the United States must provide leadership to the world to achieve the objective of reduced carnage but, in doing so, it will not apply its superior economic, political or military power unilaterally, other than in the unlikely cir-

cumstances of a defense of the continental United States, Hawaii and Alaska.[28]

The multilateral imperative was characterized as "zero-tolerance multilateralism" for the United States, indicating that the world's only remaining superpower should *never* intervene unilaterally, except "in the unlikely circumstances" of an attack on the United States Itself.[29]

"In the unlikely circumstances"—the phrase now seems bizarrely anachronistic. For whatever the likelihood or unlikelihood of an attack on the U.S. homeland in June 2001, when *Wilson's Ghost* was published—and it certainly *seemed* unlikely at the time to almost all specialists on international peace and security—the likelihood or probability no longer matters. The terrorist attacks on New York and Washington on September 11, 2001, constitute a tragic demonstration of the point made by Harvard political scientists Richard Neustadt and Graham Allison in their analysis of the Cuban missile crisis. "No event demonstrates," they wrote more than thirty years ago, "more clearly than the missile crisis that with respect to nuclear war there is an awesome crack between *unlikelihood* and *impossibility*."[30]

Robert McNamara has known since October 1962 that the supposed unlikelihood of escalation to nuclear war in October 1962 provided no comfort whatever to those charged with the responsibility for finding an escape from the crisis short of war. The key feature of this fear of a nuclear holocaust was the unspeakable totality of its *possible* destruction, not reassurance that such a catastrophe was *improbable*, simply because it was thought to be plainly irrational to initiate a nuclear war. In the same way, the 9/11 attacks, unlikely or not, occurred. Of that fact we can be 100 percent certain.

The second edition of *Wilson's Ghost* was published in the summer of 2003. In light of the 9/11 attacks, the deployment of realistic empathy was elevated in that edition to the status of a third imperative of equal stature to the moral imperative and the multilateral imperative.[31]

THE EMPATHY IMPERATIVE

The West, led by the United States, must seek by all possible means to increase its understanding of the history, culture, religion, motives and attitudes of those who have declared themselves to be its adversaries. This effort should begin by developing empathy toward the Islamic fundamentalists, specifically those groups allied with, or sympathetic to, the international terrorist network known as al-Qaeda. Empathy does *not* imply sympathy or agreement; it *does* imply curiosity, leading to deeper understanding of an adversary's mindset, as a prerequisite to resolving differences and eliminating threats to peace and security.

Why empathy? And why now? Because the 9/11 attacks were unanticipated, even unimaginable, to Americans before they occurred. They seemed to most Americans, in fact, to be unprovoked acts of "evil"—in other words, *they made no sense*. Many assumed they must therefore have been carried out by irrational zealots, or by brainwashed youth, or by people from desperate backgrounds—in any case, a group of certifiably crazy people willing to kill themselves in the act of killing others—and who therefore were *evil* people. And it is true that there can be absolutely no moral justification for the targeting of innocent civilians, as was done by those responsible for the 9/11 attacks. One can with justification therefore call the deeds "evil." The problem with labeling the perpetrators "evil," however, is that such a designation is usually taken to be an explanation for the actions—which it *is not*—warranting overwhelming military retaliation—which it *may, or it may not*. Labeling actions and actors "evil" tells us nothing about why the actions were committed.

Why did they do it? Not because they were crazy. The plan for the attacks may have taken as long as five years to implement.[32] The attackers were led by mature, well-educated men from middle-class and upper-middle-class backgrounds. Far from being odd or crazy, the attackers blended into American culture almost perfectly—some for several years—and are recalled by those who knew them in the United States, where they took their flight training, as quiet, unassuming and "normal." So the mystery deepens, along with the urgency of the need for empathy. That they hated us is clear. That the attacks were only a final step in a very detailed, daring and clever plan, and that more attacks should be anticipated—regrettably, that is also clear. But why?

The overarching lessons of the attacks of 9/11 are all related to empathy and its lack. They are identical to those derived in "The Fog of War" by McNamara from the Cuban missile crisis and Vietnam War: size is not necessarily an advantage; a small nation or group can threaten the basic security of even the world's greatest superpower; arrogance—the implicit belief that we as Americans needn't make an effort to understand an adversary, due to our asymmetrical advantage in quantifiable military capabilities—is the greatest impediment to empathy. For these reasons, "empathize with your enemy" is lesson number one in "The Fog of War." Robert McNamara, Errol Morris, and we agree: if you take away only one lesson from "The Fog of War," it should be the first lesson. "Empathize with your enemy"—without qualification. What you don't know, don't understand, or misperceive can hurt you *fundamentally*, no matter who you are, or who your enemy may be. Acceptance of this principle is the beginning—the bare beginning but a beginning all the same—of the reduction of the risk of conflict, killing and catastrophe in the 21st century.

Wilson's Ghost

The failure of empathy in the West and among its opponents has been a core reason why the 20th century was the bloodiest in all of human history and—to use Wilson's own image—a heart-breaking century.[33] He was eloquent and prophetic in conveying the sense of betrayal that would follow the incalculable sacrifices made in the war just concluded, if it were *not* "the war to end all war." Here is Wilson, sounding for all the world like a McNamaraesque "street saint," promoting what some believed was a "crazy agenda," speaking in St. Louis in September 1919, shortly before his paralyzing stroke:

> You are betrayed. You fought for something you did not get. And the glory of the armies and the navies of the United States is gone like a dream in the

night, and there ensures upon it, in the suitable darkness of the night, the nightmare of dread which lay upon the nations before this war came; and there will come some time, in the vengeful Providence of God, another war, in which not a few hundred thousand . . . will have to die, but . . . many millions.[34]

Yet by now, early in the 21st century, the deaths in war of tens of millions more of our fellow human beings have been betrayed, in the same sense: their sacrifices led not to the end of violent international conflict, but only to more (and more lethal) conflict. Neither Wilson, nor McNamara, can fairly be characterized as "crazy." Wilson turned out to be right. Can we risk betting that McNamara—Wilson's ghost—is wrong?

Before answering the question with finality, it is well to keep in mind that the stakes have risen enormously since Wilson's time. In spite of the deaths of some 160 million human beings by violent conflict in the 20th century, in spite of all that unending heartbreak, the world was not destroyed. But that was then, and this is now. We have known for at least fifty years that we, the human race, possess the physical ability to destroy ourselves and the world as we know it in a nuclear war. We have known for more than forty years, since the Cuban missile crisis, that a lack of empathy between nations can lead us to the brink of a nuclear war and, but for luck, even over the brink into total catastrophe. Now, after 9/11, we can be absolutely certain that people we do not understand, but who feel intense hatred toward us, wish to destroy us, and have proved they are well-organized, resourceful and ruthless. Such people are seeking the most efficient available means of carrying out our destruction with nuclear weapons or other weapons of mass destruction.

The Harvard scholar Michael Ignatieff has written, regarding the possibilities of empathizing with an enemy: "When it comes to political understanding, difference is always minor, comprehension is always possible."[35] Of course it is possible. But will we make the effort? And even if we do, will we do so in time? After the events of September 11, 2001, and the subsequent U.S. responses to that tragedy, two conclusions seem warranted: the deployment of empathy is the only sure path away from a monumental disaster for the

United States and the world; and, in the face of further proliferation of nuclear weapons, we may have less time to work with than we once thought we had.

In other words, we return to where we (and Robert McNamara) began, but with an addendum: "choose life over death," by empathizing with adversaries, allies, constituents—everyone, in fact. In the 21st century, this commitment must no longer be mistaken for a strategy suitable only for "Goody-Two-Shoes" idealists. Instead, it may be our best strategy for survival—as a nation, and as the human race.

"I've asked Robert McNamara to assume the responsibilities of Secretary of Defense. And I'm glad and happy to say that he has accepted this responsibility."

Chronology of the Life and Times of Robert S. McNamara

1916	Born in San Francisco, California.
1922	Enters first grade.
1933	Enrolls at the University of California, Berkeley.
1937	Graduate Studies at Harvard Business School.
1940	Marries Margaret McKinstry Craig, in Alameda, California.
1941	Joins faculty of Harvard Business School.
	First child, Margy, born.
	Japanese bomb Pearl Harbor.
	Congress declares war on Japan.
1942	Becomes a founding faculty member of the U.S. Army Air Corps Statistical Control School.
1943–45	Lieutenant Colonel in U.S. Army Air Corps during World War II. Stationed 8th Air Force in London, England; and 20th Air Force in India, China and the Marianas.
Feb–Mar 1945	Firebombing of Tokyo and other cities in Japan.
Aug 1945	U.S. drops atomic bombs on Hiroshima and Nagasaki, Japan. World War II ends.
Jan 1946	Begins work at Ford Motor Company, Detroit, Michigan.
1947	Second child, Kathleen, born.
1951	Third child, Craig, born.
1956	Senator John F. Kennedy declares, "Vietnam represents the cornerstone of the free world in Southeast Asia. We cannot abandon it."
Jan 1959	Fidel Castro's 26th of July Movement overthrows dictator Fulgencio Batista. Castro assumes power in Cuba.

Sep 1960   Fidel Castro and Soviet leader Nikita Khrushchev meet for the first time, in New York City.

Nov 1960   Assumes presidency of Ford Motor Company.

Dec 1960   Joins Kennedy administration as Secretary of Defense, the youngest to hold the position.

Jan 1961   Outgoing President Dwight Eisenhower tells Kennedy and his future cabinet that the loss of South Vietnam to the communists would mean the loss of all of Southeast Asia. John F. Kennedy sworn in as 35th President of the United States.

Apr 1961   Failed CIA-backed invasion by Cuban exiles at the Bay of Pigs, Cuba.

Jun 1961   John F. Kennedy and Nikita Khrushchev meet in Vienna.

Aug 1961   Soviets and East Germans begin building a wall to divide East and West Berlin.

Nov 1961   Kennedy refuses request by Gen. Maxwell Taylor and Walt Rostow to send 8,000 combat troops to Vietnam. Kennedy approves increase in U.S. advisers.

Oct 1962   Cuban missile crisis.

May 1963   Buddhists challenge South Vietnamese President Ngo Dinh Diem, and are brutally repressed.

Oct 1963   McNamara recommends, and President Kennedy approves, plans to withdraw all U.S. military personnel from South Vietnam by the end of 1965.

Nov 1963   Ngo Dinh Diem assassinated, following a coup in Saigon. Military junta assumes power.
President Kennedy assassinated in Dallas, Texas.
Vice President Lyndon B. Johnson sworn in as 36th U.S. president.

Aug 1964   North Vietnamese patrol boats allegedly attack two U.S. destroyers on August 2nd and August 4th in the Tonkin Gulf. U.S. retaliates with sixty-four bombing missions against targets in North Vietnam.

Sep 1964   Tonkin Gulf Resolution passes Congress; authorizes President Johnson to undertake military action in Southeast Asia.

Nov 1964   Lyndon Johnson is elected president by a landslide over Barry Goldwater.

Feb 1965   President Johnson authorizes "sustain reprisal" bombing of North Vietnam, following attacks by communist forces on U.S. advisers at Pleiku and Qhi Nhon.

Mar 1965   U.S. begins systematic bombing of North Vietnam with program called ROLLING THUNDER.
U.S. sends first Marine combat units to Danang, South Vietnam.

Jul 1965   President Johnson authorizes sending 175,000 U.S. combat troops to South Vietnam by end of the year.

Nov 1965   Gen. William Westmoreland, U.S. commander in South Vietnam, requests 200,000 additional troops in 1966. McNamara calls this "a shattering blow," coming so soon after the earlier approval for 175,000 troops.
Battle of Ia Drang Valley, first major U.S. encounter with main force units of North Vietnamese Army. The results reinforce McNamara's belief that the war in Vietnam is not winnable via U.S. military force.

1965–67   Several dozen secret peace feelers, some led by McNamara, carried to North Vietnamese authorities by intermediaries. All fail.

Aug 1967   Testifies before Senate Armed Services Committee that increase in bombing of North Vietnam will not win war, and risks escalation to wider war with China or the Soviet Union, and possible genocide of North Vietnamese.

Nov 1967   Pentagon announces that McNamara will leave to become President of World Bank.

Jan 1968   Tet Offensive launched by National Liberation Front (NLF, aka "Vietcong") on several dozen cities and provincial capitals in South Vietnam.

Feb 1968   Leaves cabinet. Receives Presidential Medal of Freedom from President Johnson. Replaced by Clark Clifford.

Mar 1968   President Johnson announces partial bombing halt of North Vietnam and willingness to begin peace negotiations. Johnson also announces he will not seek reelection.

1968–81	President of World Bank. Adds to Bank's emphasis on infrastructure in developing world a new focus on public health issues.
1969	Richard M. Nixon sworn in as 37th U.S. president. Death of Ho Chi Minh.
1970	Escalation of bombing in North and South Vietnam, and secret attacks in Cambodia and Laos, by Nixon administration.
1973	Vietnam Peace Accords signed in Paris, ending U.S. war in Vietnam.
1975	North Vietnamese and NLF forces capture Saigon, and unify the country under communist leadership in Hanoi.
1983	Publishes first of many articles arguing nuclear weapons have no military utility, except deterrence of nuclear war.
1981	Death of Margaret McNamara.
1987–2002	Leads former members of Kennedy administration and leading scholars in major retrospective reevaluation of Cuban missile crisis. Six "critical oral history" conferences occur over fifteen-year period, in U.S., Russia and Cuba.
1995–2004	Leads former members of Kennedy and Johnson administrations, along with leading scholars, in major retrospective evaluation of the escalation of the Vietnam war, modeled on Cuban missile crisis project. Five "critical oral history" conferences have occurred to date, in the U.S., Italy and Vietnam.
1995	Publishes controversial memoir, *In Retrospect: The Tragedy and Lessons of Vietnam*. Admits "we were wrong, terribly wrong" in Vietnam.
1999	Publishes (with James G. Blight and Robert K. Brigham) *Argument Without End: In Search of Answers to the Vietnam Tragedy*.
2001	Publishes (with James G. Blight) *Wilson's Ghost: Reducing the Risk of Conflict, Killing and Catastrophe in the 21st Century*.

Attack by al-Qaeda operatives on World Trade towers in New York City, and the Pentagon.

U.S. military intervention in Afghanistan; removal of Taliban regime.

2003   Publishes (with James G. Blight) expanded post-9/11 edition of *Wilson's Ghost*.

U.S. invasion of Iraq, removal of regime of Saddam Hussein, and U.S. occupation of the country.

2004   "The Fog of War" given Academy Award® for best documentary feature.

Marries Diana Masieri Byfield, in Assisi, Italy.

"LeMay said, 'If we'd lost the war, we'd all have been prosecuted as war criminals.' And I think he's right. He, and I'd say I, were behaving as war criminals."

I don't know quite what kind of a world we'll live in after we've struck Cuba.

"Cuban Missile Crisis, October, 1962"

"Vietnam, June, 1965"

We're losing...

Further Reading and Exploration

The dilemmas described at the conclusion of chapters 1–6 point to uncertainties, ambiguities and other difficulties facing those who would seek to extend or apply the "lessons from the life of Robert S. McNamara," noted in the subtitle to this book. History, it seems, yields plenty of lessons. But some are contradictory, and the successful implementation of others, while theoretically possible, may seem in practice to be little more than a pipe dream.

In this appendix, we provide some clues as to how viewers of Errol Morris' "The Fog of War," and readers of this book, might deepen their understanding of some of the central issues in the film and book. It is organized dilemma by dilemma, 1–6, that close each chapter. We offer only a "sampler" of what some of the best scholars, journalists, politicians and filmmakers have to say about these issues. Collectively, we hope, they add up to a way to approach what is to be done to "reduce the risk of conflict, killing and catastrophe in the 21st century," as the task is stated in the subtitle to *Wilson's Ghost*. Good luck in your continued explorations!

Lesson One: "Empathize with Your Enemy"

The dilemma: Empathy is essential but illusive.

We sincerely hope that the study of empathy in international affairs is "the next big thing" among those who deal professionally with foreign and defense policy. As "The Fog of War" and this book illustrate, a great deal can be explained by the presence or absence of empathy. Alas, it still lies far outside the mainstream of research in international relations, and foreign and defense policy.

The beginning of wisdom for those seeking more exposure to what has been done on empathy and international affairs is the work of Ralph K. White. See his *Fearful Warriors: A Psychological Profile of U.S.-Soviet Relations* (New York: Free Press, 1984), especially chapter 11, which is explicitly about empathy, although the entire book can be read with profit. See also White, ed., *Psychology and the Prevention of Nuclear War* (New York: NYU Press, 1986), especially chapter 6, which is a kind of synopsis of *Fearful Warriors*. More recently, we have traced the story of White's influence on the views of Robert McNamara. See James G. Blight and janet M. Lang, "Lesson Number One: 'Empathize with Your Enemy,'" *Peace and Conflict*, in press, 2005.

The great philosopher of empathy is the late Sir Isaiah Berlin. Berlin's previously unpublished writings continue to appear, several years after his death, edited by his literary executor, Henry Hardy. See *The Proper Study of Mankind: An Anthology of Essays* (New York: Farrar, Straus & Giroux, 1997), especially "Herder and the Enlightenment," pp. 359–435; and *The Sense of Reality: Studies in Ideas and Their History* (New York: Farrar, Straus & Giroux, 1996), especially the title essay, pp. 1–39. The work of Berlin's biographer, Michael Ignatieff, is also useful. See his *Isaiah Berlin: A Life* (New York: Metropolitan Books, 1998); and especially *The Warrior's Honor: Ethnic War and the Modern Conscience* (New York: Metropolitan Books, 1997), a brilliant application of the concept of empathy to ethnic warfare in 1990s Africa and the Balkans. For an attempt to integrate some of the views of Berlin and Ignatieff with the problems central to this book, see Robert S. McNamara and James G. Blight, *Wilson's Ghost: Reducing the Risk of Conflict, Killing and Catastrophe in the 21st Century*, expanded post-9/11 paperback ed. (New York: PublicAffairs, 2003), especially pp. 64–73, and the "Afterword," pp. 230–276, which deals with what the authors call "the empathy imperative."

Lesson Two: "Rationality Will Not Save Us"

The dilemma: Rationality is necessary, but insufficient.

The most disturbing finding of our seventeen-year critical oral history of the Cuban missile crisis is that the desire to "go nuclear" *is* compatible with rationality, in certain circumstances—such as those in which the Cuban government found itself during the final weekend of the intense phase of the crisis. Many still find this unbelievable: that rational human beings could actually conclude that the initiation of nuclear war is their best, or "least-worst" option. Instead, they conclude that Fidel Castro must have been "irrational," at least at the moment he requested of his Soviet allies that they launch a nuclear strike against the U.S.—if the U.S. decided to attack, invade and occupy Cuba. If Castro were "irrational," the finding would be far less troubling than what we believe is the correct conclusion: which is that Castro *was* rational, and that both the U.S. and Soviet Union had inadvertently conspired to create just the sort of situation required for a smaller, weaker country to consider nuclear war as an option.

The place to begin exploration of both the history that produced that extraordinarily dangerous moment in October 1962, and the analysis of its meaning, is in James G. Blight, Bruce J. Allyn and David A. Welch, *Cuba on the Brink: Castro, the Missile Crisis and the Soviet Collapse*, expanded paperback ed. (Lanham, MD: Rowman & Littlefield, 2002). On pp. 247–262, you will find the remarkable exchange between McNamara, Castro, and Russian General Anatoly Gribkov described in chapter two of this book. Another, related perspective, on Cuba's situation, and the psychology of its leaders, in the missile crisis may be found in James G. Blight and Philip Brenner, *Sad and Luminous Days: Cuba's Struggle with the Superpowers after the Missile Crisis* (Lanham, MD: Rowman & Littlefield, 2002). Though it focuses historically on the missile crisis, the entire book can be read as an extended analysis of the difficulties large and small countries (whether allies or adversaries) have empathizing with each other in a confrontation over security issues. The history and the history lesson have been captured succinctly in a recent documentary film, "The Other Side of Armageddon," produced by Ross Wilson and Jacqui Hayden, for the BBC, which aired in October 2002, on the 40th anniversary of the missile crisis.

As McNamara states in "The Fog of War," we still live in a world of conflict and misunderstanding, piled high with nuclear weapons—thousands of them. Moreover, the terrorist attacks of 9/11 proved that even small groups of very dedicated and resourceful people, who are willing to sacrifice themselves for a cause, can cause serious harm even to a superpower like the U.S. The new fear, therefore, is that terrorists, such as those associated with Osama bin Laden's al-Qaeda organization, may acquire a nuclear capability. If they do, then the analogy would be to a nuclear-armed Cuba, with the *Cubans* (not the Russians) in control of them, during the missile crisis. Does anyone doubt that Castro would have ordered a nuclear strike, if the U.S. had attacked?

For some historical and theoretical background on this problem, see James G. Blight and David A. Welch, "Risking 'the Destruction of Nations': Lessons of the Cuban Missile Crisis for New and Aspiring Nuclear States." *Security Studies* 4, no. 4 (Summer 1995), 811–850. See also, Jessica Stern, *The Ultimate Terrorists* (Cambridge, MA: Harvard University Press, 1999); Peter R. Lavoy, Scott D. Sagan, and James J. Wirtz, eds., *Planning the Unthinkable: How New Powers Will Use Nuclear, Biological and Chemical Weapons* (Ithaca, NY: Cornell University Press, 2000); and especially Graham Allison, *Nuclear Terrorism: The Ultimate Preventable Catastrophe* (New York: Times Books, 2004). All of these articles and books are scary—especially since they anchor their analysis in both the emerging dangers of the 21st century, and in what we might call the "psychology" of the Cuban missile crisis—what desperate leaders may do when cornered.

Lesson Three: "Belief and Seeing, They're Both Often Wrong"

The dilemma: We remain prisoners of our mindsets.

In Errol Morris' "The Fog of War," the events in the Tonkin Gulf, and their aftermath, are presented as case studies of misperception, misunderstanding and misjudgment. We agree with this interpretation, although it is controversial. Others, notably those on both margins of the U.S. political continuum, tend to see Lyndon Johnson as a conspirator who basically "manufactured" the incident, or at the very least took full advantage of it via lies and deception, in order to escalate the war in Vietnam. Those who share this view also tend to believe Robert McNamara was Johnson's chief co-conspirator.

There are, however, at least two problems with the conspiracy approach to these and other events associated with the Vietnam War—a war which seems to generate conspiracy theories at a rate unequaled by other events in American history, perhaps because Americans find it difficult, even now, to understand how they could have lost such a war. First, we believe the evidence for a conspiracy—for a campaign of lies, in the interest of escalation, is thin at best; and second, even if it were true, there is little to be learned from the study of liars, other than to try to elect those who always "tell the truth," something that, as U.S. history attests, is easier said than done.

We see two other factors as more significant. First, the episode really does have a lot to teach us about the role of mindsets and misperception—especially those of opponents who differ vastly in size and military power; second, this particular kind of confrontation—superpower versus small nation or group—has become almost paradigmatic in U.S. foreign and defense policy following the collapse of the Soviet Union, leaving the U.S. as the only superpower. This makes the study of the Tonkin Gulf incident and its aftermath instructive for the problems we face now, and are likely to face in the next decade or two.

On the Tonkin Gulf incident itself, the fundamental text is Edwin E. Moise, *Tonkin Gulf and the Escalation of the Vietnam War* (Chapel Hill, NC: University of North Carolina Press, 1996). Be forewarned, however, that the Moise book is pretty tough sledding, unless your interests run to the details of naval and air operations. A more accessible, balanced treatment is in David Kaiser, *American Tragedy: Kennedy, Johnson, and the Origins of the Vietnam War* (Cambridge, MA: Harvard University Press, 2000), pp. 312–340. To get a feel for a conspiracy theorist's approach to the same set of events, see Eric Alterman, *When Presidents Lie: A History of Official Deception and Its Consequences* (New York: Viking, 2004), pp. 160–237. Alterman's view of truth and falsehood in public officials is, in our view, simplistic, and should be read in conjunction with a reading of McNamara's account in his memoir, *In Retrospect: The Tragedy and Lessons of Vietnam*, expanded paperback ed. (New York: Vintage, 1996), pp. 127–144. For insight into how both U.S. and North Vietnamese misperceptions drove events in the Tonkin Gulf, see Robert S. McNamara, James G. Blight and Robert K. Brigham, with Thomas J. Biersteker and Col. Herbert Y. Schandler, *Argument Without End: In Search of Answers to the Vietnam Tragedy* (New York: PublicAffairs, 1999), chapter 5.

The question being asked above all others as this book is being written is: "Is Iraq another Vietnam" for the U.S.? Of course, the question is simplistic; there are many reasons to doubt that Iraq in 2003–2005 can be compared with Vietnam nearly a half century ago. If there is a basis for comparison, and thus a potential set of lessons to be learned and applied, it must be because of the nature of the U.S. decision to intervene—what the U.S. thought it was doing, what U.S. leaders may have misunderstood or ignored as unimportant, but which came back to haunt them. To put it another way: Has "terrorism," following the attacks of 9/11 come to play the role that "communism" played during the Cold War—a kind of ideological blinder through which U.S. leaders see only very imperfectly the nature of societies which may differ greatly from our own, and which may present problems to those who would intervene militarily that are difficult to foresee in Washington?

A good place to start is Seymour M. Hersh, *Chain of Command: The Road From 9/11 to Abu Ghraib* (New York: HarperCollins, 2004)—a brilliant book on why the U.S. invasion of Iraq has yielded so many surprises, and why so many of those have turned the effort in Iraq into what some are calling a "quagmire," like Vietnam. Something like a "virtual group memoir" of those who made the decision to attack, invade and occupy Iraq is in Bob Woodward, *Plan of Attack* (New York: Simon & Schuster, 2004). Woodward was granted unusual access to senior Bush administration officials, including Bush himself, in exchange for protecting the identities of those who related their stories to him regarding specific meetings, memos and other sources of information. For a relatively balanced analysis of Bush's particular applications of religious allegories and metaphors to the international political system, see Peter Singer, *The President of Good and Evil: The Ethics of George W. Bush* (New York: Dutton, 2004). The Indian architect and political writer Arundhati Roy on the other hand, is a scathing critic of the Bush administration's war on terror. See her collection *Power Politics* (Boston: South End Press, 2001), especially the essays "The Algebra of Infinite Justice" and "War is Peace." A good place to go to evaluate whether she exaggerates her accusations of high crimes and misdemeanors against the Bush administration is in a recent book by two Bush administration insiders, David Frum and Richard Perle, *An End to Evil: How to Win the War On Terror* (New York: Random House, 2003).

Lesson Four: "Proportionality Should Be a Guideline in War"

The dilemma: "How much evil must we do in order to do good?"

Probably all peoples and nations tend to view the wars they undertake as just, necessary and noble. The rhetoric of political and military officials who lead their people into violent conflicts is replete with sentiments of this sort. They—the *other*—are the guilty ones; *we*, on the other hand, must set things right and, unfortunately, sometimes one must take up arms against an enemy who cannot be persuaded by any other means. This is the usual way of arguing. It is self-serving, of course; but it is also nearly ubiquitous throughout history and around the world.

Reinhold Niebuhr, one of the most influential American theologians and philosophers of the 20th century, believed this attitude—self-righteous, self-justifying, demonizing the enemy—is the single most dangerous force associated with the American tradition of *exceptionalism*—the belief in America's unique virtuousness among nations. Niebuhr himself wrote that the combination of the American belief in its own perfect or near-perfect goodness, combined with its massive military might in the post–World War II era, meant that U.S. military interventions around the world would raise the risk of major war, even nuclear war. Why? Because the U.S. still felt, even in the wake of the horrors of the Second World War, that it had a responsibility to remake the world in its image—democratic, capitalistic, Judeo-Christian.

See Reinhold Niebuhr, *The Irony of American History* (New York: Scribner's, 1952); and Robert McAfee Brown, ed., *The Essential Reinhold Niebuhr* (New Haven: Yale University Press, 1986), especially the 1944 essay "The Children of Light and the Children of Darkness," a piece which has truly stunning relevance to the world of the first decade of the 21st century. Also helpful is a fine memoir by Niebuhr's daughter, the well-known literary editor Elisabeth Sifton, *The Serenity Prayer: Faith and Politics in Times of War and Peace* (New York: Norton, 2003). These books and essays stress the fallibility of human nature—original sin, if you like—as the first principle of international affairs. Thus, in Niebuhr's view, even though the U.S. did fight a just war in World War II that eliminated the Nazi and Japanese imperial nightmares, in the course of so doing, the U.S. also committed atrocities—for which the only appropriate personal and national response is *guilt*. Our chapter 4 focuses on one such circumstance: the firebombing of all the major and minor Japanese cities, with which Robert McNamara was involved, which killed as many as a million civilians, and which is not well known, in the U.S. or Japan. (Americans don't want to feel guilty; the Japanese don't want to advertise the fact that they more or less invented firebombing, in China, in the late 1930s.)

In the wake of the 9/11 attacks, the Bush administration embraced an image of itself of the type Niebuhr most feared: blameless, attacked and under siege, and thus fully justified in striking out at others without the restraining influence of guilt for wrongs committed in the process of carrying out retribution. In this sense, the 9/11 attacks constitute a fairly close analogy to the Japanese attack on Pearl Harbor in December 1941. For a clear-eyed, impartial, but trenchant analysis of this phenomenon, see Ivo H. Daalder and James M. Lindsay, *America Unbound: The Bush Revolution in Foreign Policy* (Washington, DC: Brookings, 2003). For a critique of the unilateralist urge that has accompanied the recent self-righteousness in American foreign policy, see Joseph S. Nye, Jr., *The Paradox of American Power: Why the World's Only Superpower Can't Go it Alone* (New York: Oxford, 2002).

But to cut perhaps a little closer to the heart of the matter— what real wars do to real human beings—see the passionate memoir by journalist Chris Hedges, *War is a Force That Gives Us Meaning* (New York: PublicAffairs, 2002). Hedges is concerned with what he calls "the collapse of the moral universe" that often attends wars-and he has covered many of the most violent ones over the past twenty years or so. In this, he is what we would call a "neo-Niebuhrian"—difficult to pronounce, perhaps, but instructive, in that Hedges would have us understand that a guilt-free war can only be achieved if those prosecuting it refuse to look at what war actually does to human beings on all sides of the conflict. This doesn't necessarily lead one to pacifism, though it might. But it should lead us to understand that war is precisely what General W. T. Sherman said it was: *hell* for all concerned, winners and losers alike!

Lesson Five: "Be Prepared to Reexamine Your Reasoning"

The dilemma: Leaders must learn from their mistakes.

Think for a moment about the discrepancy between the way President John F. Kennedy dealt with the failure of the Bay of Pigs invasion in April 1961, on the one hand; and the way President Lyndon B. Johnson dealt with the failure of U.S. and South Vietnamese military pressure to achieve U.S. objectives in Vietnam. Essentially, Kennedy made a statement on April 20, 1961, and held a press conference, in which he regretted the failure of the Cuban exile force, but reiterated that this was mainly a fight between the rival groups of Cubans and, while the U.S. might aid the anticommunists, the U.S. would not commit its own military forces to the fight. To do so, he said, would be in opposition to the norms of nonintervention established by the Organization of American States in the Western Hemisphere in the post–World War II era. Johnson, however, in an agonizing set of decisions that were protracted over several years, would never admit "defeat," would not state publicly the threshold for troops, or the level of bombing the U.S. would not exceed. In the end, he led the country incrementally into a quagmire of death and destruction. Obviously, many factors were involved in why Kennedy and Johnson diverged in their handling of news that their policies had not succeeded. But surely, the ability (or inability) to admit a mistake, take the heat, and move on is among the most important of these factors.

On the Bay of Pigs events themselves, see the National Security Archive website: www.gwu.edu/~nsarchiv/. Click on "Bay of Pigs" for access to a marvelous and comprehensive array of primary documents from the U.S. government. See also James G. Blight and Peter Kornbluh, eds., *Politics of Illusion: The Bay of Pigs Invasion*

Reexamined (Boulder, CO: Lynne Rienner, 1998). This is an account of a critical oral history conference (co-sponsored by the Watson Institute for International Studies at Brown University and the National Security Archive at George Washington University), held in 1996 with representatives of the key actors on the losing side: Cuban exiles, White House staff, the State and Defense Departments, and scholars of the period and events. Would Kennedy ultimately have pulled the plug on the U.S. effort in Vietnam, as he had in Cuba regarding the Bay of Pigs invasion? For arguments in the affirmative, see John M. Newman, *JFK and Vietnam: Deception, Intrigue, and the Struggle for Power* (New York: Warner, 1992). This book, more than any other, has helped to reshape scholarly views of Kennedy and Vietnam. Those who enter into this territory now have to deal with Newman's thesis: Kennedy had already decided to get out of Vietnam—after his reelection in 1964. This is also a powerful theme in Oliver Stone's controversial movie "JFK," which was released in 1991 to rapturous praise for its artistic merit as a film, and a good deal of outrage at Stone's playing fast and loose with the historical record. A 2003 HBO film, "Path to War," takes almost the opposite view—that a reluctant Johnson was pushed into escalating the war by McNamara and the military. This view is put forth in the scholarly literature by William Conrad Gibbons, "Lyndon Johnson and the Legacy of Vietnam," in Lloyd Gardner and Ted Gittinger, eds., *Vietnam: The Early Decisions* (Austin, TX: University of Texas Press, 1997), pp. 119–157.

There is also a dark side to the Kennedy record on Vietnam, even for those who are convinced that he had decided to abandon South Vietnam, because (like the exile effort at the Bay of Pigs) it simply was unwinnable. Kennedy, alas for his admirers, was also heavily involved in the planning for the coup that removed South Vietnamese President Ngo Dinh Diem on November 1–2, 1963, an event that opened the floodgates of chaos and mismanagement. In Lyndon Johnson's presidency, apparent South Vietnamese incompetence led the U.S. to assume responsibility for a war that ostensibly was being waged so that this virtually nonexistent entity—an independent, sovereign Republic of [South] Vietnam—could flourish. The history of the connections between Kennedy's support of the coup, and Johnson's escalation of the war in Vietnam, is in a splendid recent account by Howard Jones, *Death of a Generation: How the Assassinations of Diem and JFK Prolonged the Vietnam War* (New York: Oxford, 2003). For an analysis of the ethical and moral issues involved in Kennedy's support of the coup, and his reluctance to explain even to many close advisers that he was serious about the plan to quit Vietnam by the end of 1965, see Francis X. Winters, *The Year of the Hare: America in Vietnam, January 25, 1963–February 15, 1964* (Athens, GA: University of Georgia Press, 1997).

Finally, on a note of optimism, we welcome the appearance of a recent memoir that proves to us that honesty and self-criticism among former officials, though rare, is not extinct. The book is by retired Marine Corps General Tony Zinni (with Tom Clancy and Tony Koltz), *Battle Ready* (New York: G. P. Putnam's Sons, 2004). Zinni is a decorated Vietnam veteran, who retired recently as head of CENTCOM, or chief of the U.S. Central Command. He was involved in the operations in Somalia, Iraq and in U.S. strikes elsewhere against al-Qaeda operatives. Zinni is remarkably open, even enthusiastic, about identifying the absurdities, and mistakes, and also the inspiration he encountered in his nearly forty years in the Marine Corps. We found especially poignant his recollections of his service in Vietnam—where he learned to read and speak Vietnamese—and also his remarkable April 2003 speech at the U.S. Naval Academy, titled "The Obligation to Speak the Truth."

Chapter Six: Critical Reviews of "The Fog of War"

The Dilemma: We understand backwards, but must live forwards.

The problem of what to do about the two kinds of knowledge—from direct experience, and from books, discussions, etc.—is a vexing one, and utterly fascinating to those who share an interest in how, or whether, we can learn from history—from our mistakes. In the Western tradition, this dichotomy is most famously associated with William James' delineation of "knowledge of acquaintance" and "knowledge about." See his *The Principles of Psychology*, 2 vols. (New York: Henry Holt, 1890), vol. 1, pp. 221–223, for the basic statement. Bertrand Russell also noted the importance of the split between lived experience and retrospective knowledge in *The Problems of Philosophy* (New York: Oxford University Press), ch. 5.

In our view, however, the work of Søren Kierkegaard has the most direct relevance to the problem of how to learn from our mistakes, even though we live forwards, but must understand backwards. This is in spite of the fact that Kierkegaard wrote in the early 19th century, and ostensibly on issues unrelated to issues of war and peace. His masterpiece on the dilemma posed in chapter 6 of this book is *The Concept of Anxiety: A Simple Psychologically Orienting Deliberation on the Dogmatic Issue of Hereditary Sin,* ed. and trans. by Reidar Thomte and Albert B. Anderson (Princeton: Princeton University Press, 1980), especially chapter 5, "Anxiety as Saving Through Faith." See what we mean? Who would have believed that insight into how foreign and defense policymakers learn (or fail to learn) from their mistakes would be contained in a volume with this magnificently antique subtitle? For a specific application of Kierkegaard to the anxiety and learning that occurred in, and because of, the Cuban missile crisis, see James G. Blight, *The Shattered Crystal Ball: Fear and Learning in the Cuban Missile Crisis,* foreword by Joseph S. Nye, Jr. (Lanham, MD: Rowman & Littlefield, 1990). All the epigraphs in the book come from Kierkegaard, as did the inspiration to write the book in the first place.

As we mention in the "Prologue" to this book, the anomalous situation in which we find ourselves—living forward, understanding backwards—is central to our method of *critical oral history.* While we cannot "fix" the problem of having these two kinds of knowledge, the method of *critical oral history* is thought to have built into it ample room for knowledge of both sorts: memories by policymakers of life lived forward, without knowledge of the outcome; and retrospective scholarship, beginning with knowledge of the outcome, and proceeding to an attempt to explain that outcome.

For a sample of ways in which scholars have endeavored to interpret the application and the results of *critical oral history,* see the following: Len Scott and Steve Smith, "Lessons of October: Historians, Political Scientists, Policy-Makers and the Cuban Missile Crisis." *International Affairs* 70 (October 1994), 659–84; Mark Kramer, " The Cuban Missile Crisis and Nuclear Proliferation." *Security Studies* 5, no. 1 (Autumn 1995), 171–79; James G. Blight and David A. Welch, "On Historical Judgment and Inference: A Reply to Mark Kramer." *Security Studies*, 5, no. 4 (Summer 1996), 172–182; and James G. Blight and janet M. Lang, "Burden of Nuclear Responsibility: Reflections on the Critical Oral History of the Cuban Missile Crisis." *Peace and Conflict*, 1, no. 3 (Summer 1995), 225–264.

Each of these articles tries to grapple with the ambiguities and complexities of historical knowledge as it has emerged in the practice of *critical oral history*—knowledge of the thoughts and actions of forward-living, by backward-glancing, policymakers and scholars. The bottom line is this: certainty is unattainable (though the method regularly produces really new knowledge and interpretations); so, modesty is still the best policy, epistemologically speaking. We'd like to think Kierkegaard would approve. We are pretty sure, however, that he would not be surprised to discover that almost everything we learn gets modified subsequently, maybe perpetually.

Cover Art

The cover is based on the poster that Sony Pictures Classics developed for the film. We use it courtesy of Sony Pictures Classics Inc., © 2003 Sony Pictures Classics Inc. All Rights Reserved.

The photo-portrait of Robert S. McNamara that appears on the film poster and on the book cover is by Elsa Dorfman, © 2003 www.elsa.photo. net.

Photo Credits

All photos except those on pages 8, 55, 227, and 304 are from the film, "The Fog of War," 2004, Sony Pictures Classics. They are used courtesy of Sony Pictures Classics, Errol Morris, and Fourth Floor Productions.

Additional permission was granted by James G. Blight (page x) and Craig McNamara (page 218) for use of their personal pictures.

The top picture on page 26 is used with the permission of The UCLA Film and Television Archive. It is from their Hearst Metrotone Newsreel Collection.

Four photos are not from "The Fog of War." For the design of the logo for *critical oral history* that appears on page 8, we thank Murphy & Murphy Design Graphics of Providence, RI. The photo from the Hanoi critical oral history conference (page 55) was taken by Monica d. Church, June 1997, and is used with her permission. The cover of *Wilson's Ghost* (page 227) is used with the permission of PublicAffairs, a member of the Perseus Books Group. The picture of the authors (page 304) with Errol Morris and Julia Sheehan is from the authors' personal collection.

Permissions to reprint

Passages in Chapters One and Three from *Argument without End: In search of Answers to the Vietnam Tragedy,* Robert S. McNamara, James G. Blight, and Robert K. Brigham, with Thomas J. Biersteker and Col. Herbert Y. Schandler (New York: PublicAffairs, 1999) and passages in the Epilogue from *Wilson's Ghost: Reducing the Risk of Conflict, Killing and Catastrophe in the 21st Century,* Robert S. McNamara and James G. Blight (New York: PublicAffairs, 2001; expanded, post 9/11 paperback edition 2003) are reprinted with the permission of PublicAffairs, a member of the Perseus Books Group.

Passages in Chapter Two from *Cuba on the Brink: Castro, the Missile Crisis and the Soviet Collapse,* expanded paperback edition, James G. Blight, Bruce J. Allyn, and David A. Welch (Lanham, MD: Rowman & Littlefield, 2002) and *Sad and Luminous Days: Cuba's Struggle With the Superpowers After the Missile Crisis,* James G. Blight and Philip Brenner (Lanham, MD: Rowman & Littlefield, 2002) are reprinted with the permission of Rowman & Littlefield.

Letters from Japanese survivors of the U.S. firebombing during World War II, reprinted in Chapter Four, are from *Senso: The Japanese Remember the Pacific War. Letters to the Editor of Asahi Shimbun,* ed. Frank Gibney; trans. Beth Cary (Armonk, NY: M.E. Sharpe, 1995). English translation copyright © 1995 by the Pacific Basin Institute. Reprinted with permission of M.E. Sharpe, Inc."

Passages in Chapters Two and Four are from *Iron Eagle* by Thomas M. Coffey, copyright [add copyright symbol] by Thomas M. Coffey. Used by permission of Crown Publishers, a division of Random House, Inc.

Passages in Chapter Four are from *The Night of the New Moon* by Laurens van der Post published by Hogarth Press. Used by permission of The Random House Group Limited."

In Chapter Five, the selections from Noam Chomsky and James K. Galbraith are used by permission of the authors. Copyright 2004 by Noam Chomsky. His piece first appeared in the *Boston Review* (December 2003/January 2004), http://bostonreview.net>. Copyright 2003 and 2004 by James K. Galbraith. His pieces first appeared in the *Boston Review* (October/November 2003 and December 2003/January 2004), http://bostonreview.net>.

Articles, Interviews, and Film Reviews reprinted in Chapter Six

"Robert McNamara, Errol Morris Return to Berkeley to Share Lessons Learned from 'The Fog of War'" by Bonnie Azab Powell. Copyright © University of California regents 2004. First published in the UC Berkeley NewsCenter on February 5, 2004. Reprinted with permission.

"Interview with Errol Morris" by Terry Gross, January 5, 2004. *Fresh Air with Terry Gross,* produced in Philadelphia by WHYY. Reprinted with permission.

"Soul on Ice" by Sydney Schanberg. Reprinted with permission from *The American Prospect*, Volume 14, Number 10: November 01, 2003. The American Prospect, 11 Beacon Street, Suite 1120, Boston, MA 02108. All rights reserved."

"The Fog around Robert McNamara" by David Talbot. This article first appeared in Salon.com, at http://www.Salon.com. An online version remains in the Salon archives. Reprinted with permission.

"'Fog of War' Recalls One Man's Ultimate Protest, and Gives His Widow Hope it Changed One Mind" by Carl Schoettler. Reprinted with permission from *The Baltimore Sun*, February 29, 2004.

"A Remorseless Apology for the Horrors of Vietnam" by Andrew Lam. Reprinted with permission from The Copyright Clearance Center and *The San Francisco Chronicle*, February 2, 2004.

"War and Never Having to Say You're Sorry" by Samantha Power. Copyright © 2003 by The New York Times Co. Reprinted with permission.

Epigraph

1. Milan Kundera, *Testaments Betrayed*. Quoted in Richard Byrne, "Lyndon Agonistes," *The American Prospect*, August 2004, pp. 46–49, p. 49.

Authors' Note

1. Even those who don't ignore the history can get it wrong. For example, the G. W. Bush administration's determination to create a new generation of U.S. nuclear forces, in the absence of the East-West Cold War, seems to us to run counter to one implication of the Cuban missile crisis: reduce your forces so that if mistakes are made and escalation occurs, you don't "destroy nations." Make sure the forces are so small that it is impossible to inflict irremediable damage. Likewise, the comparisons that have been made between the war in Vietnam and the war in Iraq are too numerous to cite. Suffice it to say that in Iraq, as in Vietnam, the U.S. intervened (with tragic results) without adequately understanding the local context in which it would be operating.

2. Quoted in James G. Blight, *The Shattered Crystal Ball: Fear and Learning in the Cuban Missile Crisis* (Lanham, MD, Rowman & Littlefield Publishers, Inc., 1990), p. 55.

Prologue

1. The full texts of the eleven lessons Errol Morris derives from the life of Robert McNamara are found in Susan Graseck, James G. Blight and janet M. Lang, *Official Teacher's Guide for "The Fog of War," an Errol Morris Film*, p. 5. The guide can be downloaded from either of two websites: The movie's official website, constructed by Sony Pictures Classics, the film's principal underwriter, at www.fogofwarmovie.com; or that of the The Choices for the 21st Century Education Program at Brown University's Watson Institute for International Studies, at www.choices.edu/fogofwar. McNamara's own lessons, which are somewhat more elaborate than those Morris draws, may also be found at www.choices.edu/fogofwar.

2. This section is adapted from, Graseck, Blight and Lang, *Official Teacher's Guide to "The Fog of War,"* p. 3, Synopsis.

3. Roger Ebert, "McNamara Takes Turn in Hot Seat," *Chicago Sun-Times*, May 23, 2003.

4. Stephen Holden, "Revisiting McNamara and the War He Headed," *New York Times*, October 11, 2003, pp. B9, B17.

5. See chapter 6 in this book, especially the "dilemma" at the end of the chapter, for more on some implications of Kierkegaard's characterization of the two kinds of knowledge.

6. On the method of critical oral history as we have applied it to the Cuban missile crisis, see Len Scott and Steve Smith, "Lessons of October: Historians, Political Scientists, Policy-makers and the Cuban Missile Crisis," *International Affairs* 70 (October 1994), 659–684. On the January 1992 Havana conference (co-sponsored by the Watson Institute for International Studies at Brown University, the National Security Archive at George Washington University, and the Center for the Study of the Americas, Havana, Cuba), see J. Anthony Lukas, "Fidel Castro's Theater of Now," *New York Times*, January 20, 1992, E-17; and Arthur M. Schlesinger, Jr., "Four Days With Fidel: A Havana Diary," *New York Review of Books*, March 26, 1992, 22–29. On the October 2002 conference in Havana, see: Norman Boucher, "October, 1962: What Really Happened," *Brown Alumni Magazine*, January/February, 2003, 28–35; and Marcella Bombardieri, "Brothers in Arms: Forty years after the Cuban missile crisis, old combatants make new friends (and enemies)," *Boston Sunday Globe*, October 20, 2002.

On the application of the method to the study of the war in Vietnam, see especially David K. Shipler, "Robert McNamara and the Ghosts of Vietnam," *New York Times Magazine*, August 10, 1997, pp. 30–35, 42, 50, 56–57; and Norman Boucher, "Thinking Like the Enemy," *Brown Alumni Magazine*, November/December, 1997, 36–45. In addition, several documentary films have been made based on the June 1997 Hanoi conference (co-sponsored by the Watson Institute for International Studies at Brown University, the National Security Archive at George Washington University, and the Institute of International Relations, Ministry of Foreign Affairs, Hanoi, Vietnam), including: "Dialogue of Enemies in Vietnam," produced by Daisaku Higashi for NHK–Japan, which aired on August 6, 1998; "Fighting Blind: The Vietnam War," produced by Pamela Benson for CNN and narrated by Ralph Begleiter, which aired December 23, 1997; and "Cuba: The Other Side of Armageddon," produced for the BBC by Ross Wilson and Jacqui Hayden, which aired on October 12, 2002.

7. The basic source on everything related to the January 1992 Havana conference is: James G. Blight, Bruce J. Allyn and David A. Welch, *Cuba on the Brink: Castro, the Missile Crisis and the Soviet Collapse*, expanded paperback ed. (Lanham: MD: Rowman & Littlefield, 2002). It contains the complete, annotated and explicated transcript of the conference, along with an analysis of the political context in U.S–Cuban relations in which the conference took place. See also: James G. Blight and Philip Brenner, *Sad and Luminous Days: Cuba's Struggle with the Superpowers After the Missile Crisis* (Lanham, MD: Rowman & Littlefield, 2002). This contains the text of a fascinating secret

speech Fidel Castro gave to the Cuban leadership in January 1968, on Soviet actions in the missile crisis. Castro declassified the speech at the January 1992 Havana conference (co-sponsored by the Watson Institute for International Studies at Brown University, the National Security Archive at George Washington University, and the Center for the Study of the Americas, Havana, Cuba), during one of his interventions, and subsequently the Cuban government gave the authors both the original Spanish version, and an official English translation of the speech. See also chapters 1 and 2 in this book.

8. The basic source for the June 1997 conference in Hanoi (co-sponsored by the Watson Institute for International Studies at Brown University, the National Security Archive at George Washington University, and the Institute of International Relations, Ministry of Foreign Affairs, Hanoi, Vietnam) is Robert S. McNamara, James G. Blight and Robert K. Brigham, with Thomas J. Biersteker and Col. Herbert Y. Schandler, *Argument Without End: In Search of Answers to the Vietnam Tragedy* (New York: PublicAffairs, 1999). Aspects of the material are also dealt with in this book, in chapters 1, 3 and 5.

9. Ibid., pp. 205–212.

10. Robert S. McNamara and James G. Blight, *Wilson's Ghost: Reducing the Risk of Conflict, Killing and Catastrophe in the 21st Century* (New York: Public-Affairs, 2001). A second, expanded, post–9/11 paperback edition was published by PublicAffairs in 2003.

11. See the "Epilogue" to this book for a consideration of Robert McNamara *as* Wilson's Ghost.

12. The first set of Errol Morris' interviews with Robert McNamara was on May 1–2, 2001; the second set was on December 11–12, 2001; and the third was on April 1–2, 2002.

13. This section is adapted from Susan Graseck, James G. Blight and janet M. Lang, *Official Teacher's Guide for "The Fog of War,"* p. 22, Behind the Scenes.

14. For example, in a project on the collapse of U.S.–Soviet detente during the Carter-Brezhnev period in the late 1970s, we had to decide whether to invite former President Jimmy Carter to participate, face-to-face, with the other members of his administration, and with their Russian counterparts. It became clear that both sides—but particularly the U.S. side—would have been constrained by Carter's presence. In the end, we did not invite Carter to participate "at the table," but instead we briefed him following each major conference, and got his feedback—which was detailed and informative. We have also been told by many former members of the Kennedy and Johnson administrations that they would have felt similarly constrained if either JFK or LBJ had been present "at the table."

The limiting case of this problem has occurred during the three conferences we have organized in Havana—two on the Cuban missile crisis, and one on the Bay of Pigs invasion—in which Cuban President Fidel Castro participated fully "at the table." It is clear that all the other Cubans present await their cues from their president, who is famously expansive. Yet we also feel this trade-off has been more than worth it. Castro's memory is prodigious, and he knows things no other Cuban knows. Moreover, a surprise: in the critical oral history setting, he is remarkably amenable to interruptions, for example by people seeking clarification, or even by instructions from the chair that it is time to let others speak. We have been told by Cuban colleagues that this has never happened in Cuba, except in the critical oral history conferences.

15. We are grateful to Prof. Steve Smith of the Department of Politics, University of Wales, Aberystwyth, for raising a number of these issues at a July 1998 conference in Bellagio, Italy. See also Danny Postel, "Revisiting the Brink: The Architect of 'Critical Oral History' Sheds New Light on the Cold War," *Chronicle of Higher Education*, October 18, 2002.

16. Oliver Cromwell, quoted in Jacob Bronowski, *The Ascent of Man* (Boston: Little, Brown, 1974), p. 374.

17. Robert S. McNamara, *In Retrospect: The Tragedy and Lessons of Vietnam*, expanded paperback ed. (New York: Times Books, 1996), p. xx. The original hardcover edition appeared in April, 1995.

18. Ibid., p. xx.

19. With the publication of *In Retrospect* in 1995, McNamara broke a decades-long vow never to write about the Vietnam War. This was followed in 1999 with McNamara, Blight, and Robert K. Brigham, et. al, *Argument without End* which records and analyzes several meetings between U.S. and North Vietnamese civilian and military leaders. McNamara drew the lessons of his life and research into issues of war and peace in *Wilson's Ghost* (written with James G. Blight). "The Fog of War" draws on all three books, and on much else besides, including his experience in the Second World War and, from 1945 to 1960, at the Ford Motor Company. As always, critics focused on the war in Vietnam, McNamara's central role in it, and much speculation about why he continued to revisit the tragedy so often, and so publicly. See, on this point, the essay by Samantha Power in chapter 6 of this book.

20. Philip Dunn, *The Art of Peace: Balance Over Conflict in Sun Tzu's "The Art of War"* (New York: Tarcher/Putnam, 2003), pp. 53–54. This fascinating book includes excerpts from Sun Tzu's original, translated and interpreted by Dunn. He offers a timely corrective to the received wisdom concerning Sun Tzu—that his writings contain advice on how to defeat an opponent. According to Philip Dunn, one finds far more emphasis on preventing conflict, chiefly via self-knowledge, leading to empathetic curiosity with regard to potential antagonists which in many (though not necessarily all) cases, permits meaningful communication and compromise, rather than conflict. On this theme, see also Shannon E. French, *The Code of the Warrior: Exploring Warrior Values Past and Present* (Lanham, MD: Rowman & Littlefield, 2003), especially pp. 179–198, on "Chinese Warrior Monks: The Martial Artists of Shaolin." As French writes, "the Shaolin warrior's code is truly exceptional in that its intention is to produce warriors who have no interest in making war" (p. 197).

21. The Vietnam War still matters greatly. Critics on one side still insist that the U.S. should have, and would have, "won," if only the U.S. military had been allowed to use the full extent of its power (presumably including the use of nuclear weapons, if necessary). Others remain convinced that the fundamental error was sending U.S. combat forces in the first place and making this America's war. Vietnam, and its relevance to the war in Iraq was hotly debated during the 2004 U.S. presidential campaign. See especially the fine essay by Jackson Lears, "Why the Vietnam War Still Matters," in *In These Times*, October 22, 2004, online edition at: www.inthesetimes.com/site/main/article/1421/. In contrast, David Gelernter believes that "If this [Iraq] be Vietnam, make the most of it. Let's do it right this time." His piece is in *The Weekly Standard*, October 11, 2004, online edition at www.weeklystandard.com/Utilities/printer_ preview.asp?id/Article. On the historical issue of whether the U.S. military could have "won" in any realistic sense, see Herbert Y. Schandler, "U.S. Military Victory in Vietnam: A Dangerous Illusion?" This is chapter 7 in McNamara, Blight and Brigham et al., *Argument Without End*. Schandler, who served two tours of duty in Vietnam and is an eminent military historian, concludes that "victory" was impossible, short of a political decision to, in essence, attack North Vietnam with genocidal force, an act which he regards as morally unthinkable, and at any rate likely to have drawn the Chinese in and widened the war. See also a dialogue between Col. Schandler and Col. Quach Hai Luong, the former commander of antiaircraft batteries protecting Hanoi during the war, and now the deputy director of a military think tank in Hanoi. "The colonels" spoke at a lunch break during a critical oral history conference in Hanoi, February, 1998. Their dialogue is reprinted in chapter 1.

22. The figure 1,324 is from the December 28, 2004 posting on www.defenselink.mil/news. See also www.icasualties.org for a breakdown of deaths of all coalition forces in Iraq. For the Iraqi story, see Les Roberts, Riyadh Lafta, Richard Garfield, Jamal Khudhairi, and Gilbert Burnham, "Mortality before and after the 2003 invasion of Iraq: cluster sample survey," *The Lancet*, vol. 364, issue 9448, (2004), pp. 1857-1864; posted online on October 29, 2004, at: http://image.thelancet.com/extras/04art10342web.pdf. Three commentaries accompanied the Roberts et al. study: Richard Horton, "The War in Iraq: Civilian Casualties, Political Responsibilities," p. 1831; Sheila M. Bird, "Military and public-health sciences need to ally," pp. 1832-1833; and Bushra Ibraham Al-Rubeyi, "Mortality before and after the Invasion of Iraq in 2003," p. 1834. While asserting that they keep no count of Iraqi deaths (civilian or insurgent), the governments of the U.S. and the UK disputed the estimate from the Roberts et al. study. For a thoughtful review of the *Lancet* study, with comparisons to other methods of counting civilian casualties (such as the British-based group, www.iraqbodycount.net, which has estimated the death toll at roughly 15,000), see Christopher Shea, "Countless," *Boston Globe*, November 7, 2004, p. D5.

23. Richard Horton, "The War in Iraq: Civilian Casualties, Political Respon-

sibilities," *The Lancet*, vol. 364, issue 9448, (2004), p. 1831; posted online on October 29, 2004, at http://image.thelancet.co/extras/o4cmt364web.pdf.

Chapter 1

1. Ralph K. White, *Fearful Warriors: A Psychological Profile of U.S.–Soviet Relations* (New York: Free Press, 1984), p. 160, emphasis in original.

2. Ibid., p. 161, emphasis in the original.

3. Ibid., pp. 162–163. See also Robert S. McNamara and James G. Blight, *Wilson's Ghost: Reducing the Risk of Conflict, Killing and Catastrophe in the 21st Century*, expanded paperback ed. (New York: PublicAffairs, 2003), pp. 66–73, from which the material on Ralph White is adapted. More recently, we have traced the connection between Ralph White's work and Robert McNamara's views on foreign and defense policy. See James G. Blight and janet M. Lang, "Lesson Number One: 'Empathize With Your Enemy.'" *Peace and Conflict*, in press, 2005.

4. Ernest R. May and Philip D. Zelikow, eds., *The Kennedy Tapes: Inside the White House During the Cuban Missile Crisis* (Cambridge, MA: Harvard University Press, 1997), p. 499, emphasis in original.

5. Ibid., p. 554.

6. To understand better why McNamara described the writer of the letter as either "drunk, or under tremendous stress" and also the retrospective view that Khrushchev's letter poignantly describes the awesome feeling of responsibility for being at the brink of nuclear war, see see Sergei N. Khrushchev, *Nikita Khrushchev and the Creation of a Superpower* (University Park, PA: The Pennsylvannia State University Press, 2000). The author provides an illuminating description of the situation in the Kremlin when his father drafted the letter (pp. 584–585), later met with his advisors to review and revise the letter (pp. 588–589), the conditions related to sending the letter (p. 589), as well as its receipt in Washington (p. 592). Delays in the transmission of the letter resulted in the letter arriving in Washington in sections—but the sections were out of order!

7. The source is the late Richard E. Neustadt of Harvard University, who told us that he heard it directly from President Kennedy shortly after the crisis. According to Neustadt, the 26 October letter from Khrushchev was proof to Kennedy that he and Khrushchev were "in the same boat," trying to find an exit from the crisis before being overwhelmed by the onrush of events.

8. Laurence Chang and Peter Kornbluh, eds., *The Cuban Missile Crisis, 1962: A National Security Archive Documents Reader*, revised ed. (New York: The New Press, 1998), pp. 195–198.

9. For a glimpse inside the Kremlin during the missile crisis, see Sergei Khrushchev, *Nikita Khrushchev*, especially pp. 579–603 for an authoritative account of Khrushchev's thoughts and actions regarding the two letters he sent

to Kennedy. See also Aleksander Fursenko and Timothy Naftali, *"One Hell of a Gamble:" Khrushchev, Castro, and Kennedy, 1958–1964* (New York: Norton, 1997), where an argument is presented that "[i]n Soviet eyes the Jupiters legitimated the missiles in Cuba" (p. 196).

10. Chang and Kornbluh, eds., *The Cuban Missile Crisis, 1962*, pp. 207–209.

11. Ibid., pp. 233–235.

12. Ibid., pp. 236–239.

13. Ibid., pp. 240–242.

14. James G. Blight and David A. Welch, *On the Brink: Americans and Soviets Reexamine the Cuban Missile Crisis*, 2nd ed. (New York: Hill and Wang/Farrar, Straus & Giroux, 1990), pp. 249–250, emphasis in original.

15. Bruce J. Allyn, James G. Blight, and David A. Welch, eds., *Back to the Brink: Proceedings of the Moscow Conference on the Cuban Missile Crisis, January 27–28, 1989* (Lanham, MD: University Press of America, 1992), p. 7–9, 14.

16. Nguyen Duy Trinh, cited in Robert S. McNamara, James G. Blight and Robert K. Brigham, with Thomas J. Biersteker and Col. Herbert Y. Schandler, *Argument Without End: In Search of Answers to the Vietnam Tragedy* (New York: PublicAffairs, 1999), p. 278.

17. Lyndon Baines Johnson, *The Vantage Point: Perspectives on the Presidency, 1963–1969* (New York: Holt, Rinehart and Winston, 1971), pp. 592–593.

18. Ibid., pp. 594–595.

19. Ibid., p. 596.

20. McNamara, Blight and Brigham et al., *Argument without End*, pp. 193–195, emphasis in original.

21. Robert S. McNamara, *In Retrospect: The Tragedy and Lessons of Vietnam*, expanded paperback ed. (New York: Vintage, 1996). The hardback was published in April 1995.

22. McNamara, Blight, and Brigham et al., *Argument without End*, pp. 254–256, emphasis in original.

Chapter 2

1. The literature deriving from the Cuban missile crisis project, in which McNamara has been a central participant, is vast. An introduction to both the findings and the method of critical oral history used in the investigation of the crisis may be found in the following: James G. Blight, *The Shattered Crystal Ball: Fear and Learning in the Cuban Missile Crisis*, foreword by Joseph S. Nye, Jr. (Lanham, MD: Roman & Littlefield, 1990); James G. Blight and David A. Welch, *On the Brink: Americans and Soviets Reexamine the Cuban Missile Crisis*, rev. paperback ed. (New York: Hill and Wang, 1990); James G. Blight,

Bruce J. Allyn and David A. Welch, *Cuba on the Brink: Castro, the Missile Crisis and the Soviet Collapse*, expanded paperback ed. (Lanham, MD: Rowman and Littlefield, 2002); James G. Blight and Philip Brenner, *Sad and Luminous Days: Cuba's Struggle With the Superpowers After the Missile Crisis* (Lanham, MD: Rowman and Littlefield, 2002); and James G. Blight and David A. Welch, eds., *Intelligence and the Cuban Missile Crisis* (London: Frank Cass, 1998). In addition, the Soviet side of the equation has been greatly clarified by Gen. Anatoly I. Gribkov and Gen. William Y. Smith, *Operation Anadyr: U.S. and Soviet Generals Recount the Cuban Missile Crisis*, ed. by Alfred Friendly, Jr., foreword by Michael Beschloss (Chicago: Edition Q, 1994); Aleksandr Fursenko and Timothy Naftali, *"One Hell of a Gamble": Khrushchev, Castro, & Kennedy, 1958–1964* (New York: Norton, 1997); and Sergei N. Khrushchev, *Nikita Khrushchev and the Creation of a Superpower* (University Park, PA: The Pennsylvania State University Press, 2000).

2. The literature from which McNamara draws this conclusion is summarized in James G. Blight and janet M. Lang, "Burden of Nuclear Responsibility: Reflections on the Critical Oral History of the Cuban Missile Crisis," *Peace and Conflict*, Vol. 1, No. 3 (1995), pp. 225–264. See also Blight, Allyn and Welch, *Cuba on the Brink*; and Blight and Brenner, *Sad and Luminous Days*. Both *Cuba on the Brink* and *Sad and Luminous Days* address what had long been *terra incognita* to U.S. scholars, the nature of the Soviet–Cuban relationship before, during and after the missile crisis.

3. The notion of the evolution of situational perversity was introduced into the literature in Blight, *The Shattered Crystal Ball*, especially pp. 107–116.

4. U.S. intelligence never confirmed that nuclear warheads had, in fact, already arrived in Cuba before the U.S. quarantine was set up. Some, though far from all, analysts and policy-makers prudently assumed their presence on the island. McNamara states in "The Fog of War," that "[i]t wasn't until January, 1992, in a meeting chaired by Castro in Havana, Cuba, that I learned 162 nuclear warheads, including 90 tactical warheads, were on the island at the time of this critical moment of the crisis." (He is referring to the critical oral history conference co-sponsored by the Watson Institute for International Studies at Brown University, the National Security Archive at George Washington University, and the Center for the Study of the Americas, Havana, Cuba.) U.S. intelligence also underestimated, by orders of magnitude, the size of the Soviet military force on the island. Again, it was only in 1992, at that same critical oral history conference in Havana, that we learned that there were over 40,000 troops there, rather than 8–10,000. With a U.S. airstrike, followed by an invasion, there was undoubtedly the risk that Soviet commanders in Cuba would use the tactical nuclear weapons against U.S. troops as they approached the beaches of Cuba. See Blight and Welch, *Cuba on the Brink*, pp. 54–71; Blight and Welch, eds., *Intelligence and the Cuban Missile Crisis*, pp. 26–31. See also Thomas S. Blanton and James G. Blight, "A Conversation in Havana," *Arms Control Today*, pp. 6–7 where Nikolai S. Leonov, chief of the KGB's Depart-

ment of Cuban Affairs for thirty years, Georgy M. Kornienko, former first deputy foreign minister of the U.S.S.R., and Robert McNamara discuss the danger of escalation during the crisis.

5. Timothy Naftali and Philip D. Zelikow, eds., *The Presidential Recordings, John F. Kennedy: The Great Crises*, vol. 2 (New York: Norton, 2001), pp. 584–598. A helpful narrative summary of this discussion may be found in Sheldon M. Stern, *Averting the "Final Failure": John F. Kennedy and the Secret Cuban Missile Crisis Meetings* (Stanford, CA: Stanford University Press, 2003), pp. 121–129.

6. The missile crisis correspondence between Fidel Castro and Nikita Khrushchev was published by the Cubans in November 1990, just prior to a U.S.–Soviet–Cuban "critical oral history" conference on the crisis on the Caribbean island of Antigua, which took place in early January 1991, and was co-sponsored by the Watson Institute for International Studies at Brown University, the National Security Archive at George Washington University, and the Center for the Study of the Americas, Havana, Cuba. The full correspondence, corroborated against both the Cuban and Soviet archival copies, first appeared in the U.S. as an appendix to Blight, Allyn and Welch, *Cuba on the Brink*, pp. 474–491. The letter of October 26, 1962 from Castro to Khrushchev cited in the text is on pp. 481–482. See also James G. Blight, janet M. Lang and Aaron Belkin, "Why Castro Released the Armageddon Letters," *Miami Herald*, January 20, 1991, Sunday Supplement, p. 1.

7. The quotation from Aleksandr Alekseev's cable of October 26–27 from Havana to Khrushchev is in Blight and Lang, "Burden of Nuclear Responsibility," 225–264, p. 238. The existence of the document was first revealed at the January 1991 conference on the missile crisis in Antigua by Oleg Darusenkov, a long time Cuba specialist within the Soviet Foreign Ministry and Central Committee of the Communist Party of the Soviet Union.

8. Ernesto "Che" Guevara, quoted in Carla Anne Robbins, *The Cuban Threat* (New York: McGraw-Hill, 1983), p. 47. See also James G. Blight and David A. Welch, "Risking 'The Destruction of Nations': Lessons of the Cuban Missile Crisis for New and Aspiring Nuclear States," *Security Studies*, Vol. 4, No. 4 (Summer 1995), pp. 811–850, especially pp. 841–845; and Blight and Brenner, *Sad and Luminous Days*, pp. 73–84.

9. Blight, Allyn and Welch, *Cuba on the Brink*, pp. 509–510.

10. See Sergei Khrushchev, *Nikita Khrushchev and the Creation of a Superpower*, pp. 26–32 for further details.

11. Blight, Allyn and Welch, *Cuba on the Brink*, pp. 510–511.

12. Fidel Castro to Anastas Mikoyan, November 19, 1962. Quoted in Blight and Brenner, *Sad and Luminous Days*, p. 79.

13. Anastas Mikoyan to Fidel Castro. Quoted in Ibid., p. 80.

14. Ernesto ("Che") Guevara, comment to Anastacio Cruz Mancilla, November 13, 1964. Quoted in ibid., p. 81.

15. Blight, Allyn and Welch, *Cuba on the Brink*, pp. 517–519.

16. The entire text of the Five Points may be found in ibid., p. 508.

17. Different names for the crisis reflect the divergent national perspectives on the event. To the U.S., the *Cuban missile crisis* connotes that the problem was the placement of missiles in Cuba; to the Soviet Union, the *Caribbean crisis* indicates that in their view, it was not "the missiles" that caused the crisis, but U.S. aggression in the Caribbean; to Cuba, the *October crisis* implies that this was just one of many crises with the U.S.—it is the one that happened to come in October. For further analysis of the "three crises/three names" phenomenon, see Blight and Brenner, *Sad and Luminous Days*, pp. 1–31. This trichotomy of crises was first noted in Bruce J. Allyn, James G. Blight, and David A. Welch, "Essence of Revision: Moscow, Havana, and the Cuban Missile Crisis." *International Security* 14, no.3 (winter 1989/90), pp. 136–172.

18. Fidel Castro to U Thant, November 15, 1962. In Blight and Brenner, *Sad and Luminous Days*, pp. 210–213.

19. These comments were made by Nikolai Leonev, the former long time chief KGB officer with responsibility for Cuba, who was present in Havana, when, during the crisis, the Soviets changed their uniforms. See Thomas S. Blanton and James G. Blight, "A Conversation in Havana," *Arms Control Today*, November 2002, pp. 6–7.

20. Blight, Allyn and Welch, *Cuba on the Brink,* pp. 108–109.

21. One of us (JGB) was personally involved with these U.S.–Russian efforts to reduce the risk of nuclear war: The Project on Avoiding Nuclear War, at the Belfer Center for Science and International Affairs, at Harvard's Kennedy School of Government. See especially the following volumes that issued from that project: Albert Carnesale, Paul Doty, Stanley Hoffmann, Samuel P. Huntington, Joseph S. Nye, Jr., and Scott D. Sagan, *Living With Nuclear Weapons* (New York: Bantam, 1983); Graham Allison, Albert Carnesale and Joseph S. Nye, Jr., eds., *Hawks, Doves & Owls: An Agenda for Avoiding Nuclear War* (New York: Norton, 1985); Joseph S. Nye, Jr., *Nuclear Ethics* (New York: Free Press, 1986); and James G. Blight, *The Shattered Crystal Ball: Fear and Learning in the Cuban Missile Crisis* (Lanham, MD: Rowman & Littlefield, 1990).

22. Blight, Allyn and Welch, *Cuba on the Brink,* pp. 250–253.

23. Blight, Allyn and Welch, *Cuba on the Brink,* pp. 255–256.

24. Gen. Maxwell Taylor, videotaped interview with Richard E. Neustadt, June 1983. Quoted in Blight, *Shattered Crystal Ball*, p. 74.

25. Thomas M. Coffey, *Iron Eagle: The Turbulent Life of General Curtis LeMay* (New York: Crown, 1986), pp. 369–372, 391–392. Coffey interviewed LeMay for more than 100 hours in the preparation of this quasi-"official" biography. All quotes are from Coffey, as indicated in the endnotes. The bulk of material quoted below from LeMay is from an interview LeMay gave to Coffey on February 2, 1984 at LeMay's home in Newport Beach, CA.

26. Gen. Curtis E. LeMay (with Mackinlay Kantor), *Mission With LeMay*

(Garden City, NY: Doubleday, 1965), p. 8. Quoted in Ibid., pp. 369–370.

27. LeMay, *Mission With LeMay*, quoted in ibid., p. 8.

28. General Curtis LeMay, interview with Thomas M. Coffey, February 2, 1984, Newport Beach, CA. Quote in Coffey, *Iron Eagle*, p. 372.

29. Ibid., pp. 372–373.

30. Ibid., pp. 392–393.

Chapter 3

1. NSAM 273, cited in Robert S. McNamara, *In Retrospect: The Tragedy and Lessons of Vietnam*, expanded paperback ed. (New York: Vintage, 1996), pp. 102–103.

2. Maxwell D. Taylor to Dean Rusk, 3 August 1964. Cited in Michael Beschloss, ed., *Taking Charge: The Johnson White House Tapes, 1963–1964* (New York: Simon & Schuster, 1997), p. 493.

3. The phrase "probable but not certain" is McNamara's. See *In Retrospect*, p. 128.

4. This section is adapted from Robert S. McNamara, James G. Blight and Robert K. Brigham, with Thomas J. Biersteker and Col. Herbert Y. Schandler, *Argument Without End: In Search of Answers to the Vietnam Tragedy* (New York: PublicAffairs, 1999), pp. 165–167. For additional documents and commentary related to the events in the Gulf of Tonkin in August 1964, see John Prados, ed., "Gulf of Tonkin Incident, 40 Years Later: Flawed Intelligence and the Decision for War in Vietnam," National Security Archive Electronic Briefing Book #131, available online at www.gwu.edu/~nsarchiv/ (under the U.S. Intelligence Community, in the Documents section). See also Edwin E. Moise, *Tonkin Gulf and the Escalation of the Vietnam War* (Chapel Hill, NC: University of North Carolina Press, 1996).

5. These excerpts are from Beschloss, ed., *Taking Charge*, pp. 494–495, 498, and 509–510. This is the first volume of a projected multi-volume series, expertly but unobtrusively edited by Michael Beschloss. In the volumes published so far, the personality of LBJ, and his manner of interacting with his advisers, comes through in all its richness, caginess and humor.

6. Ibid., pp. 494–495.

7. Admiral Ulysses S. Grant Sharp was the Commander in Chief of the Central Command in the Pacific, or CINCPAC. In the telephone conversations, he is referred to by his nickname, "Ollie."

8. Beschloss, ed., *Taking Charge*, p. 498.

9. "The ICC" refers to the International Control Commission, a three-person body created by the Geneva Accords of 1954, consisting of one diplomat each from a communist country, a noncommunist Western country, and a neutral. At key points throughout the 1960s, the ICC was involved behind the

scenes—one Pole, one Canadian and one Indian—in trying to get all sides to the negotiating table. Typically, members of the ICC were the only people allowed to fly directly from Saigon to Hanoi and vice versa.

10. Beschloss, ed., *Taking Charge,* pp. 509–510.

11. These formerly classified telephone logs were obtained from the Lyndon B. Johnson Presidential Library, Austin, Texas. These "raw data" yield a good deal of insight into the ad hoc nature of the decision to launch an air strike against North Vietnam, at the operational level.

12. Lyndon B. Johnson, "Radio and Television Report to the American People Following Renewed Aggression in the Gulf of Tonkin." In *Public Papers of the Presidents,* 1963–64, 2 vols. (Washington, DC: U.S. Government Printing Office, 1965), vol. 2, pp. 927–928.

13. "Joint Resolution of the Maintenance of Peace and Security in Southeast Asia." Reprinted in Susan Graseck, James G. Blight and janet M. Lang, *Official Teacher's Guide for "The Fog of War,"* p. 12. (Available at www.choices.edu/fogofwar, and www.fogofwarmovie.com. The document can be downloaded from either website.)

14. *The Great Anti-U.S. Resistance War for National Salvation of the Fatherland, 1954–1975—Military Events [Cuoc Khang Chien Chong My, Cuu Nuoc, 1954–1975]* (Hanoi: Nha Xuat Ban Doi Nhan Dan, 1988), p. 61. See also McNamara, Blight and Brigham et al., *Argument without End,* p. 185.

15. *The Great Anti-U.S. Resistance War,* p. 60. While not lacking in overheated anti-imperialist rhetoric, this chronology of military events, assembled by officials and scholars in Hanoi, with an official English translation by the Vietnamese government, offers a good deal of insight into Hanoi's perceptions (including its misperceptions) of U.S. motives and capabilities during the escalation of the U.S. war. See also, McNamara, Blight and Brigham, *Argument without End,* pp. 184–186.

16. *The Great Anti-U.S. Resistance War,* p. 60. See also William S. Turley, *The Second Indochina War: A Short Political and Military History,* 1954–1975 (Boulder, CO: Westview/NAL, 1986), pp. 60–61.

17. Bao Ninh, *The Sorrow of War: A Novel of North Vietnam,* trans. by Phan Tanh Hao, ed. by Frank Palmos (New York: Pantheon, 1993), pp. 226, 232.

18. McNamara, Blight and Brigham et al., *Argument without End,* pp. 23–24. This is an excerpt from the transcript of the audio-taped exchange between Robert McNamara and Gen. Vo Nguyen Giap, Ministry of Defense, Hanoi, Vietnam, 9 November 1995. Translation by Pham Sanh Chau.

19. Ibid., pp. 202–205.

Chapter 4

1. Studs Terkel, *"The Good War": An Oral History of World War Two* (New York: Pantheon, 1991). See also Tom Brokaw, *The Greatest Generation* (New

York: Random House, 1998); and *An Album of Memories: Personal Histories from the Greatest Generation* (New York: Random House, 2001). Among the many other examples are the Stephen Spielberg film "Saving Private Ryan," and the TV series "Band of Brothers."

2. This cartoon also provides the title of one of the most illuminating books ever written on the Pacific War, by the MIT historian John Dower, *War Without Mercy: Race and Power in the Pacific War* (New York: Pantheon, 1986). The cartoon, by Carey Orr in the *Chicago Tribune*, appears on p. 181 of Dower's book.

3. Ibid., p. 180.

4. Terkel, *"The Good War,"* pp. 107–108. The issue played by racism is dealt with definitively by Dower, in *War without Mercy*. See also Ronald Takaki, *Hiroshima: Why America Dropped the Atomic Bomb* (Boston: Little, Brown, 1995).

5. See Michael Walzer, *Just and Unjust Wars*, 2nd ed. (New York: Basic Books, 1992), pp. 255–268. Walzer states that, regarding the decision to bomb German cities, "There have been few decisions more important than this one in the history of warfare" (p. 255).

6. See Peter Calvocoressi, Guy Wint and John Pritchard, *The Penguin History of the Second World War* (London: Penguin, 1999), pp. 519–520. This brilliant history of the war was first published in 1972, and has been updated in several editions since then. It is the best one-volume history of the war we have encountered. On the firebombing of Dresden, see the recent book by Frederick Taylor, *Dresden: Tuesday February 13, 1945* (New York: Harper-Collins, 2004). See also the novel by the German-American writer Kurt Vonnegut, Jr., *Slaughterhouse-Five: The Children's Crusade, a Duty-Dance with Death* (New York: Dell, 1968). Vonnegut survived the firebombing of Dresden as a German prisoner-of-war because at the moment the firebombs hit Dresden, he was being held, along with several dozen others, underground in what had been a slaughterhouse for pigs. It is not always easy to follow the twists and turns of the "magic realism" of this singular American novelist. But he has few equals in his ability to convey not only the horror of war, but also the absurdities that are uttered and written to justify the slaughter.

7. McNamara first posed this question in print in the context of intervention into communal conflicts, such as Bosnia or Rwanda, in order to prevent genocide. See Robert S. McNamara and James G. Blight, *Wilson's Ghost: Reducing the Risk of Conflict, Killing and Conflict in the 21st Century*, expanded, post-9/11, pb. ed. (New York: PublicAffairs, 2003), especially pp. 122–131.

8. Calvocoressi et al., *Penguin History of the Second World War*, p. 1174.

9. Dower, *War without Mercy*, pp. 40–41.

10. E. Bartlett Kerr, *Flames Over Tokyo: The U.S. Army Air Forces' Incendiary Campaign Against Japan, 1944–1945* (New York: Donald I. Fine, 1991), pp. 324–325.

11. This declassified memorandum was obtained from the National Archives, Washington, DC. We especially thank Errol Morris and Adam Kosberg for bringing it to our attention.

12. Hannah Arendt, *Eichmann in Jerusalem: A Report on the Banality of Evil*, rev. ed. (Hammondsworth, Eng.: Penguin, 1977), pp. 287–288. The book first appeared as a five-part essay in *The New Yorker* in 1963, and was published in enlarged book form in 1965. The citation is to the paperback edition of the 1977 revised text.

13. Frank Gibney, ed., and Beth Cary, trans., *Senso, The Japanese Remember the Pacific War: Letters to the Editor of Asahi Shimbun* (Armonk, NY: M. E. Sharpe, 1995). *Asahi Shimbun* is Japan's leading newspaper. In 1986, the editors invited readers to submit recollections of their World War II experiences. For many who responded, these were their first public statements about their horrific experiences. The series was controversial, sparking a debate about the value of dredging up these memories. The editors summarized their view as follows: " . . . it is quite natural to want an unpleasant past erased from memory. Indeed, for individuals to forget a bad past amounts to a healthy act of self-purification. But the history of a country is a different matter. . . . " (p. viii).

14. Ibid., pp. 204–205.

15. Ibid., pp. 207–208.

16. Ibid., p. 208.

17. See R. A. C Parker, *The Second World War*, rev. ed. (New York: Oxford, 1997), pp. 232–233; and Walzer, *Just and Unjust Wars*, pp. 266–267.

18. Thomas M. Coffey, *Iron Eagle: The Turbulent Life of General Curtis LeMay* (New York: Crown, 1986), pp. 160–165. Coffey interviewed many of LeMay's former associates in the Air Force. LeMay also granted Coffey more than one hundred hours of interviews at LeMay's home in Newport Beach, California. In addition, LeMay recorded six separate U.S. Air Force oral histories, to which Coffey also had access. (See pp. 451–455, "Sources.") Comments by LeMay are set off in quotation marks, and derive from discussions between LeMay and Thomas Coffey, unless otherwise indicated. Passages not in quotation marks are comments made by Coffey to add context to LeMay's statements.

19. Curtis E. LeMay (with MacKinlay Kantor), *Mission with LeMay* (New York: Garden City, NY, 1965), p. 352.

20. From an interview with LeMay by Thomas M. Coffey, 14 December 1983, at LeMay's home in Newport Beach, California, in Coffee, *Iron Eagle*, p. 162.

21. Thomas Coffey points out that the mission had to be delayed for twenty-four hours. As LeMay told him in an interview, "My idea of what was humanly possible sometimes did not coincide with the opinion of others" (Ibid., p. 167).

22. Harry Truman, "Address to the American People on the Atomic Bombing of Japan," quoted in Michael Walzer, *Just and Unjust Wars*, p. 264.

23. See Dower, *War without Mercy*, pp. 33–73 for a catalogue of what he calls "war hates and war crimes" associated with Japanese behavior in the Pacific War.

24. Laurens van der Post, *The Night of the New Moon* (London: Hogarth, 1970), pp. 27–36, 143–146. This remarkable memoir of life in a Japanese prison camp is devoid of the bitterness, even hatred, that often (and understandably) characterizes recollections of life as a POW under the Japanese in the Second World War. The writer, born in South Africa into an Afrikans family, became a British citizen, and spent three years imprisoned in various locations on the island of Java (which would become part of a newly independent Indonesia after the war). After writing this memoir, he would achieve worldwide fame as an interpreter of the psychological theories of the Swiss psychoanalyst, Carl G. Jung. We are grateful to Jeanet H. Irwin for bringing this unusual memoir to our attention.

25. We have used standardized American spelling throughout this excerpt, to avoid confusion among readers. For example, "programme" is rendered "program," etc.

26. van der Post, *The Night of the New Moon*, pp. 27–36.

27. Field Marshal Terauchi Hisaichi was Supreme Commander of all Japanese forces in Southeast Asia.

28. The Japanese Emperor Hirohito, speaking for the people and government of Japan, unconditionally surrendered to U.S. forces and their allies on August 15, 1945, following a week of intense infighting in the Tokyo government between those who were prepared to surrender and those who were not. See Parker, *The Second World War*, pp. 239–242.

29. van der Post, *The Night of the New Moon*, pp. 143–146.

Chapter 5

1. On the significance of the Geneva conference and agreement of 1954, see Robert S. McNamara, James G. Blight, and Robert K. Brigham, with Thomas J. Biersteker and Col. Herbert Y. Schandler, *Argument without End: In Search of Answers to the Vietnam Tragedy* (New York: PublicAffairs, 1999), pp. 60–92.

2. Barbara Tuchman, *The March of Folly* (New York: Random House, 1984). See pp. 4–33 for Tuchman's general remarks on her "theory" of wooden-headedness, which is actually far more interesting and compelling than its label might otherwise suggest. And see pp. 234–387 for her analysis of America in Vietnam.

3. Serious U.S. financial involvement in Vietnam began in 1950, when the

Truman administration, spearheaded by Secretary of State Dean Acheson, agreed to underwrite the French effort to subdue the guerrilla movement known as the Vietminh, led by Ho Chi Minh. U.S. physical presence in Vietnam was however limited to some CIA operatives and some low-level officials who dealt with the French colonial governor. After the Geneva conference adjourned in July 1954, American involvement changed qualitatively. A command headquarters was established in Saigon. Military advisers to the Saigon government began to arrive. And South Vietnam became the "poster-child" for U.S. academic and governmental advocates of "nation-building"—the attempt to create democracies where none existed before, as a counterweight to what was perceived at the time to be the forward march of communist guerrilla movements in Asia, Africa and Latin America. On this, see George McT. Kahin, *Intervention: How America Became Involved in Vietnam* (New York: Anchor, 1986), pp. 66–92.

4. This term, "the best and the brightest," is now used almost exclusively in an ironic sense, due to the success of the book that made the phrase a household term of irony, even derision: David Halberstam, *The Best and the Brightest* (New York: Random House, 1972).

5. John F. Kennedy was born on May 29, 1917; Robert S. McNamara was born on June 9, 1916.

6. Stanley I. Kutler, ed., *Encylopedia of the Vietnam War* (New York: MacMillan, 1996), pp. 103–104.

7. John F. Kennedy, *Why England Slept,* Introduction by Henry R. Luce (New York: Wilfred Funk, 1940), pp. 226, 229–230. The book began as Kennedy's senior thesis at Harvard, which he had completed in March, 1940. He sent a copy of the thesis to his father, Joseph P. Kennedy, Sr., who was then the U.S. Ambassador to Great Britain, who forwarded it to Arthur Krock of the *New York Times*. Krock found a publisher for the book and helped shape it. Krock also suggested the title, as a contrast to Winston Churchill's *While England Slept*. JFK finished the book in two months, and it was published in July 1940, just two months after his twenty-third birthday. As Kennedy biographer and historian Doris Kearns Goodwin has written, "the young author became an instant celebrity." See her *The Fitzgeralds and the Kennedys: An American Saga* (New York: Simon and Schuster, 1987), p. 605.

8. The italics are Kennedy's.

9. Sen. John F. Kennedy, "America's Stake in Vietnam," the keynote speech to a June 1956 symposium sponsored by the American Friends of Vietnam. In William Conrad Gibbons, *The U.S. Government and the Vietnam War: Executive and Legislative Roles and Relationships, part II, 1961–1964* (Princeton: Princeton University Press, 1986), pp. 5–6. The background on the American Friends of Vietnam and Kennedy's affiliation with it may be found in part I, pp. 301–305, of Gibbons' monumental documentary history of U.S. decisionmaking with regard to the Vietnam War, which covers the period 1945–1960.

10. President John F. Kennedy, "Inaugural Address," January 20, 1961. In Gibbons, *The U.S. Government and the Vietnam War, part II,* pp. 3–4.

11. Theodore Draper, *Castro's Revolution: Myths and Realities* (New York: Praeger, 1962), p. 59.

12. John F. Kennedy, quoted in Theodore C. Sorensen, *Kennedy* (New York: Harper & Row, 1965), p. 309. On the details of the planning, execution and aftermath of the invasion itself, see James G. Blight and Peter Kornbluh, eds., *Politics of Illusion: The Bay of Pigs Invasion Reexamined* (Boulder, CO: Lynne Rienner, 1998). The book contains key documents relating to the events, and chronologies of what took place, and when. It also contains the most comprehensive account in English of the internal Cuban resistance, which was crushed as a result of the invasion.

13. Undersecretary of State Chester Bowles participated in the first postmortem discussion of the Bay of Pigs fiasco on April 20, 1961. This excerpt is from his notes of that meeting, which he labeled "Personal," and which he wrote up approximately two weeks after the meeting. The document is available from the National Security Archive, Washington, DC: www.gwu.edu/~nsarchiv/. These next three documents—memoranda by Chester Bowles, McGeorge Bundy and Arthur Schlesinger, Jr.—can usefully be regarded as a unit, exemplifying various aspects of Kennedy's humiliation due to the Bay of Pigs debacle. All three documents, along with hundreds of others, were included in the briefing notebooks for participants in a groundbreaking conference on the Bay of Pigs invasion in Havana, Cuba, March 22–24, 2001, co-sponsored by the National Security Archive at George Washington University, the Watson Institute for International Studies at Brown University, and the University of Havana. Participants included members of the invasion brigade of Cuban exiles, former U.S. government officials, and Cuban civilian and military leaders involved in repelling the invasion, including Cuban President Fidel Castro and former Cuban Militia leader (and current Vice President) Jose Ramon Fernandez.

14. The selection presented here is the concluding section. The entire document is well worth studying. The prescience of Bundy's analysis, just four days after the fiasco of the Bay of Pigs, is stunning. The document is available from the National Security Archive, Washington, DC: www.gwu.edu/~nsarchiv/.

15. This memorandum, classified "Confidential," was requested of Schlesinger, then a White House aide, by Kennedy. Schlesinger drafted it immediately after returning from a whirlwind tour of European cities, April 22–May 3, 1961. It is available from the National Security Archive, Washington, DC: www.gwu.edu/~nsarchiv/.

16. Drew Middleton was a foreign affairs and military affairs correspondent for the New York Times. Robert Boothby was an independent member of the House of Lords.

17. One opinion Kennedy seems to have valued particularly is that of Harvard economist and Kennedy's ambassador to India, John Kenneth Galbraith. In November 1961, Kennedy asked Galbraith to stop in Saigon for an independent assessment, on his way from Washington to New Delhi. Galbraith wrote to Kennedy with an irreverent, caustic, sardonic wit that resembled Kennedy's own. Galbraith told Kennedy, for example, the nearly quarter-of-a-million-man, well-armed South Vietnamese army appeared to be running scared from the 15–18,000-man insurgency of the National Liberation Front. "If this were equality," Galbraith said, "the United States would hardly be safe against the Sioux." He concluded:

"A time of crisis in our policy on South Vietnam will come when it becomes evident that the reforms we have asked have not come off and that our presently proffered aid is not accomplishing anything. Troops will be urged to back up Diem. It will be sufficiently clear that I think this must be resisted. Our soldiers would not deal with the vital weakness. They could perpetuate it." Ambassador John Kenneth Galbraith to President John F. Kennedy, 20–21 November 1961. In *The Pentagon Papers (Sen. Gravel Edition)*, Vol. 2, pp. 121–124).

This letter, and one from April 5, 1962, from Galbraith to Kennedy are reprinted in full in John Kenneth Galbraith, *Letters to Kennedy*, ed. by James Goodman (Cambridge, MA: Harvard University Press, 1998), pp. 89–94, and pp. 100–103. The letters are a delight to read. It is easy to see why, as has been reported by some of Kennedy's associates, Kennedy loved to hear from Galbraith.

18. A very illuminating account of the debate between Kennedy and his advisers on November 15, 1961 may be found in Lawrence Freedman, *Kennedy's Wars: Berlin, Cuba, Laos, and Vietnam* (New York: Oxford, 2000), pp. 330–334.

19. Robert S. McNamara, "Memorandum for the President." In Gibbons, *The U.S. Government and the Vietnam War, part II*, pp. 86–87. It may also be found, with useful commentary in *The Pentagon Papers, (The Senator Gravel Edition): The Defense Department History of the United States Decisionmaking on Vietnam* (4 vols.), (Boston: Beacon Press, 1971), pp. 108–109.

20. "Notes on National Security Council Meeting, 15 November 1961." In Gibbons, *The U.S. Government and the Vietnam War, part II*, pp. 96–98. This document is located in the LBJ Library, Austin, Texas, but not the JFK Library in Boston. The notes are unattributed, but were taken by Col. Howard Burris, of Johnson's staff, who often served as note-taker for the Vice President.

21. See Francis X. Winters, *The Year of the Hare: America in Vietnam, January 25, 1963–February 15, 1964* (Athens, GA: University of Georgia Press, 1997), pp. 29–39; and Howard Jones, *Death of a Generation: How the Assassination of Diem and JFK Prolonged the Vietnam War* (NY: Oxford, 2003), pp. 247–267.

22. See the excerpts from James K. Galbraith, below, in the "Dialogues," and the notes associated with them, for more information on the institutional

preparations, going back to the spring of 1963, for a withdrawal of U.S. military personnel from South Vietnam.

The drafter of the McNamara-Taylor Report was William Bundy, then an Assistant Secretary of Defense. In an unpublished memoir of the Vietnam War, Bundy wrote that he noticed, in retrospect, a "clear internal inconsistency" in the report: begin to withdraw U.S. military personnel, while at the same time note that the political situation in South Vietnam is bound to get worse, not better, in ways that would seem to require a larger U.S. presence, if South Vietnam is not to be taken over by the communist insurgents of the National Liberation Front (or "Vietcong"). His comments are quoted in Gibbons, *The U.S. Government and the Vietnam War, part II,* p. 186. Bundy wrote that he later regretted letting this "inconsistency" remain in the report, unaddressed. He attributed it to exhaustion, having drafted the report on the long flight back to Washington from Saigon. Yet it should be noted that the "inconsistency" regretted by William Bundy is troubling only if one doubts Kennedy's commitment to withdrawal whether or not the Diem regime survives—and, in fact, whether or not the communists take over in the South. We are inclined to believe Kennedy had made this decision, in his own mind, though it is of course impossible to know for certain.

23. Robert S. McNamara and Gen. Maxwell D. Taylor, "Report to the President on the Situation in South Vietnam." In Robert S. McNamara, *In Retrospect: The Tragedy and Lessons of Vietnam,* expanded paperback ed. (New York: Vintage, 1996), pp. 77–79. McNamara has excerpted the most important parts of the report, and presented them in his memoir. The complete text is in *The Pentagon Papers* (the Senator Gravel Edition), pp. 751–766.

24. Transcripts of audiotaped discussions between President John F. Kennedy, Robert S. McNamara, and McGeorge Bundy. These are taken from John F. Kennedy Library Tape 114A49. They were transcribed by George Eliades, and are included as appendices to James K. Galbraith, "Kennedy, Vietnam and Iraq," Salon.com, November 22, 2003. See also Galbraith's companion piece, "Exit Strategy: In 1963 JFK Ordered a Complete Withdrawal From Vietnam," *Boston Review,* October–November, 2003; online edition is at http://www.bostonreview.net/BR28.5/galbraith.html.

25. James K. Galbraith notes that this may be a mistranscription. The context suggests to him that McNamara is referring to the four "Corps" areas of South Vietnam, of which the Fourth was the Mekong Delta. If Galbraith is right, then the transcription should read something like the following: " . . . first, I believe we can complete the military campaign in the first three Corps in '64, and the Fourth Corps in '65." While the meaning doesn't change substantially, it shows how difficult it is to be confident in the exactness of the transcriptions of many of the Kennedy tapes.

26. The transcriber, historian George Eliades, believes that McGeorge Bundy is the speaker, but is not certain.

27. When Kennedy says: "Let's just go ahead and do it without making a

public statement about it," he appears to tell McNamara to announce the fact of the 1,000-troop withdrawal by 31 December 1963, but not to elaborate on its *implementation*. Presumably, this would allow Kennedy the political space to later claim that the troops were withdrawn as a normal part of rotation of advisors. While this interpretation is necessarily speculative, such a motive as we attribute to Kennedy would have allowed him to hedge in the 1964 presidential campaign as to whether he had actually ordered a decrease in the size of the deployment or not. (Republican hawks were bound to accuse him of doing so.) If this was more or less what Kennedy was up to—keeping his options open, inserting a measure of ambiguity into his actions—then one begins to appreciate the problem that Lyndon Johnson is faced with when he unexpectedly assumes the presidency. The actions required to "continue Kennedy's policy" are ambiguous at best, contradictory at worst.

28. Together with our colleague David A. Welch of the University of Toronto, we have launched a project the objective of which is to look as deeply and dispassionately as possible into the available documentation, as well as memoirs and oral testimony from both former associates of Kennedy and Johnson and leading scholars of U.S. decisionmaking during the Vietnam War.

29. John F. Kennedy, in an interview with Chet Huntley and David Brinkley of NBC Television News, September 9, 1963. Quoted in *Pentagon Papers* (Sen. Gravel Edition), vol. II, p. 828.

30. John F. Kennedy, in an interview with Walter Cronkite of CBS Television News, September 25, 1963. Quoted in ibid., p. 827.

31. Tuchman, *March of Folly,* p. 303.

32. Jared Diamond, in his *Collapse: How Societies Choose to Fail or Succeed* (New York: Viking, 2005), concludes that the manner in which President John F. Kennedy "reexamined his reasoning" after the Bay of Pigs fiasco, as McNamara puts the proposition in "The Fog of War," may have been essential to the peaceful outcome of the Cuban missile crisis a year and a half later. In a key chapter, "Why Do Some Societies Make Disastrous Decisions," Diamond states:

> Why did decision-making in these two Cuban crises unfold so differently? Much of the reason is that Kennedy himself thought long and hard about the 1961 Bay of Pigs fiasco, and he charged his advisors to think hard, about what had gone wrong with their decision-making. Based on that thinking, he purposely changed how he operated the advisory discussions in 1962 (p. 439).

Diamond's purpose is to illuminate nothing less than why societies (like that of Easter Island) seem to engage in self-destructive, virtually suicidal, annihilation of their environment, while others (like that of Japan) have been (for example) preserving green spaces for more than 400 years, in spite of the press of increasing population. Diamond concludes: "By reflecting deeply on causes of past failures, we too, like President Kennedy in 1961 and 1962, may be able to mend our ways and increase our chances for future success" (p. 440).

We leave it to others to determine whether Diamond's comparative analysis of the "destructiveness" of societies is sound. But we are convinced that the Kennedy "learning curve" that helped avoid nuclear catastrophe in October 1962 would also have been applied, had he lived, to the prevention of a kind of "catastrophe in slow-motion" underway in southeast Asia.

33. Anthony Lewis, Robert S. McNamara and Theodore C. Sorensen, discussion on Kennedy and Vietnam, October 22, 2003 on National Public Radio. Quoted in Galbraith, "Kennedy, Vietnam and Iraq." Lewis, the former New York Times columnist and Harvard Law School professor, interviewed McNamara and Sorensen about the implications of the McNamara-Taylor Report of October 2, 1963.

34. Noam Chomsky, *Rethinking Camelot: JFK, the Vietnam War, and US Political Culture* (Boston: South End Press, 1993), pp. 36–38. Chomsky's book is in part a reply to a book and a film, which he characterizes as the leading edge of "a Kennedy revival"—in Chomsky's view, a misleadingly positive stance with regard to Kennedy's actions and intentions on the Vietnam question. The book is: John M. Newman, *JFK and Vietnam: Deception, Intrigue, and the Struggle for Power* (New York: Warner, 1992). The book was very widely reviewed when it appeared, and advocates what Newman (and others since) have called the "discontinuity thesis"—that Kennedy had no intention of Americanizing the war in Vietnam, which is what Johnson of course did, thus discontinuing the Kennedy approach. Newman became an adviser to a widely discussed film by Oliver Stone, "JFK," which was released in 1991, and which strongly implied that a conspiracy to assassinate Kennedy was rooted in unhappiness with his resistance to escalating the war in Vietnam. The controversy in the popular press ignited by Newman's book and Stone's film also led to a scholarly reassessment, at a conference held at the LBJ Library in Austin, Texas, in October 1993, eventually published as Lloyd C. Gardner and Ted Gittinger, eds., *Vietnam: The Early Decisions* (Austin: University of Texas Press, 1997). Newman is among the contributors, as is William Conrad Gibbons of Princeton, who takes a view of the Kennedy-Johnson transition that is more or less the antithesis of Newman's. The book is highly illuminating, in large part because proponents of various opposing views were able to cross-question one another face-to-face, in the process of preparing the book.

35. As Galbraith notes, Johnson's task was made even more difficult than it might otherwise have been, due to the coup in Saigon on November 1, 1963. On the effect of that coup, and the murder of Diem and Nhu on the escalation of the war, see McNamara, Blight and Brigham et al. *Argument without End,*

(New York: PublicAffairs, 1999), especially pp. 163–164, and the notes to those pages.

36. James K. Galbraith, "Exit Strategy: In 1963, JFK Ordered a Complete Withdrawal From Vietnam." *Boston Review,* October–November 2003. Available online at: http://www.bostonreview.net/BR28.5/galbraith.html. Due to space constraints, the authors of *The Fog of War* have had to focus solely on James K. Galbraith's conclusions, rather than the way he develops his argument or uses his sources. Reference to Galbraith's data base has thus been omitted, regrettably, including the documentary evidence with which he buttresses his conclusions about National Security Action Memorandum (NSAM) 263, signed by President Kennedy on October 11, 1963. We therefore recommend reading Galbraith's entire *Boston Review* and *Salon.com* articles to appreciate the force of his argument.

In this summation of Kennedy's decisions on Vietnam in the fall of 1963, and the way the coup in Saigon ruined everything for Lyndon Johnson, Galbraith relies in large part on a recent, comprehensive, well-argued book by historian Howard Jones: *Death of a Generation: How the Assassinations of Diem and JFK Prolonged the Vietnam War* (New York: Oxford, 2003). But see also Newman, *JFK and Vietnam,* and Peter Dale Scott, *Deep Politics and the Death of JFK,* paperback ed., with a new preface by the author (Berkeley: University of California Press, 1993). The Newman and Scott books are highly controversial, in large part because each moves beyond the question of what JFK did; and might have done with regard to Vietnam, to a consideration of the possible links between Kennedy's decisions and inclinations about Vietnam and motives underlying his assassination. As mentioned previously, Newman for example was an adviser to Oliver Stone for the film "JFK," which implies that Kennedy was killed by forces wishing to expand the war in Vietnam. But Galbraith (and Newman) have argued that Stone's decidedly paranoid view of recent U.S. history is not Newman's responsibility, nor did he derive it from Newman.

Cornell University historian Fredrik Logevall has explored all sides of the Kennedy counterfactual, or "what-if," regarding Vietnam, and he has done so in a courageous manner, given the evident distaste many of his fellow historians have for counterfactuals in general, and the polarized nature of debate about the Kennedy-Vietnam counterfactual, in particular. See Logevall's *Choosing War: The Lost Chance for Peace and the Escalation of the War in Vietnam* (Berkeley, CA: University of California Press, 1999), especially pp. 395–413. See also his full-bore assault on some of the specific issues raised by the counterfactual in his fine, comprehensive essay, "Vietnam and the Question of What Might Have Been," in Mark J. White, ed., *Kennedy: The New Frontier Revisited* (New York: New York University Press, 1998), pp. 19–62. Finally, to get a feel for the intensity with which Logevall's treatment of the Kennedy counterfactual was greeted by professional historians, as well as Logevall's spirited and indefatigable defense of his position, see the website that has become the most frequently visited "chat-room" of specialists in diplomatic history, H-DIPLO: <hdiplo@YorkU.CA>. See the entries for the entire month of February, 2000, when the site was inundated with reactions to Logevall's (then) newly published *Choosing War.*

37. National Security Action Memorandum 263 was signed by Kennedy on October 11, 1963. It enacted the recommendations in the McNamara-Taylor Report of October 2 (which are summarized in the above selection by McNamara, in his memoir, In Retrospect.) The full McNamara-Taylor Report is in *The Pentagon Papers* (Sen. Gravel Edition), vol. II, pp. 751–766. For the report's very pessimistic assessment of the "Political Situation and Trends," see Part IV of the McNamara-Taylor Report (pp. 758–760 in vol. II of the Sen. Gravel Edition of *The Pentagon Papers*). In addition, the White House issued a press release on October 2, 1963, containing five points, including the intention to withdraw 1,000 U.S. advisers from South Vietnam by the end of the calendar year, 1963 (point 3), but also containing the admission that "the political situation in South Vietnam remains deeply serious" (point 4). The press release is in Gibbons, *The U.S. Government and the Vietnam War,* part II, p. 185.

38. Henry Cabot Lodge was the U.S. ambassador to South Vietnam, having taken up the post earlier in 1963.

39. Arthur Schlesinger, Jr., *A Thousand Days: John F. Kennedy in the White House* (New York: Fawcett, 1965).

40. George Ball was the undersecretary of state; Mike Mansfield, Democrat of Montana, was the Senate Majority Leader; Wayne Morse was a Democratic Senator from Oregon and a member of the Senate Foreign Relations Committee.

41. Peter Dale Scott, *Deep Politics and the Death of JFK.*

42. Noam Chomsky and Howard Zinn, eds., *Pentagon Papers*, vol. 5, Analytic Essays and Index (Boston: Beacon Press, 1972).

43. Newman, *JFK and Vietnam.*

44. Noam Chomsky, Letter to the editor, *Boston Review*, December 2003–January 2004. Online edition available at http://bostonreview.net/ BR28.6/ letters.html.

45. Jones, *Death of a Generation.*

46. James K. Galbraith, Reply to Noam Chomsky. *Boston Review*, December 2003–January 2004. Online edition is available at http://bostonreview.net/ BR28.6/letters.html.

47. Secretary of State Colin Powell's testimony before the United Nations on February 5, 2003, was aimed at demonstrating the evidence for the first two claims—Iraq's weapons of mass destruction and Iraq's links to al-Qaeda. The background to that presentation, along with the development of the evidence behind the claims, is described in Bob Woodward's *Plan of Attack* (New York: Simon & Schuster, 2004), pp. 297–301, 309–312. For the third claim—the fostering of democracy in postwar Iraq—see page 328 in Woodward's book for

a summary of the March 4, 2003, briefing of President Bush and members of the National Security Counsel by Douglas Feith, Undersecretary of Defense, on "U.S. and Coalition Objectives" for postwar Iraq. Two op-ed pieces by Kenneth Adelman, a former assistant to Rumsfield and a member of the National Defense Advisory Board, succinctly capture the views of the administration prior to the war and immediately after the capture of Baghdad. In the August 27, 2002 *Wall Street Journal* piece, Adelman wrote: "Every day Mr. Bush holds off liberating Iraq is another day endangering America. Posing as a 'patient man,' he risks a catastrophic attack" (quoted in *Plan of Attack*, p. 165). The headline of Adelman's April 10, 2003 *Washington Post* piece read "Cakewalk Revisited." He castigated those "frightful forecasters" who had predicted disaster (quoted in *Plan of Attack*, p. 409).

48. See Jessica T. Matthews, George Perkovich, and Joseph Cirincioni, *WMD in Iraq: Evidence and Implications* (Washington, DC: Carnegie Endowment for Peace, 2004) for data that conflicts with the first two claims of the Bush Administration, available at www.ceip.org/files/projects/npp/resources/iraqintell/name.htm. See also Charles Duelfer, *Comprehensive Report of the Special Advisor to the DCI on Iraq's WMD*, 30 September 2004, issued by the CIA, and available at www.cia.gov/cia/reports/iraq_wmd_2004. See also *The 9/11 Commission Report: Final Report of the National Commission on Terrorist Attacks Upon the United States,* Authorized Edition (New York: Norton, 2004), p. 334, where the Commission cites an internal National Security Council memo that found no "compelling case" that Iraq was involved in the planning or execution of the 9/11 attacks. See also Seymour M. Hersh, *Chain of Command: The Road from 9/11 to Abu Ghraib,* (New York, HarperCollins, 2004), especially Chapter IV "The Iraq Hawks," and Chapter V "Who Lied to Whom?"

49. Weapons expert David Kay—who originally headed the U.S. government Iraq Survey Group, which had responsibility for searching Iraq for WMD—appeared before the Senate Armed Services Committee on January 28, 2004, shortly after he had resigned. He stated, "We were almost all wrong, and I certainly include myself." (Quoted in Woodward, *Plan of Attack*, p. 434.)

Chapter 6

1. See, for example, the entries from 1987 to the present in the Brief Chronology of the Life and Times of Robert S. McNamara (Appendix A). For a description of the research methods and results from the inquiries into the Cuban missile crisis and the Vietnam War that McNamara participated in, see the "Prologue" to this book. See also James G. Blight, Bruce J. Allyn and David A. Welch, *Cuba on the Brink: Castro, the Missile Crisis and the Soviet Collapse,* expanded paperback ed. (Lanham, MD: Rowman and Littlefield, 2002) and

Robert S. McNamara, James G. Blight, and Robert K. Brigham, with Thomas J. Biersteker and Col. Herbert Y. Schandler, *Argument without End: In Search of Answers to the Vietnam Tragedy* (New York: PublicAffairs, 1999), pp. 60–92.

2. David Talbot, "The Fog Around Robert McNamara," Salon.com, February 28, 2004.

3. One measure of the interest in "The Fog of War" is that *The New York Times* chose to review and comment on the film several times. See, for example: Stephen Holden, "Revisiting McNamara and the War He Headed," October 11, 2003, pp. B9, B17 (and reprinted as "McNamara, Looking Back at Vietnam and Other Battles," on December 19th, 2003, p. B16); Samantha Power, "War and Never Having to Say You're Sorry," December 14th, 2003, Section 2, pp. 1, 33 (reprinted in this chapter); Nancy Ramsey, "Oddly Hopeful in a World of War," reprinted in the *International Herald Tribune*, December 26, 2003, p. 14; and Frank Rich, "Oldest Living Whiz Kid Tells All," January 25, 2004, Section 2, pp. 1, 20.

4. Errol Morris' interviews with Robert McNamara were conducted on May 1 & 2, 2001, December 11 &12, 2001, and April 1 & 2, 2002.

5. For additional reviews, see www.rottentomatoes.com/m/fog_of_war/.

6. See Doug Saunders, "It's Just Wrong What We're Doing," *Toronto Globe and Mail*, January 25, 2004.

7. The "three memoirs" that Powell refers to are: Robert S. McNamara, *In Retrospect: The Tragedy and Lessons of Vietnam*, expanded paperback ed. (New York: Vintage, 1996); McNamara, Blight and Brigham et al., *Argument without End*; and Robert S. McNamara and James G. Blight, *Wilson's Ghost: Reducing the Risk of Conflict, Killing and Catastrophe in the 21st Century* (New York: PublicAffairs, 2001). The expanded, post–9/11 paperback edition was published in June 2003. Only *In Retrospect* is a memoir. *Argument without End* is mainly a work of history, while *Wilson's Ghost* applies the lessons of history to the world of the 21st century. Both books do, however, include some autobiographical material by McNamara.

8. The full text of Errol Morris' "Director's Statement" is available on www.fogofwarmovie.com and www.errolmorris.com.

9. On February 29, 2004, in Los Angeles, "The Fog of War" received the Academy Award® for Best Documentary Feature.

10. See endnote #6, above.

11. McNamara's own eleven lessons are available at www.choices.edu/fogofwar. Also available at this website is Susan Graseck, James G. Blight and janet M. Lang, *Official Teacher's Guide for "The Fog of War,"* as well as supplementary material. All material can be downloaded without charge from the website.

12. "The Pentagon Papers" is the commonly used term for *The Defense Department History of United States Decisionmaking on Vietnam*. It exists in sev-

eral formats, the best of which is the so-called "Senator Gravel Edition," 4 vols. (Boston: Beacon Press, 1971). On June 29, 1971, Sen. Mike Gravel of Alaska entered 4,100 pages from the papers into the *Congressional Record,* in defiance of the Nixon Administration, which had tried to suppress their publication.

13. See chapter 4 for further discussion of war and war crimes during World War II and see the next section in this chapter for additional excerpts about Robert McNamara and World War II from the Terry Gross interview of Errol Morris.

14. "The Fog of War" opened in New York City and Los Angeles on December 19, 2003.

15. See endnote #6, above, for McNamara's exception to his rule, as well as the piece by Bonnie Azab Powell, "Robert McNamara, Errol Morris Return to Berkeley to Share Lessons Learned From 'The Fog of War,'" reprinted as the first review in this chapter.

16. This subject is taken up in detail in the Epilogue. See also McNamara and Blight, *Wilson's Ghost,* pages 29–49 on the moral imperative, pages 49–54 on the multilateral imperative, and pages 234–239 on the empathy imperative.

Epilogue

1. The phrase "how wrong he was" does not appear in the final cut of the film, having been edited out of the several takes in which McNamara concludes with variations on the theme: "how wrong he was," or sometimes "how wrong we were." It is included here because McNamara puts great stress on the similarities between the post–World War I era of false optimism, epitomized by Wilson, and our own post–Cold War era, which is turning out to be anything but an era of peace among nations and peoples, such as some thought would follow the demise of Soviet communism following the relatively peaceful transition in the countries of the former Soviet Union.

2. Robert S. McNamara and James G. Blight, *Wilson's Ghost: Reducing the Risk of Conflict, Killing and Catastrophe in the 21st Century* (New York: Public-Affairs, 2001). The expanded, post–9/11 paperback edition was published in June 2003.

3. Those wishing to learn more of the facts that make up the chronology of the life of Robert McNamara should consult two biographical studies: Deborah Shapley, *Promise and Power: The Life and Times of Robert McNamara* (Boston: Little, Brown, 1993); and Paul Hendrickson, *The Living and the Dead: Robert McNamara and Five Lives of a Lost War* (New York: Knopf, 1996). Both books provide interesting perspectives on their subject. Yet both are deeply flawed. Shapley seems concerned, more than anything else, to "catch" McNamara—either the historical McNamara or the McNamara who agreed to submit to be interviewed by her—when he is lying. This obsession leads the

author, in our view, down many an irrelevant garden path. In addition, we disagree with her criteria for truth-telling among public officials, which must be rather different than criteria used to evaluate personal honesty. Hendrickson's book also suffers from the intrusion of too much author and not enough subject. The author seems to be using the book to work through his own feelings about the Vietnam era, the war, and the man who directed the Pentagon as the war escalated. That said, both books are the product of exhaustive research, and much can be learned from them about McNamara, and the context in which he rose to high office.

4. McNamara and Blight, *Wilson's Ghost,* pp. xvii–xviii.

5. One of us (JGB) co-authored *Wilson's Ghost* with Robert McNamara. The collaboration was thoroughgoing, in that both authors had to agree, in the end, on every word in the book. But it is in the nature of most collaborations that one author assumes primary responsibility for some parts, the other author for other parts. The "Manifesto" included here was one aspect of the book for which Bob McNamara took primary responsibility. In addition, both authors owe a debt of gratitude to Peter Osnos, the publisher and head of PublicAffairs, for suggesting to both authors that the book begin with a manifesto of some sort.

6. The comment was made during the question-and-answer period in Telluride, following the screening. The song the viewer referred to, "MTA" (Metropolitan Transit Authority), was a hit for the Kingston Trio in 1959. The song was originally written, however, as a campaign jingle in support of a candidate named George O'Brien, in the 1948 mayoral campaign in Boston. (The song, as sung by the Kingston Trio, contains the line, "Vote for George O'Brien and get Charlie off the MTA.") The panelists following the Telluride premiere were Robert McNamara, Errol Morris and journalist Mark Danner, who acted as moderator. One might infer by the repeated references to "the old man"—McNamara—that the person making the comment was young. But she wasn't. When asked her age after the screening, she replied only, "not quite as old as Bob McNamara." Still, she was old enough to remember a hit song from almost a half century ago.

7. See Samuel P. Huntington, *The Clash of Civilizations and the Remaking of World Order* (New York: Simon & Schuster, 1996). See also McNamara and Blight, *Wilson's Ghost.* The first edition was published in June 2001, just months before the attacks of 9/11. This chapter expands on several points made in *Wilson's Ghost,* especially the 2003 afterword, "Wilson's Ghost in the Post–9/11 World," pp. 230–276.

8. Samantha Power, "War and Never Having to Say You're Sorry," New York Times, December 14, 2003, pp. 1, 33. This article is reprinted in chapter 6.

9. See, for example, the following: Robert S. McNamara, *In Retrospect: The Tragedy and Lessons of Vietnam,* expanded paperback ed. (New York: Vintage, 1996), pp. 3–4; Robert S. McNamara, James G. Blight and Robert K.

Brigham, with Thomas J. Biersteker and Col. Herbert Y. Schandler, *Argument without End: In Search of Answers to the Vietnam Tragedy* (New York: Public-Affairs, 1999), p. 2; and the impact of this earliest memory of McNamara's suffuses all of McNamara and Blight, *Wilson's Ghost.*

10. Woodrow Wilson, speech in Sioux Falls, SD, September 8, 1919. Quoted in Herbert Hoover, *The Ordeal of Woodrow Wilson* (Washington, DC: Woodrow Wilson Center Press, 1992), p. ix. This quite moving and admiring portrait of Wilson was first published in 1958. It may perhaps come as a surprise to some readers to learn that Herbert Hoover, a Republican president from Iowa (1929–1933), was an unstinting admirer of Wilson. Hoover worked for Wilson in the last days and aftermath of the First World War coordinating the distribution of food to the ravaged Europeans. It was said by many at the time that Hoover's job description was to find a way to feed four hundred million starving people. Wilson, for his part, appreciated Hoover's organizational and administrative talent, qualities with which Wilson was less endowed.

11. David Lloyd George, quoted in ibid., p. 254.

12. Woodrow Wilson appeared to many to be a stiff, moralistic, cold fish of a politician. There is some truth in each of these descriptions. But Wilson was also a fascinating and multifaceted man. To get a better sense of Wilson the man, see especially the "American Experience," two-part documentary, called simply "Woodrow Wilson," a Carl Byker film, which aired on PBS in 2002. See also the short recent biography, *Woodrow Wilson,* by Louis Auchincloss (New York: Penguin, 2000), and the very moving book by John Milton Cooper, *Breaking the Heart of the World: Woodrow Wilson and the Fight for the League of Nations* (New York: Cambridge University Press, 2001).

13. Woodrow Wilson, quoted in Frank Ninkovich, *The Wilsonian Century: American Foreign Policy Since 1900* (Chicago: University of Chicago Press, 1999), p. 72. (Emphasis added)

14. Ibid., pp. 48–49.

15. Roger Angell, "Late Review," *The New Yorker,* January 19, 2004, pp. 31–32, p. 32.

16. "McNamara's Century" was briefly considered at a very early point as a possible title for the film that became "The Fog of War." Interestingly (to us), the title was eventually rejected by both Errol Morris and Robert McNamara. Morris didn't like it because, he said, it sounded too much like "one of those boring public television documentaries." McNamara, on the other hand, hated it because it sounded "like the ravings of an egomaniac." (McNamara had no veto over the title, or anything else that went into the movie, though Morris was careful to consult him on matters of fact and interpretation at each stage of production.)

17. This section draws on material in McNamara and Blight, *Wilson's Ghost,* pp. 21–27.

18. Lewis H. Lapham, "War Movie," *Harper's Magazine* (July 1999), pp. 12–15, p. 12.

19. Dan Smith, ed., *The State of War and Peace Atlas*, 3rd ed. (New York: Penguin, 1997), p. 14.

20. Josef Joffe, "The Worst of Times," *New York Times Book Review*, November 21, 1999, p. 22.

21. As of 1996, the official death toll from the bombing of Hiroshima was 197,045. The official death toll of the Nagasaki bombing, also by 1996, was 108,039. See Charles J. Moxley, Jr., *Nuclear Weapons and International Law in the Post–Cold War World* (Lanham, MD: Austin & Winfield, 2000), p. 433. Moxley cites official Japanese government figures published on the 50th anniversary of the bombings.

22. Carnegie Commission on Preventing Deadly Conflict, *Preventing Deadly Conflict: Final Report with Executive Summary* (Washington, DC: Carnegie Commission, 1997), p. 13.

23. Smith, ed., *State of War and Peace Atlas,* p. 13.

24. United Nations demographers estimate that the world population grew from approximately 2.3 billion in 1945 to approximately 6 billion by the end of the 20th century. In 1982, they predicted that the world's population would reach 10.2 billion by the end of the 21st century, with an essentially zero growth rate. They also predict that 94% of population growth in the 21st century will occur in the poorest countries. See Commission on Global Governance, *Our Global Neighborhood* (New York: Oxford University Press, 1998), pp. 27–28, 139.

25. Graham Allison, *Nuclear Terrorism: The Ultimate Preventable Catastrophe* (New York: Times Books, 2004), pp. 6–8. Allison's book steers a useful middle course between alarmism—although much of what he reveals in the book is alarming—and strategies for preventing a nuclear terrorist attack. It reads like a Tom Clancy thriller and, in fact, the book's introduction gives an analysis of Clancy's 1991 novel, *The Sum of All Fears,* which deals with a stolen nuclear warhead being detonated at the Superbowl.

26. Suleiman Abe Gheith, quoted in Allison, *Nuclear Terrorism,* p. 12.

27. Errol Morris' interviews with Robert McNamara were conducted on May 1 & 2, 2001, December 11 & 12, 2001, and April 1 & 2, 2002.

28. See McNamara and Blight, *Wilson's Ghost,* p. 2.

29. See Ibid., pp. 164–166, on "zero-tolerance multilateralism."

30. Richard E. Neustadt and Graham T. Allison, "Afterword" to Robert F. Kennedy, *Thirteen Days: A Memoir of the Cuban Missile Crisis* (New York: Norton, 1971), pp. 107–150, p. 112, emphasis in original.

31. See McNamara and Blight, *Wilson's Ghost,* pp. 64–73 and 257–274, for a discussion of realistic empathy and its potential for reducing the risk of conflict, killing and catastrophe. See also James G. Blight and janet M. Lange, "Lesson Number One: Empathize with Your 'Enemy,'" in *Peace and Conflict,* in press, 2005.

32. On these issues, see especially the two following essays: Fouad Ajami, "The Uneasy Imperium," in James F. Hoge, Jr. and Gideon Rose, eds., *How*

Did This Happen?: Terrorism and the New War (New York: PublicAffairs, 2001), pp. 15–30; and Abbas Amanat, "Empowered Through Violence: The Reinventing of Islamic Extremism," in Strobe Talbott and Nayan Chanda, eds., *The Age of Terror: America and the World After September 11* (New York: Basic Books, 2001), pp. 23–52.

33. Woodrow Wilson is quoted to this effect in Cooper, *Breaking the Heart of the World: Woodrow Wilson and the Fight for the League of Nations*, p. 9.

34. Woodrow Wilson, speech in St. Louis, Missouri, September 1919. Quoted in Louis Auchincloss, *Woodrow Wilson* (New York: Penguin, 2000), p. 116. In section 23 of the extras in the DVD version of "The Fog of War," McNamara reads this passage and comments on it.

35. Michael Ignatieff, *The Warrior's Honor: Ethnic War and the Modern Conscience* (New York: Metropolitan Books, 1997), p. 60.

AAF	Army Air Force
AF	Air Force
BC	Bomber Command
CIA	Central Intelligence Agency
CINCPAC	Commander in Chief of U.S. Forces in the Pacific
DRV	Democratic Republic of Vietnam
EDT	Eastern Daylight Time
GVN	Government of South Vietnam
HE	High Explosives
I	Incendiaries (firebombs)
ICC	International Control Commission
JCS	Joint Chiefs of Staff
M	Mines
MIT	Massachusetts Institute of Technology
NATO	North Atlantic Treaty Organization
NLF	National Liberation Front
NSAM	National Security Action Memorandum
OPLAN	Operational Plan
POW	Prisoner of War
RAF	Royal Air Force
SOP	Standard Operating Procedure
UN	United Nations
USSR	Union of Soviet Socialist Republics
WMD	Weapons of Mass Destruction

This book would not exist had not Errol Morris and Robert McNamara collaborated on "The Fog of War," Morris' Academy Award®–winning documentary. Nor would it exist if they had they not invited us to advise both of them throughout the three-year period during which the movie was produced and distributed.

When we first visited Errol Morris' production company, The Globe Department Store, in Cambridge, Massachusetts, we felt as if we had stepped onto the set of a science fiction thriller, complete with equipment we could not name, let alone use, and a "cast" of very young people, dressed mainly in black, who seemed to know what they were doing—which buttons to push on the intimidating control panels that fill most of the rooms. Without exception, the members of Errol's team took us in, taught us as much as we could absorb, and did so with kindness, humor and patience. We are especially grateful to Steven Hath, Adam Kosberg, Ann Petrone, and Karen Schmeer. Jackpot Junior, Errol's four-footed Director of Officeland Security, unfailingly lifted our spirits (whether or not he was stealing Robert McNamara's cookies). Coproducer Michael Williams of Scoutvision had the patience of Job, as he probably logged more phone hours with Robert McNamara than any other single person in history, *and* lived to tell about it. He quickly learned that McNamara's "no's" were most often calls for further discussion. To all: well done!

We also received a crash course in the administrative end of filmmaking, due to the unusually intense interest taken in the film, and in Bob McNamara, by the executives at the principal underwriter of "The Fog of War," Sony Pictures Classics. For generosity of spirit and patience with us, we thank the Sony copresidents, Michael Barker and Tom Bernard, the "Felix and Oscar" of serious filmmaking. We also thank Jennifer Anderson, Nana Brew-Hammond, Tracy Garvin, Sal Ladestro, Stephanie Lynch, Carmelo Pirrone, and Gloria Witham. We worked with this bicoastal group to develop and publicize the many educational aspects of "The Fog of

War." Thanks for bringing us into the digital age—"The Fog of War" is the first DVD that we ever bought. And thanks for encouraging us to work with you on the design of the liner for that DVD.

The entire team of "Fog Warriors," as all of us began calling ourselves, came together for the first time in France, at the Cannes Film Festival, in May 2003. Errol Morris' team and Sony's team were both present at what was, for all of us, a busman's holiday *in extremis*. It was at Cannes that we began to see that, as Michael Barker and Tom Bernard had told us, pursuing an Oscar is more or less analogous to running a political campaign. In this context, we met the people whom Sony had hired to promote the film, known in shorthand as the "IHOP-ers," after "IHOP"—the International House of Publicity—from New York. (We would team up twice more: at the Telluride, Colorado Film Festival, in September 2003; and at the New York Film Festival the following month.) They answered our never-ending questions about critics, publications, etc., under the most stressful conditions, in the heat of battle, so to speak, as "The Fog of War" competed for the attention of the film critics and honors from the festivals. Many thanks to R. Jeffrey Hill, Kitty Bowe Hearty, Jessica Uzzan, and Catherine Escandell for helping us in so many ways. (And to Cathy: may the Little Blue Buddha continue to work his magic for you.)

While at Cannes, we not only took an intensive "course," so to speak, in "Film Festivals 101," we also met people who helped us understand the special place that Errol Morris occupies in the world of documentary filmmaking. We are particularly grateful to Richard Corliss, Mary Corliss, Roger Ebert and Kenneth Turan for enlightening us during one very long, very late dinner, following the world premiere of the film in Cannes. We will never forget Roger Ebert's single reservation about "The Fog of War." He said: "I am not sure Robert Strange McNamara is 'strange' enough for an Errol Morris film."

And so a "draft" of a movie came into existence, was revised dozens of times, screened at the major film festivals, and released on December 19, 2003, in New York and Los Angeles, to rave reviews. At this point, typically, we would have departed the scene, gone back to our documents, interviews, teaching, etc., because the need for our advising would have ended. But not this time. This

film, great as it is, seemed to us to cry out for a book to complement it—a book focused on the foreign and defense policy issues
raised in its 107 minutes of intensely and complexly rendered (as
one critic called it) "Morris on McNamara on McNamara." It had
to be a book that synergistically melded with the film, yet provided
its own kind of stimulation and provocation—something that pro-
fessors, teachers and their students might find useful, but sufficiently accessible for anyone to read with profit.

But what kind of book, exactly? In helping us to sort all this out,
and in the transformation of the material from one medium to another, we received much assistance from the team at Rowman &
Littlefield, our publisher. We are grateful to CEO Jonathan Sisk
and his team at R&L: Andrew Boney, Mary Carpenter, Stephen Dri-
ver, Laura Roberts Gottlieb, Susan McEachern and Christopher
Ruel. What a year: the film wins the Oscar, the book comes out,
and Jon Sisk's Boston Red Sox finally win it all.

When the intention to write a book to accompany "The Fog of
War" was firm, but the writing had not yet begun, we received a
tremendous boost from an organization at Brown University's Watson Institute that should be declared a national treasure: The
Choices Program. Our colleagues from the Choices Program take
our research (and the research of all the scholars at the Watson Institute) and turn it into challenging and thought-provoking curric-
ula for high school teachers and their students all over the U.S. In
the fall of 2003, with the support of our institute and Sony Pictures
Classics, we collaborated with the Choices Director, Susan
Graseck, and her colleagues on the *Official Teacher's Guide to "The
Fog of War."* By the time of the release of the film on December 19,
2003, the twenty-four-page *Teacher's Guide* had been distributed to
almost 100,000 teachers in the U.S., and it was made available for
downloading from the Sony website—www.fogofwarmovie.com—
and the Choices website—www.choices.edu/fogofwar. We extend a
deeply felt "thank you" to our colleagues at the Choices Program
who played key roles in the creation of the *Teacher's Guide*: Andrew
Blackadar, Langan Courtney, Sarah Cleveland Fox, Susan Graseck,
Lucy Mueller, and Madeline Otis.

Following the creation of the *Teacher's Guide*, we have screened
the entire film (or in some instances edited sections of the film) for

a wide variety of audiences, and led postscreening discussions. This process, which is ongoing, has helped us crystallize our thoughts and try out ideas, and it has given us a forum in which to listen to what thoughtful people have to say about the film. The first such screening occurred a month after the December 19, 2003, premiere. We are especially grateful to the director of the Watson Institute, Thomas J. Biersteker, and to board member Lucinda Watson for arranging this first screening.

We are also grateful to the following institutions and organizations for inviting us to screen the film (or portions of it) and lead discussions of its content (in chronological order of screening): Hudson (Massachusetts) High School; the annual convention of the Organization of American Historians, in Boston; the Jepson School of Leadership at the University of Richmond (Virginia); the Cable Car Cinema (Providence, RI); the Francis Wayland Collegium for Liberal Learning at Brown University; the annual meeting of the New England Association of Independent Schools at Westminster School in Simsbury, CT; the annual meeting of the Society for the History of American Foreign Relations in Austin, Texas (special thanks to Philip Brenner, of American University, for pinch-hitting for us in Austin); a workshop on "Teaching American History" in Omaha, Nebraska; the annual convention of the American Political Science Association, in Chicago; Vassar College; and the annual meeting of the National Conference of Social Studies, in Baltimore. Thanks to all for inviting us to take our ideas on the road and field-test them, before we issued forth with a book.

Few books are written without a supportive local environment. This one is no exception. For help and advice of all sorts, we thank the following colleagues at our home base, the Watson Institute for International Studies at Brown University: Peter Andreas, Thomas J. Biersteker, Ellen Carney, Susan Costa, Neta C. Crawford, James Der Derian, Sheila Fournier, Frederick Fullerton, Elizabeth Garrison, Mark Garrison, Abbott Gleason, Elizabeth Goodfriend, Geoffrey Kirkman, Sergei Khrushchev, Jean Lawlor, Margareta Levitsky, Amy Langlais Smith, Nancy Hamlin Soukup, Nina Tannenwald, Caleb Waldorf, and Daniel Widome, as well as the members of the "Tuesday Seminar." Thanks for everything, including keeping the secret about the "B&B" on the second floor.

Over the last three years, in our seminars on the Cuban missile crisis and the Vietnam War, we have used portions of the film to stimulate discussion. During the past year, we have also distributed and discussed drafts of this book. We thank our students, one and all, for their comments, criticism, and outright enthusiasm for the issues that found their way into the book. Their 21st century outlook gave our 20th-century minds much to think about.

With us based at Brown, and Bob McNamara in Washington (when not travelling to Africa or Asia or Europe or who knows where), the only way that we could reliably communicate when it was absolutely necessary was to rely on the many talents of Linda Brown, who always knew where Bob was and how to get our packages to him. Thanks, Linda, for putting our FedEx packages on the top of Bob's piles of mail.

Those familiar with the movie will notice that Lesson #5, "Be prepared to reexamine your reasoning," is given a different emphasis here from that in the film. Our own application of this lesson concerns the extent to which John F. Kennedy may have reexamined his position—several times—on whether to send U.S. combat troops to Vietnam. Robert McNamara says in "The Fog of War" that he believes Kennedy probably would not have Americanized the war, but many disagree with his assessment. For help in sorting through the documents, memoirs, audiotapes and other materials relevant to this issue, we thank the following friends and colleagues: Thomas Blanton, Robert K. Brigham, Malcolm Byrne, Daniel Ellsberg, Frances FitzGerald, James K. Galbraith, Gordon Goldstein, Paul Golob, Fredrik Logevall, Christian Ostermann, John Prados, Mary Ann Schwenk, and David A. Welch. We have appreciated your good advice and equanimity on an issue known for the vehemence with which it is often debated.

We have been blessed with help from two young people, both former students of ours at Brown, who have worked for us as research assistants. Barbara Elias and Kingston Reif have been creative, hard-working colleagues whose enthusiasm—Barbara's in Washington, at our sister institution, the National Security Archive at George Washington University; Kingston's here at Brown—has been infectious, and whose contributions have been important to us and to the book. Thanks, kids!

Finally, we thank Errol Morris and Robert S. McNamara. We thank them for inviting us to play supporting roles in a collaboration that is surely unique in the history of documentary filmmaking. Errol and Bob both had a lot to lose if this project failed, and it could have crashed at any one of a dozen different junctures. Errol had constantly to listen—not just pretend to listen, but really listen—to Bob's "preferences." He also had to avoid the twin dangers of, on the one hand, appearing to be a shill for McNamara or, on the other, appearing to have carried out a hatchet job on him. Bob, for his part, has always been, is now, and probably will remain, a control freak. In a way, granting Errol Morris the freedom to make his own movie, his way—which would be a perfectly sensible approach for most people—required of Bob McNamara almost the equivalent of an unnatural act.

The existence of the final product, the film itself, seems to us almost a miracle, yet the process was anything but miraculous. It was accomplished by hard work and courage displayed by a controversial public figure and a gifted filmmaker. The film is a testament to the dedication of each man to the same larger message, best summed up in the subtitle of McNamara's latest book: *Wilson's Ghost: Reducing the Risk of Conflict, Killing and Catastrophe in the 21st Century*. Because of this mutual dedication, the two guys we, as advisers, came to call "Mr. Induction" (EM) and "Mr. Deduction" (RMcN) found common ground. Thanks to both Errol and Bob for seeing it through to the conclusion. Thanks, too, for asking us to help out.

absentees, and critical oral history, 12
Abu Ghraib, 137
Academy Award®, 176, 247
Afghanistan, 224, 247
agendas, in critical oral history, 10
Albert, Carl, 91
Alekseev, Aleksandr, 68
Allison, Graham, 235, 237
al-Qaeda, 170, 224, 235–36, 246
Alvarez, Everett, Jr., 95
Anderson, George, 62
Anderson, Jeffrey M., 172
Angell, Roger, 231
appeasement: and Kennedy mindset, 142,
    145, 197–98; LeMay on, 63
Arendt, Hannah, 122
atomic bomb: LeMay and, 119; Truman
    on, 130–31

Ball, George, 30, 166
Bao Ninh, 105
Bataan Death March, 131
Batista, Fulgencio, 243
Bay of Pigs invasion, 17, 40–41, 147–50;
    and Cuban missile crisis, 169; further
    reading on, 257–58
belief. *See* misperception/misjudgment
Berlin, Isaiah, 250
bin Laden, Osama, 111, 224
Blight, James, 8, 221–22, 246–47
bombing, in World War II, 113–37
Boothby, Robert, 149
Bowles, Chester, 148–49
Boyar, Jay, 172
Brigham, Robert K., 246
Brinkley, David, 160
Brokaw, Tom, 114
Buddhism, in Vietnam, 154
Bundy, McGeorge, 30, 39–40, 93, 149,
    153, 157
Burchinal, David, 94, 96–98

Bush, George W., 111, 170–71, 225; Mc-
    Namara on, 182–83
Byfield, Diana Masieri, 247

Carroll, Larry, 172
Castro, Fidel, 243; at conferences, 7,
    75–81; and Cuban missile crisis,
    67–74; McNamara on, 59
casualties: of bomber pilots, 119; in fire-
    bombing of Japan, 113; in twentieth
    century, 4, 222, 232–34; in twenty-
    first century, 234–35
Catholicism, in Vietnam, 154
Chamberlain, Neville, 142
Chomsky, Noam, 163–68, 202, 204
Clancy, Tom, 259
Clark, Mike, 172
Cleaver, Eldridge, 199
Clifford, Clark, 245
Coffey, Thomas M., 82, 125–26
Cold War, 195–97; Kennedy mindset on,
    142
Constellation, 98
control: Gross on, 190–91; McNamara
    and, 173–76; Schanberg on, 200
Corliss, Richard, 172
counterfactuals, in critical oral history,
    12–13
courage, and empathy, 14
Craig, Margaret McKinstry, 243, 246
crimes against humanity: Arendt on, 122;
    McNamara on, 8; Power on, 208, 211
critical oral history, 3–25; development
    of, 5–8; empathy and, 14; FAQs on,
    8–13. *See also* dialogues
Cromwell, Oliver, 14
Cronkite, Walter, 160
Cuban missile crisis, 5, 244; and Bay of
    Pigs invasion, 169; Castro on, 75–76;
    conferences on, 6–7; empathy and,
    29–42; mistakes on, 17–18; momen-

tum of, 60–61; rationality and, 59–85; reviews of "The Fog of War" and, 195–99

Cultural Revolution, 233

curiosity: of decision-makers, 7; Kennedy and, 148

Dang Vu Hiep, 7

Danner, Mark, 177, 181–83

Dao Huy Ngoc, 52, 54

decision-makers, 5; and critical oral history, 6–7; McNamara as, 8

dialogues: on Cuban missile crisis, 39–42, 74–84; on Vietnam War, 48–55, 104–9, 159–68; on World War II, 125–35

dilemmas: on empathy, 55–57; on historical perspective, 214–17; on misperception/misjudgment, 109–11; on mistakes, 169–71; on proportionality, 135–37; on rationality, 84–85

Dirksen, Everett, 92

documents: and critical oral history, 6, 11; on Cuban missile crisis, 29–39, 62–74; on Vietnam War, 42–55, 91–104, 144–58; on World War II, 117–25

domino theory, Kennedy on, 142, 160, 162

Dower, John, 115

Dresden, 116

Dunn, Philip, 23

Ebert, Roger, 4, 172

Eichmann, Adolf, 122

Eisenhower, Dwight D., 162, 244

empathy, 4, 27–57; definition of, 13–14; dilemma on, 55–57; further reading on, 249–50; imperative, in twenty-first century, 238–39; lack of, and evil, 122; McNamara on, 27; Welsh and, 202–3

evil: Arendt on, 122; Bush on, 225; dilemma on, 135–37; further reading on, 255–57; Power on, 208–14; and September 11, 2001, 238. *See also* moral choices

exceptionalism, Niebuhr on, 255

firebombing of Japan, 117–18, 126, 233; eyewitness accounts of, 123–25; Mc-Namara on, 113; Schanberg on, 192–93

Five Points, Cuban government, 73

fog of war, definition of, vii, 207

"The Fog of War," 22–23, 174; critical reception of, 4–5, 172–217, 259–61; development of, McNamara and, 3–25; lessons of, 4, 13–21; premiere of, 224–25;

Ford Motor Company, 84, 195, 243–44

French, and Vietnam, 49, 140

Fresh Air, 184–91, 193–95

Galbraith, James K., 161, 163–68

Geneva Accords, 140

Gheith, Suleiman Abu, 236

Gilpatric, Roswell, 150–51

Glass, Philip, 174

Goldwater, Barry, 89, 91–92, 100–101, 245

Gorbachev, Mikhail, 40

Gordon, Lincoln, 167

Great Leap Forward, 233

Gribkov, Anatoly, 7

Gross, Terry, 184–91, 193–95, 216

Guantanamo base, 73

Guevara, Ernesto "Che," 68, 71

guilt, Niebuhr on, 136

Hamburg, 116

Hanoi Hilton, 95

Harding, Warren G., 226

Harkins, Paul, 156

Hayden, Tom, 199

Hedges, Chris, 256–57

hindsight, in critical oral history, 10

Hirohito, emperor of Japan, 134

Hiroshima, 194

historical insight: dilemma on, 214–17; Kierkegaard on, 6, 214; Kundera on, vii

Hitler, Adolf, 142, 229

Hoa Lo Prison, 95

Ho Chi Minh, 44–47, 108, 246
Ho Chi Minh Trail, 43
Holden, Stephen, 4
Horton, Richard, 24–25
Hunter, Stephen, 172
Hussein, Saddam, 111, 247

Ignatieff, Michael, 240
International Control Commission, 94
International Criminal Court, 137
international system, Kennedy mindset
    on, 142
Iraq war, 24–25, 247; further reading on,
    254–55; McNamara and, 176–77,
    181–83; misperception/misjudgment
    and, 111; mistakes and, 170–71;
    moral choices and, 137
Iwo Jima, firebombing of, 118

James, William, 215, 259
Japanese, character of, 120–21, 131–35
JFK, 163
Joffe, Josef, 233
Johnson, Lyndon B., 42–47, 88–95,
    159–68, 244–45; announcement of
    Tonkin Gulf strike, 95, 99–101; Gal-
    braith on, 163–64; and Tonkin Gulf
    Resolution, 101–2
Joint Chiefs of Staff, 62, 81–82, 150–51,
    169

Kennedy, John F., 244; assassination of,
    88, 141, 164; Chomsky and Gal-
    braith on, 163–68; and Cuban mis-
    sile crisis, 29–39, 60, 62–66; Inau-
    gural Address, 146–47; mindset of,
    141–47; mistakes of, 141–43,
    159–60, 169–70; and Vietnam, 141,
    145–46, 150–58
Kennedy, Joseph P., Sr., 197
Kennedy, Robert F., 81, 166
Khrushchev, Nikita, and Cuban missile
    crisis, 29–42, 60, 67–73, 244
Kierkegaard, Søren, 6, 214, 260
Kobe, firebombing of, 118
Kundera, Milan, vii

Lam, Andrew, 206–8
Larsen, Josh, 172
Le, Kathy, 48, 50
Le Hong Truong, 48, 50
LeMay, Curtis: background of, 126; and
    Cuban missile crisis, 60, 62–67; and
    McNamara, 59, 82–84, 113, 129;
    Morris on, 194; and World War II,
    116–19, 125–30
Lemnitzer, Lyman L., 153
Lewis, Anthony, 161–62
life, McNamara on, 222–23, 241
Lippmann, Walter, 81
Lloyd George, David, 228
Lodge, Henry Cabot, 165
Lowerison, Jean, 172
luck, McNamara on, 59, 84
Luu Doan Huynh, 107–9
Lybarger, Dan, 172

Maddox, 88–89, 92–94, 103–4, 108
Mansfield, Mike, 91, 166
Mao Tsetung, 233
Marder, Murray, 94
Martin, Glen W., 128
McCone, John, 94
McKelway, St. Clair "Mac," 129
McNamara, Craig, 243
McNamara, Kathleen, 243
McNamara, Margaret McKinstry Craig,
    243, 246
McNamara, Margy, 243
McNamara, Robert S.: character of,
    220–22, 230–32; chronology of life
    and times of, 243–47; on Cuban mis-
    sile crisis, 40–42, 77–81; on Kennedy,
    161–62; and LeMay on, 59, 82–84,
    113, 129; lessons of, 13–21; and
    Morrison, 202–5; road to "The Fog of
    War," 3–25; on Vietnam War, 52–53,
    91–94, 96–98, 104–7, 150–52; and
    World War I, 226–30; and World War
    II, 120–21
McNamara-Taylor Report to the Presi-
    dent, 154–56, 161–62, 164
memory, in critical oral history, 9–10
Middleton, Drew, 149

Mikoyan, Anastas, 40, 71
Mikoyan, Sergo, 39–40
military force, Kennedy mindset on, 142
misperception/misjudgment, 4, 87–111;
    dilemma on, 109–11; further reading
    on, 252–55; lack of empathy and,
    13–14, 28; McNamara on, 87
mistakes, 139–71; Bush (G. W.) adminis-
    tration and, 170–71; dilemma on,
    169–71;
    further reading on, 257–59; Kennedy
    and, 141–43, 159–60, 169–70; and
    lack of empathy, 28; McNamara on,
    15–21
moral choices in wartime, 4, 113–37;
    dilemma on, 135–37; further reading
    on, 255–57; Power on, 208–14
moral imperative, for twenty-first century,
    236–37
Morris, Errol, 4, 8, 122, 174–76; on
    Fresh Air, 184–91, 193–95;
    Salon.com interview, 197–99
Morrison, Emily, 203
Morrison, Norman, 202–5
Morse, Wayne, 166
multilateral imperative, for twenty-first
    century, 236–37
Munich, and Kennedy mindset, 142

Nagasaki, 130, 194
Nagoya, firebombing of, 118
National Liberation Front (NLF), 19, 43,
    90, 245
National Security Action Memoranda
    (NSAM): 88, 164–65, 263, 273
National Security Council, November 15,
    1961 meeting, 152–53
Neustadt, Richard, 237
Newman, John M., 166–67
Ngo Dinh Diem, 101, 151–52, 154–55,
    159, 244
Ngo Dinh Nhu, 154–55, 159
Nguyen Co Thach, 52, 54–55
Nguyen Dinh Uoc, 107–8
Nguyen Duy Trinh, 43–44
Niebuhr, Reinhold, 117, 135–36, 255–56
Ninkovich, Frank, 230

Nixon, Richard M., 246
Norstad, Lauris, 120
nuclear danger, 5, 85; Castro on, 79–81;
    and Cuban missile crisis, 17–18; Mc-
    Namara on, 15, 59; rationality and,
    76–77
Nye, Joseph S., Jr., 40–41

October crisis, term, 73
Okinawa, 126
Okubo Michiko, 123–24
Operational Plan 34-A, 88, 91–92, 94
Operation Mongoose, 40–41
Osaka, firebombing of, 118
Otsubo Hiroaki, 124–25

Pacific War, 113–37; characteristics of,
    120–21, 131–35
participant selection, in critical oral his-
    tory, 11–12
politics, in critical oral history, 10–11
Powell, Bonnie Azab, 177–83
Powell, Colin, 182
Power, Samantha, 208–14, 216, 225–26
Power, Thomas S., 128–29
prevention of war, 4; Dunn on, 23; empa-
    thy and, 28
prisoners of war (POWs): contemporary
    treatment of, 137; Japanese and,
    120–21, 131–35
proportionality, 113–37; dilemma on,
    135–37; further reading on, 255–57

Quach Hai Luong, 48–51

racism, in World War II, 115
Radio Moscow, 37–38
Railroad of Death, 131
rationality, limits of, 4, 59–85; dilemma
    on, 84–85; further reading on,
    250–52
Reedy, George, 92
responsibility, McNamara on, 139, 173
Rich, Frank, 172
Risquet, Jorge, 41–42
Rolling Thunder, 245
Rostown, Walt, 244

Roy, Arundhati, 254
Rumsfled, Donald, 213–14
Rusk, Dean, 30, 88, 91, 93, 152–53

Schanberg, Sydney, 192–93, 199–202, 216
Schandler, Herbert Y., 48–51
Schell, Orville, 180
Schlesinger, Arthur, Jr., 149–50, 163, 166
Schmeer, Karen, 191
Schoettler, Carl, 203
scholars: and critical oral history, 6; Mc-Namara as, 8
Schweitzer, Albert, 222–23
Scott, Peter Dale, 166
seeing. *See* misperception/misjudgment
self-deception: Lam on, 206; Tuchman on, 140
self-reflection: McNamara and, 23–24. *See also* mistakes
September 11, 2001, 224, 238, 246
Shakhnazarov, Georgy, 40–41
Sharp, U. S. G. "Ollie," 93–98
Shinoda Tomoko, 123
Shoup, David, 62–63, 66–67
Sifton, Elisabeth, 256
situational perversity, 60–61
Sorenson, Theodore C., 21–22, 39–40, 147, 161–62
Southeast Asia Resolution. *See* Tonkin Gulf Resolution
South Vietnamese, reactions to "The Fog of War," 205–8
Stalin, Joseph, 233
Stone, Oliver, 163
success, Kennedy on, 170
Sun Tzu, 23
surveillance technology, 77
sympathy, versus empathy, 28

Talbot, David, 197–99
Taylor, Maxwell, 62, 64, 82, 88–89, 150, 244. *See also* McNamara-Taylor Report to the President
Terauchi Hisaichi, 134–35
Terkel, Studs, 114

terrorism, 224–25, 233, 235–36
Terry, Peggy, 115
Tet Offensive, 245
Thant, U, 36, 73–74
Thompson, Llewellyn "Tommy," 31–32, 60
Ticonderoga, 88
Tokyo, firebombing of, 117–18, 211, 233
Tonkin Gulf events, 88;
    further reading on, 253–54;
    Vietnamese view of, 103–4
Tonkin Gulf Resolution, 89, 101–2, 244
Tran Quang Co, 52–54
Trollope ploy, 35
Truman, Harry S, 130–31, 194
Tuchman, Barbara, 140, 160
Turkey, 34
Turner Joy, 89, 108
twentieth century, 4; McNamara on, 222; tragic reality of, 232–34
twenty-first century: dangers of, 234–36; imperatives for, 236–39; McNamara on, 222–23; reviews of "The Fog of War" and, 208–14

United Nations Security Council, 85
United States: Kennedy mindset on, 143; Niebuhr on, 136
U-2 plane, shot down over Cuba, 36, 69

Versailles, Treaty of, 228–29
Vietcong, 19, 43, 90, 245
Vietnam War, 244–46; empathy and, 42–55; further reading on, 253–54, 258–59; misperception/misjudgment and, 87–111; mistakes on, 18–20, 139–71; Morris on, 184–87; reviews of "The Fog of War" and, 199–208
Vo Nguyen Giap, 104–6, 108

war: of attrition, Vietnam as, 49–51, 90; fog of, definition of, vii, 207; further reading on, 255–57; McNamara and, 15, 22; moral choices in, 4, 113–37, 208–14; prevention of, 4, 23, 28; rules of, 115, 131; on terror, 225; Wilson and, 228 weapons of mass destruction (WMD), in Iraq, 111

Welsh, Anne Morrison, 202–5

Westmoreland, William, 245

Wheeler, Earle, 62

White, Ralph K., 28–29

Wilmington, Michael, 172

Wilson, Woodrow: on future, 239–40; influence of, 219–41; McNamara on, 219, 226–30

Wilson's Ghost (McNamara & Blight), 8, 221–22, 247

Wolfensohn, James, 21, 24

wooden-headedness, Tuchman on, 140

Woodward, Bob, 254

World Bank, 21, 245–46

World War I, McNamara on, 219, 226–30

World War II: proportionality in, 113–37; reviews of "The Fog of War" and, 192–95

Zinni, Tony, 259

"Director Errol Morris, second from the left, with his wife, Julia Sheehan (left), and the authors, outside the theater at the world premiere of the film at the Cannes Film Festival, May, 2003."

James G. Blight is Professor of International Relations (Research) at the Watson Institute for International Studies at Brown University. He is the author of several books on the Cuban missile crisis and the Vietnam War. These books highlight the views of "the other side"—the Soviet/Russian and the Cuban sides during the missile crisis, and the Vietnamese side during the war. They document the risks that ignorance of "the other side" poses for U.S. foreign and defense policy. His most recent book (written with Robert S. McNamara) is the post–9/11 paperback edition of *Wilson's Ghost, Reducing the Risk of Conflict, Killing, and Catastrophe in the 21st Century* (2003).

janet M. Lang is Associate Professor of Epidemiology (emerita) at Boston University School of Public Health, and Adjunct Associate Professor (Research) of International Relations at the Watson Institute for International Studies at Brown University. For the past fifteen years, she has codirected (with James Blight) the Critical Oral History Project at Brown University. The project has sponsored nearly two dozen conferences, over half of which have occurred outside the U.S., in Western Europe, Russia, Cuba, and Vietnam.

The authors have been married for twenty-eight years and live in Milton, MA.